Monsters and Monstrosity in Media

Reflections on Vulnerability

Edited by

Yeojin Kim

University at Buffalo/Singapore Institute of Management

Shane Carreon

University of the Philippines Cebu

Series in Critical Media Studies

VERNON PRESS

www.vernonpress.com

In the Americas:
Vernon Press
1000 N West Street, Suite 1200
Wilmington, Delaware, 19801
United States

In the rest of the world:
Vernon Press
C/Sancti Espiritu 17,
Malaga, 29006
Spain

Series in Critical Media Studies

Library of Congress Control Number: 2024931013

ISBN: 979-8-8819-0177-6

Also available: 978-1-64889-846-4 [Hardback]; 978-1-64889-862-4 [PDF, E-book]

Cover design by Greys Compuesto, UP Cebu.

Table of Contents

List of Figures

Introduction

Anson Koch-Rein

University of North Carolina

Shane Carreon

University of the Philippines Cebu

Yeojin Kim

University at Buffalo/Singapore Institute of Management

From Creature to Culture

While monster studies as a distinct academic field is relatively recent, monsters and the fascination with them have deep historical roots. Before their study as cultural constructs, there were monsters as beings and stories. Monster figures can be traced back to ancient mythologies and folklore from cultures worldwide. Tales of mythical creatures and extraordinary, inexplicable, or supernatural beings were a crucial part of oral traditions passed down from generation to generation. Monsters were described as beings and worked as signs. Etymologically, the term monster is derived from the Latin *monere*, "to remind, bring to (one's) recollection, tell (of); admonish, advise, warn, instruct, teach" (Online Etymology Dictionary). Monsters have always pointed beyond themselves and carried messages. The narratives spun around their messages historically served to explain natural phenomena, delineate social norms, and instill moral order. Monsters were used to grapple with the unknown, forbidden, or mysterious and to understand the human condition. The study of monsters in these contexts was often situated in theology, metaphysics, and cosmology.

With the rise of scientific ways of knowing, the monster as a being disappears, in a sense, into different objects of knowledge. In the *Abnormal* lectures, Michel Foucault explains the beginning of the disappearance of the monster with the advent of the "abnormal individual" (Foucault 2003, 66f.). Disability studies scholar Rosemarie Garland-Thomson discusses this shift in the narrative framing and terminology of extraordinary bodies. Forms of embodiment that used to signal wonder and religious mystery became scientific pathologies (Garland-Thomson 2018, 91). Stephen Asma notes that the pejorative meaning of the term 'monster' intensified with this decline of the wonderous or religious study of the monster because, with the rise of modern science, "there is no longer any truly *literal* sense of the term" (Asma 2009, 15). Without 'literal' monsters in authoritative descriptions of the world, the focus of the study of monsters shifted to the stories.

As cultural figures, monsters became the object of analysis for scholars seeking to understand human beings on an individual and collective level. Such work explored the universality of certain monster archetypes or the role of monsters in various societies (e.g., Frazer 1922). This early period laid the foundation for studying monsters as cultural constructs. With scholars from ever more disciplines, including literature, cultural studies, anthropology, history, art history, psychology, and sociology, beginning to delve more sustainedly into the significance of monsters and to move them from the periphery into the central focus, monster studies as its own field started to take shape in the 1980s (Mittman and Hensel 2018, x). Throughout the changes in the approaches and objectives of their scholarly pursuers, monsters have continued to thrive across cultures, genres, and media.

In the mid-1990s, Jeffrey Jerome Cohen's influential essay "Monster Culture (Seven Theses)" helped put the academic study of monsters as its own interdisciplinary field more visibly on the map (Mittman 2012, 2). Based on Cohen's seven "breakable" theses that approach the monstrous body as "pure culture," the monster can be read as the embodiment of cultural conflict, individual fears, epistemic crises, desire, cultural moments, and historical forces. Importantly, for Cohen, the monster "exists only to be read" is a mode of reading. At the same time, monster studies takes seriously the monster's "uncanny independence" (Cohen 2018, 44). Reading the monster offers a means to understand the culture or context that made it (or the one that circulates it). Reading the monster can also give insight into the bodies and subjects that take on monstrous meaning. However, since "[m]onsters are meaning machines," their interpretability can never be fully exhausted (Halberstam 2018, 87). Monsters are independent and uncannily exceed their uses. Pejorative uses of the term can be reclaimed. A monster can circulate between media, cultures, authors, and audiences and take on new meanings along the way. Monster studies as an interdisciplinary field evolves with the ways monsters are read in each instance and with the lenses brought to the task. Vulnerability plays an important role in many approaches to the monster.

Monster as Metaphor

Mary Shelley's creature in *Frankenstein* may have started as one of the great literary monsters of nineteenth-century gothic fiction, but he keeps wandering on independently as one of the most prolific monster metaphors. He appears not just in theatrical or film adaptations of the novel; he has left Shelley's novel and crossed over into many other media, genres, original works, toys, and visual culture, reaching different audiences wherever he goes (Hitchcock 2007).

This monster, man-made and of questionable creation, is a prime example of the monster as pure culture. The novel makes him wear this fact on his body, as seen through the alienated reactions of others. The processes of his literal and social construction are "laid bare for the reader's condemnation" (Young 2008, 22). Not only is the reader in on these processes of construction but so is the creature. He is independent of his creator as he becomes explicitly self-aware as a monster. He is vulnerable to rejection and social misrecognition. He critically reflects on his becoming a monster, on learning the meaning of his embodiment, and he rages against the injustice of the way he is treated. His level of meta-monstrosity makes him "a metaphor for metaphor itself" (Young 2008, 12). As such, Frankenstein's monster will serve as a recurring example throughout this introduction for various interpretations of the monster.

While most scholarship, like Young's, read monsters as metaphors (Erle and Hendry 2020; Lecercle 2019; Hamilton 2020), sometimes scholars themselves introduce the monster. Peter Adams, for example, investigates metaphors as monsters. He defines "monster metaphors" as ones that forcefully dominate their discourse and "turn nasty" (Adams 2023, 3, 70). Adams recognizes that calling such metaphors monstrous "is a rhetorical maneuver in its own right" (Adams 2023, 8), a scholarly exercise in metaphor usage and monster-making rather than in their analysis. Calling metaphors that are forceful, nasty, and dominating monsters activates a powerful metaphor to draw on its negative meaning.

While also deploying the monster, Henriksen et al.'s exercise of "monster writing" uses the monster "to think with and through vulnerability in writing practices" (Henriksen et al. 2022, 563). They discuss the act of writing as one of creating and living with "text monsters" (Henriksen et al. 2022, 565). This use of the monster draws on a sense of creation and co-existence. Of course, this monster metaphor for the text itself is already present in Mary Shelley's preface to the 1831 edition of *Frankenstein*, when she famously bids her "hideous progeny go forth and prosper" (Shelley 2017, 193), leaving a rich ambiguity of referent between the book and its monster. Such "text monsters" make the monster a figure for the process and product of writing itself. From nineteenth-century novelists to twenty-first-century rhetorical scholars, these writers turn to the monster to mark the idea that vulnerability (to the independence of the text monster or the text's monster) is inherent in writing and publishing.

Symbolic and Mediated Vulnerabilities

One particularly prominent tool for interpreting the meaning of monsters has been psychoanalysis. Anthropologist David Gilmore, for instance, argues that "monsters are universal" in a psychogenetic sense and that "a psychoanalytic approach is unavoidable" (Gilmore 2009, 15f.). He uses cultural comparison to arrive at a universalized psychogenesis of monsters emerging with human civilization and self-consciousness: for him, monsters originate in "the urge for self-punishment and a unified metaphor for both sadism and victimization" (Gilmore 2009, 4f.). Other approaches are critical of universalizing or tautological tendencies in some psychoanalytic criticism (Corstorphine 2023, 14) and favor the close analysis of monsters in their specificity, be that regarding cultural, social, or historical contexts. Jack Halberstam, for example, urges scholars to "avoid psychoanalytic" interpretations of Gothic fiction long enough to allow for historicizing monstrosity in terms of the production of subjectivity, otherness, and embodied deviance (Halberstam 2018, 80).

Feminist theorist Margrit Shildrick offers a psychoanalytic approach to monstrosity that explores the centrality of vulnerability: being "always and everywhere vulnerable" is central to "the constant condition of becoming" (Shildrick 2002, 11). Therefore, "as we reflect on the meaning of the monstrous, and on its confusion of boundaries, the notion of vulnerability emerges precisely as *the* problematic" (Shildrick 2002, 15). The monster embodies this vulnerability of the subject as much as it is a figure of, necessarily incompletely, disavowing and rejecting it in the form of monsterized 'others.' Shildrick's approach shows that a careful handling of psychoanalytic conceptual tools can deploy them in nuanced ways that center vulnerability and explain the unstable production of both self and 'other' through the monster.

Where psychoanalytic approaches tend to be interested in the symbolic vulnerability that monsters reveal, some affect-oriented approaches focus on the vulnerability of the audience's body to the monster as a mediated experience (Hart 2019, 8). Making the case for such an "affective-corporeal model" of horror, Xavier Aldana Reyes argues that what is specific to horror is how the audience's bodies are affected by the genre's cinematic techniques (Reyes 2016, 15). In addition to film studies, the place of the audience's affective, embodied engagement with monsters has garnered particular attention in the study of video games.

For many scholars in media and game studies, what sets monsters in "videoludic horror" apart is the place of the (embodied) player (Marak 2021, 187). Compared to the audiences, viewers, or readers of other media, the level of immersion, engagement, and the interactive intensification positions players differently in relation to the monster (Krzywinska 2002, 13). On the one hand, this means players are vulnerable to the affective effects of game worlds in which they face, move toward, or run away from monsters, play from the monster's point of view, or play in monstrous ways. On the other hand, games can bolster a sense of player mastery that reduces monstrous independence to fit into tightly controlled computational logics, game stats, and boss fights (Švelch 2013, 194). In such scenarios, monsters are objects of play that give players a sense of control and function as nothing more than carefully calibrated challenges in a game's design (Švelch 2013, 202).

The tension between these two argumentative poles, game monsters as examples of players' immersive loss of control and game design that provides an experience of controlling and defeating monsters, is precisely the kind of unstable dynamic that characterizes and animates monsters. Rather than two distinct categories of games or gaming experiences, this tension is often dynamic and shifting within one and the same game. In fact, Tanya Krzywinska argues that the sense of mastery that players cultivate in moments of game activity is what makes the experience of loss of control in more passive or constrained moments of facing game monsters so acute (Krzywinska 2002, 20). The 'boss fight' with the monster sets up a sense of self-determination that the monster cutscene tears down. There is no doubt that the great variety of game genres, design approaches, and varying degrees of interactivity and player immersion populate gaming with a rich array of monsters. They range from generic cannon fodder to more powerful monsters that provide players with an experience of vulnerability that makes video games "the art of failure" (Juul 2013, 30). However, whether players position the monster as self or 'other' as a point of identification, desire, or fear arguably depends more on the monster's cultural than on its software-coded construction. Regardless of the medium under discussion, approaches that are centered on affect and the embodied experience of the audience, rather than the characteristics of the monster's body, add an important tool to the analysis of how monsters are made and acquire meaning.

Monster Studies from the Margins

Monsters defy temporality and expose linear chronologies as lies (Cohen 2017, 451). It is perhaps fitting, then, that they are studied in a field with ancient beginnings but a short history. Among monster studies' multiple origin stories within that short history, it is important to highlight the pivotal role of fields like feminist, queer, black, disability, and postcolonial studies. Asa Mittman calls monster studies "the most recent in a long series" of these thematic fields (Mittman 2012, 3). This version of the origin story places monster studies as the most recent of a list of thematic fields, which are notably all intersectionally related, to begin with. A more sharply pointed version of the story might claim these fields as part of its very foundation. Literary scholar Audrey Fisch, for example, argues in *Frankenstein: Icon of Modern Culture* that the proliferation of scholarly readings of *Frankenstein* starts with its feminist canonization in the 1970s (Fisch 2009, 202). If Shelley's novel became "a suitable subject for academic inquiry" through feminist work (Fisch 2009, 8), monster studies does not merely arrive chronologically in the wake of but is critically shaped by such work.

Concerns central to monster studies, such as who counts as human, the mechanisms of dehumanization, the cultural coding of marked embodiment, resistance, and "the unpredictability of categories" (Hellstrand et al. 2018, 144f.) are of urgent interest to and pursued outside of monster-related topics in fields investigating social categories. Their contributions have directly and indirectly pushed the boundaries of analysis and brought monsters into the view of disciplines and canons that had traditionally dismissed monsters and monster genres from serious scholarship.

We can only briefly touch on some examples of their approaches and contributions to monster studies to flag their continuing importance. Critical attention to monstrosity and race analyzes the monster both as a tool of racist dehumanization and as a means of antiracist critique (Young 2008, 5). As part of that work, scholars trace the long history of the adaptation, reception, and intertextuality of Frankenstein as a Black American metaphor (Lacy 2015, 231). The history of that metaphor continues to unfold: in Bomani J. Story's 2023 film *The Angry Black Girl and Her Monster,* teenage science enthusiast Vicaria frankensteins her murdered older brother Chris back to life as a monster embodying and enacting violence, injustice, and community trauma.

Disability studies perspectives, as seen in Garland-Thomson's work on extraordinary bodies mentioned above, analyze ableist constructions of mental and physical diversity as monstrosities and interpret the monster, including in *Frankenstein,* as a disabled subject (Knight 2020). Feminist and queer studies perspectives shed light on the gendered and sexual aspects of monstrous beings. Analyzing the portrayal of monstrous women, mother figures, or feminine-coded creatures exposes underlying patriarchal norms and biases in cultural narratives (e.g., Palko and O'Reilly 2021). Queer studies also examine how monsters can serve as vehicles for subverting heteronormative ideals of sociality and embodiment or as figures of queer experiences of social exclusion. Non-heteronormative ways of being, embodying, or desiring are often dehumanized in monstrous media depictions (e.g., Benshoff 1997).

Through a postcolonial studies lens, scholars make visible the colonial legacies of monsters and connect monstrosity to the portrayal of the colonial 'other.' By analyzing how indigenous or non-Western cultures are represented in relation to monsters in the colonial imaginary constructions of peoples, places, and geographies, these perspectives challenge Western-centric narratives and highlight the importance of decolonizing monster studies (e.g., Davies 2016).

From all these perspectives and their intersections, monsters are of interest as symbols of vulnerability and resilience. They are claimed as cultural figures inviting identification and affective affiliation with the likes of *Frankenstein's* creature, whose "blood boils" at the injustice of his rejection (Shelley 2017, 186). The monster's liminal and non-normative characteristics carry a history of symbolic violence at the same time that they offer a sense of validation and representation that resonates with marginalized audiences and critics. Of course, the ambivalent resonance of the monster as a figure of 'othering'/dehumanization AND self-recognition/resistance potentially characterizes all encounters with monstrosity to varying degrees. After all, "*everyone* is a little hard to categorize" (Asma 2009, 40), and "[w]e are all one another's monsters" (Mittmann and Hensel 2018, xiv). The monster surely speaks to widely shared, even constitutive, experiences of embodiment and subjectivity. Nevertheless, the long history of using monsters to "exclude, disempower, and dehumanize a range of groups and individuals" in targeted ways gives them particular resonance with those groups and individuals (Mittman and Hensel 2018, xiii). It is no coincidence, for instance, that transgender monsters, both as figures of dehumanization and of reclamation, shape trans representation in the media as much as they recur in transgender studies (Stryker 2006; Nordmarken 2014; Zigarovich 2018).

As monster studies continue to evolve, it relies on diverse perspectives that "give voice to the things that dwelled on the fringes" (Newman-Stille 2018, 2) to deepen our understanding of the significance and construction of monstrous bodies, beings, and feelings.

About this Anthology

This anthology project began sometime during the global lockdowns when various forms of isolation, categorizations, and border controls were enforced in many ways. During this period, we observed across various media platforms the emergence of novel types of monsters related to issues of unidentified disease and infection, uncontrollable natural disasters, regional wars, intensified nationalism, and the influence of neoliberalism that naturalized the categorizing of persons and exacerbated profound disparities. We noted how the normative primacy of sight applies a biopolitical perspective and acts to separate constructed notions of human and monster.

Considering dynamics of power that socially and politically shape interpretations and understandings of what is visible, we ask, on the one hand, how constructions of the monster and monstrosity related to visuality and sight constantly prop up logic that protects borders and sustain binaries to maintain the power and the system that positions subjects in a chain of binaries subverting and transpositing with each other. On the other hand, we also ask how sight can be undermined in ways that disrupt traditional understandings of identity and human beings as humans and monsters become difficult to tell apart. In other words, how can sight blur a vision of who is seen as human or deemed as the monster. We noted how monster figures on-screen can signal a wide range of subversive destabilizations on the construction of the monster and the meaning/value of monstrosity, including who gets to define them.

Considering the COVID-19 situation as a point of departure, wherein contemporary nation-states seek to redefine and establish the meaning of "new normals" in order to sustain power hierarchies, we want to connect monsters and monstrosity to vulnerabilities through which tensions in understanding identity primarily constructed through sight are surfaced. As monsters are conjured by a society into existence, imbued with meanings and values based on what the society seeks to defend itself from, and positioned as antithetical embodiment of social norms, this volume looks into reimaginations of the notion of monstrosity and of monstrous subjects within society. Through collective scholarly effort, we rethink the monster on-screen as well as the notion of monstrosity not only as it represents perceived difference, (non)belongings, and disruptions of traditional identity markers but also as it either implicitly endorses violence towards or conceals varying vulnerabilities of the labeled Other.

The collection begins with chapters that analyze how authoritative social systems produce monstrous other(s) as a social apparatus to maintain power and structure and offer a critical perspective on monstrosity as an opposite component of the dominant within social systems. In the first chapter, "The Enemy as Monster, the Monster as Neighbor: Anticommunist Propaganda in South Korea and Kwŏn Chŏng-saeng's Korean War Trilogy," Youn Soo Kim Goldstein examines how nation-states create the image of monstrous Otherness to solidify ideological binarism as a mechanism to uphold its hegemony. By analyzing Kwŏn Chŏng-saeng's Korean War trilogy—*Mongsil ŏnni* (My sister Mongsil, 1984), *Ch'ogajibi ittŏn maul* (The village with thatched houses, 1985), and *Chŏmdŭgine* (Chŏmdŭk's family, 1990)—Youn Soo focuses on how the South Korean authoritarian state created the 'division system,' an anti-communist dichotomous structurer to reforge the ideological divide between South and North Korea, thereby constructing North Korea as an ethnic Other. Also, as a means to establish post-war South Korean subjectivity, North Korea's imagery is portrayed as monstrous in propaganda materials to recast it as the monstrous Other. However, by illustrating how the genre rhetoric of children's fiction can unveil the vulnerability of the structured system, the chapter challenges binary oppositions between South Korea and North Korea, comrades and enemies, and notions of good and bad. Furthermore, it exposes the true monstrous facet within the context by the child protagonist's perspective: the system itself.

In the following chapter, "Weaponizing Monstrosity: Starz's *Black Sails* and the Power of Monstrous Narrative," Min-Chi Chen discusses how the British Empire portrayed pirates as 'hostis humani generis' (enemies of all humankind) to legitimize the empire's status as a civilized nation in the early eighteenth century. Min-Chi reveals how the discourse of power necessitates the concept of monster(s) to establish a binary boundary between civilization and the uncivilized, allowing the utilization of monstrosity as a mechanism to support the colonial system and social hierarchies. By looking into the narration of the story from the perspective of the pirates, this chapter challenges the social construction of monstrous subjects and explores the significance of their ontological presence in social narratives, as depicted in Starz's *Black Sails* (2014-2017).

In the chapter titled "The Move to Innocence: Reframing Monstrosity in Colin Trevorrow's *Jurassic World*," Angie Fazekas and Aarzoo Singh discuss how the ongoing investment in heteronormative whiteness in the *Jurassic Park* film series inevitably produces monstrosity as a means to sustain white heroism. By exploring how the monstrous dinosaurs in the film represent social anxieties regarding science and capitalism, posing a threat to the heteronormative system, this chapter delves into how monstrosity and racial subordination are constructed to uphold the heteronormative system. Introducing the concept of the 'race to innocence,' Angie and Aarzoo reimagine the filmic narratives of white dominance as the real monster, positioning racialized others as a subsidiary subject and creating monsters as a way of protecting the 'ordinary' subject.

Shifting gears from viewing monstrosity as a socially created concept to maintaining the hegemony's status quo, the following chapters subvert the anthropocentric understanding of monsters and monstrosity. Joshua Nieubuurt's "Dark Zombiecologies: Trekking through the Transformative Zombie Forest" examines the rhetorical transformation of cinematic zombies as a projection of societal anxieties and collective fears. While zombies are a relatively new monster in Western culture, they are established as a cultural metaphor representing the social anxieties of their respective time period. The chapter proposes that contemporary renditions of zombies serve as a form of eco-apocalyptic projection involving both human and non-human threats. It analyzes how the ontological nature and applications of the zombie undergo transitions, ultimately reshaping culture and redefining distinctions between the human and the non-human in societies where they emerge. This chapter offers an essential opportunity for readers to contemplate how we should interpret the recurring presence of monsters on screen, who or what causes their resurgence in history, and the roles they represent within the anthropocentric world.

The subsequent chapters bring in technology and the engagement with it as part of rethinking the idea of monster. In the chapter titled "Monstrous Gatekeepers – Eco-gothic Bodies in Video Games," Morgan Kate Pinder explores how ecogothic monsters are presented as transgressive and abject 'others' and analyzes the deep-seated anxieties related to the intricate barriers between the human and the non-human, as well as between video players and their objectives. By thoroughly examining video games—*Sekiro: Shadows Die*

Twice, Inscryption (Daniel Mullins Games 2021), *Return of the Obra Dinn* (2018), and *Until Dawn* (Supermassive Games 2015)—Morgan offers a significant perspective on ecophobia and eco-gothic bodies, which manifest as hybridized, mutated, or otherwise transgressive species. Morgan challenges the anthropocentric perspective of categorization and reimagines eco-gothic monsters as victims, portrayed through their experiences of trauma and otherness. This chapter holds particular significance in discussing how ecosystems have been relegated to the role of ecological 'others,' positioned in contrast to human civilization or technology; it is especially pertinent as we edge closer to the looming ecological crisis of the Late Anthropocene and the fragility of the structures that insulate humans from the unpredictable violence of nature have become increasingly apparent.

In "The Monstrous Gaze: Examining the Camera In Horror Film," Mychal Reiff-Shanks looks into slasher films and presents the hybridity of the camera as inhabiting a heterotopic space where the "tension of horror resides." Drawing from Patricia MacCormack's definition of monstrosity, Mychal argues how the camera created a new form of the monstrous in the horror film genre in the way it controls the precarious viewing position of the audience and turns it into a "subversive gaze of hybridity." In other words, the audience is made to identify with the POV of the camera that can take on not only the gaze of the killer and the gaze of the victim, which are both in the cinematic world, but also the simultaneous contradiction of indestructible killer, who is invincible so long as the audience is made to be their extension, as well as the indestructible victim, the final girl who has the potential agency against the killer. This chapter points at the implications of how technology can mediate the perception of monstrosity on-screen and the experience of it beyond the screen.

Later essays in this collection place gender and sexuality in conversation with the notion of monster/monstrosity. As the previous chapter notes how the camera in slasher films can shift the audience or the spectator's identification, Adam P. Wadenius, in the chapter "You are Trespassing in My House: Subverting the Gaze in Jennifer Kent's *Monster* and *The Babadook*," carefully unpacks shots and cinematographic techniques to show how counter cinema frees the female protagonist from typical representations in the horror genre, confronts and contests conventional symbolic structures that may take the form of a monster, and reveals the fiction of the Other.

Female protagonists in the horror film genre are also analyzed by Eleanor Gratz in, "Ladies of the Night What Pop Music They Make: The Monstrous Adolescent in *Jennifer's Body* and *Blue My Mind*." In particular, Eleanor looks into these films to see how women filmmakers explore the experience of female adolescence in relation to both the female body at the cusp of adulthood and the concept and figure of the monstrous adolescent. Eleanor argues that women filmmakers cinematically revise and reclaim female monstrosity by showing complexities in the feminine coming-of-age in terms of interiority, corporeality, and sexuality.

In "Watch Out Boys, She'll Chew You Up: Feminine Monstrosity's Linguistic Traps," Ryanne Probst points out disparities in the general reception of female monsters and male monsters and notes how perceptions of gender influence language that facilitates discussions on monstrosity. Using elements from Media Theory, Ryanne analyzes the etymology and (non)shifts in the meaning of the words *hero, heroine,* and *monster* from classical stories to contemporary popular culture that led to a distortion not only preventing meaningful and critical discourse on feminine monstrosity but also impacting views on real-life women. Central to discussions and story-telling surrounding monstrosity is who is chosen to be empathized with, how this empathy was arrived at, and, conversely, who is denied. This chapter's important contribution is an argument drawn from Suzanne Keen's theory of Narrative Empathy. Ryanne puts forward that in certain "valued emotional states" the audience is primed to prioritize gendered in ways that lead towards male monsters being understood, even empathized with as female monsters are ostracized; Ryanne calls for seeing the linguistic trap and for unlearning the vocabulary that sets up the general reception of woman as monster and feminine monstrosity.

Drawing theoretical foundations from Butler on the performance of gender and from José Esteban Muñoz on disidentification, Sheridyn Villarreal in "Trans/futurities: Queering the Cyborg as a Strategy of Transgender Disidentification" analyzes the connection between the transgender experience and the cyborg figure through three works of art: a French film by Julia Decornau; an immersive virtual reality environment by Tabitha Nikolai; and a music video by Arca. Villareal reads these works as acts of political disidentification wherein the notion and figure of the cyborg are invoked to probe conceptions of gender, sex, embodiment, and the body, particularly as mediated by technologies. Villareal argues that marginalized trans subjects in these works of art align with cyborgs, typically considered as monsters, to reject oppressive dominant scripts on gender and sexual deviancy and reclaim the cyborg as a symbol of radical self-determinacy and emancipatory transformation.

In the final chapter of this collection, "Boulet Brothers' Drag Supermonster: Goth, Macabre, and Queer Excellence," Charlito O. Codizar champions horror drag both for invoking responses that oscillate between terror and enchantment and for creating an afterlife for drag characters. By afterlife, Charlito means to exist as one's own entity, meaning, to have an aliveness beyond presumably repressive structures of lived realities. The chapter suggests performativity as well as transnational flows of representations of the monstrous. It also opens up multiple and varied conversations on potential other imaginings of the notion of monstrous or that which is truly feared, desired, or simultaneously both in relation to dominant ideological structures. Altogether, the chapters in this collection not only challenge the conventional notions of monster/monstrosity with their attending racial, ethical, sexual, and gendered binary systems but also deconstruct representations of monster/monstrosity on-screen to reveal various lived vulnerabilities.

Bibliography

Adams, Peter J. 2023. *Monster Metaphors: When Rhetoric Runs Amok.* Taylor & Francis.

Asma, Stephen. 2009. *On Monsters: An Unnatural History of Our Worst Fears.* Oxford: Oxford University Press.

Benshoff, Harry. 1997. *Monsters in the Closet: Homosexuality and the Horror Film.* Neptune City, NJ: Manchester University Press.

Cohen, Jeffrey Jerome. 2017. "Postscript: The Promise of Monsters." In *The Ashgate Research Companion to Monsters and the Monstrous*, 449–64. Taylor and Francis. https://www.routledgehandbooks.com/doi/10.4324/97813152 41197. post.

———. 2018. "'Monster Culture (Seven Theses).'" In *Classic Readings on Monster Theory*, edited by Asa Simon Mittman and Marcus Hensel, 43–54. Demonstrare, Volume One. Arc Humanities Press. https://doi.org/10.2307/j.ctvfxvc3p.10.

Corstorphine, Kevin. 2023. "Horror Theory Now: Thinking about Horror." In *The Evolution of Horror in the Twenty-First Century*, edited by Simon Bacon. Lanham, KY: Lexington Books/Fortress Academic. http://ebookcentral.proq uest.com/lib/uncsa-ebooks/detail.action?docID=7216737.

Davies, Surekha. 2016. *Renaissance Ethnography and the Invention of the Human: New Worlds, Maps and Monsters.* Cambridge Social and Cultural Histories. Cambridge: Cambridge University Press. https://doi.org/10.1017/CBO 9781139568128.

Erle, Sibylle, and Helen Hendry. 2020. "Monsters: Interdisciplinary Explorations in Monstrosity." *Palgrave Communications* 6 (1): 1–7. https://doi.org/10.105 7/s41599-020-0428-1.

Fisch, Audrey A. 2009. *Frankenstein: Icon of Modern Culture.* Helm Information.

Foucault, Michel. 2003. *Abnormal: Lectures at the College de France 1974-1975.* Edited by Valeria Marchetti and Antonella Salomoni. New York: Picador.

Frazer, James George. 1922. *The Golden Bough: A Study of Magic and Religion.* Project Gutenberg, 2003. https://www.gutenberg.org/ebooks/3623.

Garland-Thomson, Rosemarie. 2018. "'From Wonder to Error: A Genealogy of Freak Discourse in Modernity,' from Freakery: Cultural Spectacles of the Extraordinary Body." In *Classic Readings on Monster Theory*, edited by Asa Simon Mittman and Marcus Hensel, 89–98. Demonstrare, Volume One. Arc Humanities Press. https://doi.org/10.2307/j.ctvfxvc3p.14.

Gilmore, David D. 2009. *Monsters: Evil Beings, Mythical Beasts, and All Manner of Imaginary Terrors.* Philadelphia, UNITED STATES: University of Pennsylvania Press. http://ebookcentral.proquest.com/lib/uncsa-ebooks/detail.action?d ocID=3441642.

Halberstam, J. 2018. "'Parasites and Perverts: An Introduction to Gothic Monstrosity,' from Skin Shows: Gothic Horror and the Technology of

Monsters." In *Classic Readings on Monster Theory*, edited by Asa Simon Mittman and Marcus Hensel, 75–88. Demonstrare, Volume One. Arc Humanities Press. https://doi.org/10.2307/j.ctvfxvc3p.13.

Hamilton, Jenny. 2020. "Monsters and Posttraumatic Stress: An Experiential-Processing Model of Monster Imagery in Psychological Therapy, Film and Television." *Humanities and Social Sciences Communications* 7 (1): 1–8. https://doi.org/10.1057/s41599-020-00628-2.

Hart, Adam. 2019. *Monstrous Forms: Moving Image Horror Across Media*. Oxford: Oxford University Press.

Hellstrand, Ingvil, Line Henriksen, Aino-Kaisa Koistinen, Donna McCormack, and Sara Orning. 2018. "Promises, Monsters and Methodologies: The Ethics, Politics and Poetics of the Monstrous." *Somatechnics* 8 (2): 143–62. https://doi.org/10.3366/soma.2018.0247.

Henriksen, Line, Katrine Meldgaard Kjær, Marie Blønd, Marisa Cohn, Baki Cakici, Rachel Douglas-Jones, Pedro Ferreira, Viktoriya Feshak, Simy Kaur Gahoonia, and Sunniva Sandbukt. 2022. "Writing Bodies and Bodies of Text: Thinking Vulnerability through Monsters." *Gender, Work & Organization* 29 (2): 561–74. https://doi.org/10.1111/gwao.12782.

Hitchcock, Susan Tyler. 2007. *Frankenstein: A Cultural History*. New York: W.W. Norton. http://www.loc.gov/catdir/toc/ecip0720/2007025466.html.

Juul, Jesper. 2013. *The Art of Failure: An Essay on the Pain of Playing Video Games*. 1st Edition, 1st Printing. Cambridge, Mass: The MIT Press.

Knight, Amber. 2020. "Mary Shelley's Frankenstein, Disability, and the Injustice of Misrecognition." *Disability Studies Quarterly* 40 (4). https://doi.org/10.18061/dsq.v40i4.7109.

Krzywinska, Tanya. 2002. "Hands-On Horror." In *Axes to Grind: Re-Imagining the Horrific in Visual Media and Culture*, 2:12–23. Special Issue of Spectator 22. University of Southern California, School of Cinema Television, Division of Critical Studies.

Lacy, Michael G. 2015. "Black Frankenstein and Racial Neoliberalism in Contemporary American Cinema: Reanimating Racial Monsters in Changing Lanes." In *The Routledge Companion to Global Popular Culture*. Routledge.

Lecercle, Jean-Jacques. 2019. "What's in a Monster?" *Anglistik* 30 (3): 17–26. https://doi.org/10.33675/ANGL/2019/3/4.

Marak, Katarzyna. 2021. "Independent Horror Games between 2010 and 2020: Selected Characteristic Features and Discernible Trends." *Images. The International Journal of European Film, Performing Arts and Audiovisual Communication* 29 (38): 175–90. https://doi.org/10.14746/i.2021.38.11.

Mittman, Asa Simon. 2012. "Introduction: The Impact of Monsters and Monster Studies." In *The Ashgate Research Companion to Monsters and the Monstrous*. Routledge.

Mittman, Asa Simon, and Marcus Hensel. 2018. "Introduction: 'A Marvel of Monsters.'" In *Classic Readings on Monster Theory*, ix–xvi. Demonstrare, Volume One. Arc Humanities Press. https://doi.org/10.2307/j.ctvfxvc3p.5.

Newman-Stille, Derek. 2018. *We Shall Be Monsters: Mary Shelley's Frankenstein 200 Years On*. Renaissance.

Nordmarken, Sonny. 2014. "Becoming Ever More Monstrous: Feeling Transgender In-Betweenness." *Qualitative Inquiry* 20 (1): 37–50. https://doi.org/10.1177/1077800413508531.

"Monster (n.)." n.d. In *Online Etymology Dictionary*. Accessed August 14, 2023. https://www.etymonline.com/search?q=monster.

Palko, Abigail, and Andrea O'Reilly, eds. 2021. *Monstrous Mothers: Troubling Tropes*. First Edition. Bradford, Ontario: Demeter Press.

Reyes, Xavier Aldana. 2016. "Introduction: The Affective-Corporeal Dimensions of Horror." In *Horror Film and Affect*. Routledge.

Shelley, Mary. 2017. *Frankenstein: Annotated for Scientists, Engineers, and Creators of All Kinds*. Edited by David H. Guston, Ed Finn, Jason Scott Robert, and Charles E. Robinson. Cambridge: The MIT Press. https://muse.jhu.edu/pub/6/oa_edited_volume/book/51933.

Shildrick, Margrit. 2002. *Embodying the Monster: Encounters with the Vulnerable Self*. London: SAGE Publications Ltd.

Story, Bomani J., director. *The Angry Black Girl and Her Monster*. Crypt TV, 2023.

Stryker, Susan. 2006. "My Words to Victor Frankenstein above the Village of Chamounix: Performing Transgender Rage (1994)." In *The Transgender Studies Reader*, edited by Susan Stryker and Stephen Whittle, 244–56. New York: Routledge.

Švelch, Jaroslav. 2013. "Monsters by the Numbers: Controlling Monstrosity in Video Games." In *Monster Culture in the 21st Century: A Reader*, edited by Marina Levina and Diem-My T. Bui, 193–208. New York: Bloomsbury Academic. https://doi.org/10.5040/9781628928198.

Young, Elizabeth. 2008. *Black Frankenstein: The Making of an American Metaphor*. New York and London: New York University Press.

Zigarovich, Jolene. 2018. "The Trans Legacy of Frankenstein." *Science Fiction Studies* 45 (2): 260–72. https://doi.org/10.5621/sciefictstud.45.2.0260.

Chapter 1

The Enemy as Monster, the Monster as Neighbor: Anticommunist Propaganda in South Korea and Kwŏn Chŏng-saeng's Korean War Trilogy

Youn Soo Kim Goldstein

Weber State University

Abstract: Kwŏn Chŏng-saeng's Korean War trilogy—*Mongsil ŏnni* (My sister Mongsil, 1984), *Ch'ogajibi ittŏn maul* (The village with thatched houses, 1985), and *Chŏmdŭgine* (Chŏmdŭk's family, 1990)—challenges the monstrous portrayals of North Korea, as produced in South Korea's anticommunist propaganda material, exposing the ambiguities of the Korean division and Korean War. Under the "division system," a concept developed by sociologist Paik Nak-chung, the rhetoric of anticommunism was used by the South Korean authoritarian state as a disciplinary mechanism to solidify its hegemony in the post-1945 period. This essay examines such monstrous images of North Korea in the propaganda materials produced in South Korea alongside episodes from Kwŏn's children's fiction that depict the South Korean state's "enemy." This analysis exposes the intricacies of living through a civil war embedded in an ideological and externally imposed division in which the monstrous Other is indistinct and multifarious. In his three novels centered on the Korean War experience, Kwŏn tells stories of protagonists who are exposed to vulnerable situations in the midst of the division and war, revealing the complexities of human relationships. With children as protagonists, Kwŏn brings attention to various forms of violence resulting from the physical and ideological division on the Korean peninsula under the global Cold War structure. Kwŏn points out that in war, there is no singular monster that perpetrates violence; there are multiple entities that kill, bomb, and destroy, and there are various victims of such violence. Furthermore, in a war, anyone can become a monster who commits or participates in violent incidents due to the circumstances. Ultimately, Kwŏn's novels illustrate that in the realities of the war, the "good" side and the "bad" side are not as clear as they are portrayed in the propaganda images.

Keywords: Kwŏn Chŏng-saeng; Korean War; anticommunist propaganda; division system; counter-narrative; children's literature

***

Kwŏn Chŏng-saeng's Korean War trilogy—*Mongsil ŏnni* (My sister Mongsil, 1984), *Ch'ogajibi ittŏn maŭl* (The village with thatched houses, 1985), and *Chŏmdŭgine* (Chŏmdŭk's family, 1990)—focuses on the experiences of children during the Korean War.[1] All three youth novels are based on Kwŏn's own experiences of the war, as well as those of his family members and stories he heard from his neighbors. Kwŏn became a prominent South Korean children's literature author in the 1980s, known for his stories, novels, and poems promoting peace and non-violence. With children as protagonists in these three youth novels, Kwŏn brings attention to various forms of violence resulting from the physical and ideological division on the Korean peninsula under the global Cold War structure. Anticommunism has been a major component of the South Korean state's nation-building master narrative since the division of the Korean peninsula. Under the "division system," a concept developed by sociologist Paik Nak-chung (Paek Nak-ch'ŏng), the rhetoric of anticommunism was used by the authoritarian state as a disciplinary mechanism to solidify its hegemony. People who did not fit into the state's agenda and imagination of the South Korean nation were often depicted as "monsters" that needed to be fought and eliminated.

Kwŏn's novels challenge the monstrous portrayal of South Korea's enemy, North Korea, as produced by the anticommunist propaganda, exposing the ambiguities of the Korean division and the Korean War. *Mongsil ŏnni* follows the story of a young girl through the chaos of post-liberation Korea and the Korean War.[2] The plot of *Ch'ogajibi ittŏn maul* revolves around a group of children in a small village.[3] *Chŏmdŭgine* focuses on the story of a boy named Chŏmdŭk and his family who return to Korea from Manchuria after Korea's

---

[1] Scholars of Korean children's literature have grouped the three novels. Sung-Jin Kim (2008) called the three novels "trilogy of the Korean War." The publisher's website notes how Wŏn Chong-ch'an grouped them as "Kwŏn Chŏng-saeng 6.25 *sonyŏn sosŏl* (youth novel) trilogy" (Changbi Publishers, 2022).

[2] The story of Mongsil was first published as a series of installments, initially in a monthly youth journal of a small church starting in 1981, but it was quickly picked up by the Christian women's monthly magazine *Saegajŏng* (New family) in which it was published from January 1982 to March 1984.

[3] *Ch'ogajibi ittŏn maul* was first serialized in the youth magazine *Sonyŏn* in 1978. The full-length novel was published in 1985, after *Mongsil ŏnni*.

liberation.[4] In these novels, Kwŏn tells stories of the experiences of the protagonists who are exposed to vulnerable situations in the midst of the division and war. Though monsters appear to simplify good and evil, particularly when featured in propaganda, closer inspection into narratives of lived experiences in these novels reveals the complexities of human behaviors and relationships. This essay seeks to juxtapose Kwŏn's depictions of the South Korean state's "enemy" in his children's fiction with the images of North Korea in the state's propaganda materials to examine the intricacies of living through a civil war embedded in an ideological and externally imposed division in which the monstrous Other is indistinct and multifarious.

The Enemy as the Monster: North Koreans in Propaganda within the Division System

Paik Nak-chung's "division system" discourse explains the political condition in which the South Korean state's monster was created. According to Paik, the concept of the division system is an effort "to understand more clearly the complicated (and structured) way the two different systems—that is, sets of social institutions—of the North and the South reproduce themselves in a curious entanglement with each other" (2011, 4). It explains how each system of North Korea and South Korea, neither of which can operate alone, operates within the world system of nation-states that exist in relation to one another. At the same time, the division system mediates the operation of the world system on the Korean peninsula and the participation of each of the sides in the larger Cold War-determined geopolitics.

The monster that is the Other living among us is manifested during the civil war in Korea. Since the end of the Japanese colonial period, the master narrative of the homogenous ethnonation was prominent in both Koreas after the division. Leaders of both sides of the thirty-eighth parallel, Kim Il Sung (Kim Il-sŏng) in North Korea and Syngman Rhee (Yi Sŭng-man) in South Korea, "agreed that the Korean people belonged to the same ethnic nation, or *minjok*, and shared a single bloodline" (Shin 2006, 152). At the same time, each of the sides had to emphasize that the other side was different. In "Monster Culture (Seven Theses)," Jeffrey Jerome Cohen posits, "The monster is difference made flesh, come to dwell among us. In its function as dialectical Other or third-term supplement, the monster is an incorporation of the Outside, the Beyond—of all those loci that are rhetorically placed as distant and distinct but originate Within" (2020, 41). The "monstrous difference" comes from the political divide caused by the division system on the Korean peninsula within the larger global

---

[4] Chŏmdŭgine was first serialized in the Buddhist magazine *Haein* from March 1987 to January 1989.

Cold War; and the existence of the other Korea as the monster was essential to the identity of both Koreas. As Namhee Lee points out, "The birth and sovereignty of the South Korean state were contingent upon the existence of North Korea as the Other," and this othering of North Korea was also used to justify the violence of the authoritarian rule in South Korea (2002, 44). The division ideology of anti-communism in South Korea served to maintain the status quo of the division and became essential to its governance, and the South Korean state's master narrative depicted North Korea as the monstrous Other for this purpose.

The most observable instances of depicting the enemy as a monster occurred in war propaganda posters. In wartime, propaganda posters have always been used to dehumanize the enemy. For example, during World War II, in addition to depicting Adolf Hitler as a threat, British and American propaganda posters portrayed him as an object of contempt or ridicule and dehumanized him by representing him as a non-human objects and animals, creating an image that is "a combination of monster and clown" (Vallée 2012, 148). With the Pacific theater of World War II expanding, the United States produced propaganda posters that showed Nazi Germany and Japan as two heads of the same monster seeking to destroy freedom and urging people to contribute to the war efforts by increasing their production, as shown in the propaganda poster produced by the Office for Emergency Management below in figure 1 (UNO Digital Humanities Project, 2016).

Figure 1.1. U.S. Propaganda Poster, "Stop This Monster"

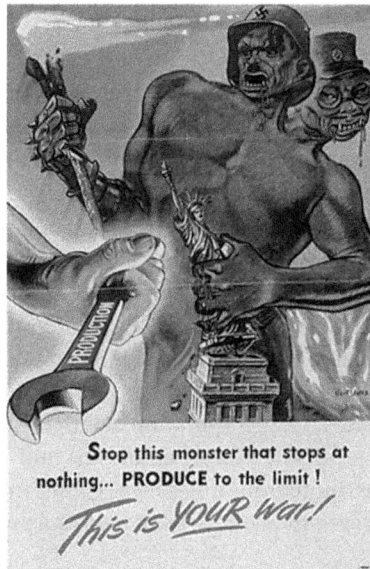

U.S. Propaganda poster from World War II portraying Nazi Germany and Japan as a two-headed monster; retrieved from UNO Digital Humanities Projects

Nazi Germany also produced propaganda posters that portrayed different nationalities, ethnicities, and ideologies as monsters. For example, the 1994 poster *Kultur-Terror* by Leest Storm portrays the United States and the American lifestyle and culture as threats to Nazi Germany (Backer 2007). As such, the imagery of monsters in propaganda posters has been frequently used in wars to create the perfect Other.

Similarly, in South Korea, the enemy was portrayed as non-human monsters and animals in propaganda leaflets during the Korean War as well as in propaganda materials produced in the decades following the armistice agreement. According to Seungsook Moon, the elites in postcolonial South Korea "adopted the notion of modernity associated with a strong military and high productivity based on advanced technology," and that Park Chung Hee's (Pak Chŏng-hŭi) regime set forth "this interpretation of modernity as a nation-building project" which was made possible "[i]n the context of the Cold War rivalry and military confrontation with North Korea" (Moon 2005, 2). Depicting the enemy Other as the monster in propaganda materials serves a military purpose in the ongoing division system. According to Cohen, "monsters born of political expedience and self-justifying nationalism functions as living invitations to action, usually military (invasions, usurpations, colonizations)" (2020, 46). Within the division system, the South Korean state's monstrous portrayals of North Korea were invitations to military action, not just during the active battle years in the early 1950s but in the perpetual dreadlock of the "Armistice" that made the division and unendingness of the war permanent on the Korean peninsula.

During wartime, the production of propaganda leaflets was led by the U.S. Army's 1st Radio Broadcasting and Leaflet (RB&L) Group under its Psywar Division. As shown in figures 2, 3, 4, and 5, these propaganda leaflets portrayed the North Korean regime, Stalin and the Soviet Union, and Communism as monsters that cause suffering and prevent freedom (U.S. Army Special Operations Command History Office, 2020). The intended effect of such dehumanization was so that South Koreans did not feel any guilt about killing the enemy because they would be killing evil monsters and animals (Yi 2021).

Figure 1.2. Korean War Propaganda Leaflet 1

A propaganda leaflet produced by the U.S. Army's RB&L Group portraying North Korea and Communism as a snake-like monster devouring soldiers; retrieved from U.S. Army Special Operations Command History Office

Figure 1.3. Korean War Propaganda Leaflet 2

A propaganda leaflet produced by the U.S. Army's RB&L Group portraying Communism as a multi-headed and multi-limbed monster broadcasting lies and gagging its people; retrieved from U.S. Army Special Operations Command History Office

Figure 1.4. Korean War Propaganda Leaflet 3

A propaganda leaflet produced by the U.S. Army's RB&L Group portraying North Korea and Communism as a snake-like monster squeezing its people of all their possessions; retrieved from U.S. Army Special Operations Command History Office

Figure 1.5. Korean War Propaganda Leaflet 4

A propaganda leaflet produced by the U.S. Army's RB&L Group portraying Communism as an ape-like monster preventing people from speaking and burning their freedom; retrieved from U.S. Army Special Operations Command History Office

In figure 2, the banner above the head of the monster has the North Korean flag and text that says "Democratic People's Republic of Korea." The monster's face resembles Stalin and has fangs and two tongues. Its body is long and winding like a snake's and has the text "Communism" written on it. There are two rows of soldiers marching into the mouth of the monster. The leaflet in figure 3 features a green monster with multiple heads and limbs. One hand is carrying the hammer and sickle symbol of Communism, and a couple of the other hands are carrying two megaphones, each to one of the heads that seem to be screaming about something. The heads are wearing Soviet military hats, and one of the heads resembles Stalin. One of the other hands has four different microphones at the fingertips. Underneath the monster, there is a row of people whose tongues have been nailed to a wooden plank. The text on the leaflet reads, "With the people's mouths shut, the Communist Party is busy with only broadcasting their lies." Figure 4 features another snake-like monster with a human's head wearing a military hat with the North Korean flag. The snake's body has the hammer and sickle symbol of Communism. The monster has two arms, with which it is holding and squeezing a person, and the person is spewing out various objects, including a sack of rice, an ox, farming equipment, clothes, and a pot. The text reads, "The Communist Party squeezes sweat and blood of the farmers!" In figure 5, a dark-colored shadow-like monster in the shape of an ape is holding a person in its arms. The face of the monster is the sickle and hammer symbol. The monster is covering the person's mouth with one hand while burning a piece of paper that reads "people's freedom" with the other hand. The text in red underneath the monster reads, "The evil claws of Communism that strips away freedom." In these posters, the North Korean regime is tied to the Soviet Union and the larger Communist bloc within the Cold War and is portrayed as monsters torturing people, taking away their freedom, and propagating lies.

Anticommunism was a mechanism for state power and discipline in South Korea since the division, as reflected in the widespread application of the National Security Law (NSL) and Anticommunist Law, the establishment of the Chungang Chŏngbobu (Korean Central Intelligence Agency, KCIA), Hakto Hoguktan (National Student Defense Corps, NSDC), and the emergency decrees (Lee 2007, 82-90). The anticommunist position of the South Korean state strengthened after Park Chung Hee's May 16 coup d'état in 1961, after a short-lived hope for change to move towards peace and democracy following the April Revolution just a year earlier. The strengthened position is particularly notable, as Namhee Lee (2007) mentions, in the state's institutionalization of anti-communist education. With the reform of the national school curriculum in 1963 (제2차 교육과정, *Che 2-ch'a kyoyuk kwajŏng*), school textbooks like *Sŭnggong* [Victory over Communism] and *Kyoryŏn* [Military training] became a mandatory part of the school. In 1968, by order of the President, the Charter of National Education (*Kungmin kyoyuk hŏnjang*) was promulgated; one of the main tenets of this charter was to instill a sense of "anticommunist ethics" (*pan'gong todŏk*) in schoolchildren. Additionally, schools regularly held anticommunist speech contests and anticommunist poster drawing contests. Through the change in the education policies, the state's objective was to make children view North Koreans and communists as the enemy.

Outside of the school setting, media was used for propaganda aimed towards children. The South Korean state imposed strict censorship through state security laws to reinforce anticommunism: "it is impossible to ignore the cumulative influence of anti-communist ideology in Korea because this ideology guided and limited all immediate post-war cultural production including the historical fiction written for children about the Korean War" (Zur 2009, 194). The Ministry of Public Information produced a comic strip shown in figure 6 in which a North Korean child realizes how horrible the conditions are in North Korea compared to South Korea and seeks to escape from North Korea (Ministry of Public Information 1966).

Figure 1.6. South Korea's Anticommunist Comic Strip

An anti-communist comic strip produced by the Ministry of Public Information in the 1960s for children titled "Boknam's Story of Vicious Communists" retrieved from the National Museum of Korean Contemporary History digital archives

This comic was produced with the intention of anticommunist education. The poster carries the message of how Communists are "vicious" and that children in North Korea must be "rescued" by children of the "free" South Korea. It portrays North Korean children being forced to labor and depicts North Koreans in ragged clothing compared to South Koreans in new and clean-looking clothing. The developmentalist pursuit and economic success of South Korea are contrasted with the poverty and backwardness of North Korea, brought on by communism.

The anticommunist rhetoric for children was also produced in the private sector. According to Theodore Hughes, "The visual and the biopolitical were mutually constitutive, the production of the visible linked at once to the promotion of South Korean developmentalist life and its citizen-subjects and the rendering invisible of the North signaled in the well-known slogan 'eradicate communism' (*myŏlgong*)" (2012, 3). In the 1960s, '70s, and '80s, films and cartoons were used as a means of education for young viewers to further strengthen the anticommunist cultural policies and internalize anticommunist ideology, a product of the division (Kim and Kim 2007). Figure 7 shows the poster of a series of cartoon films called "Ttori changgun" (General Ttori), directed by Kim Ch'ŏng-ki, which premiered in 1978 (Dong-a Kwanggo, Inc. 1978).

Figure 1.7. "Ttori Changgun" Poster

A poster of the "Ttori Changgun" animated film series produced in the 1970s; retrieved from the National Museum of Korean Contemporary History digital archives

The poster includes phrases like "Come on, fight, destroy the red gang" and "full-length anticommunist cartoon film in full colors." The enemy is portrayed in non-human forms as a pig-looking monster wearing a red cloak (top right) and a pack of wolves (bottom left), among other zoomorphic representations. The director's personal experience of having watched the Communists taking away his father during the Korean War influenced him to produce anti-communist animations. This film was the first anti-communist animation to be shown in theaters and played a significant role in instilling anticommunist sentiments in children (Jang 2009). Under the division system, visual culture was mobilized by the anti-communist master narrative to consolidate the nation against the enemy.

These propaganda materials were intended to promote anticommunism and to keep the South Korean people, adults and children alike, vigilant and fearful about the threat of Communist North Korea so that they could always be ready to be called into battle should the conflict escalate. The condition of the division system enabled the hegemony of anticommunism, and portraying North Koreans as monsters was central to demonizing the enemy for the young South Korean audience living in the division system.

The Monster as Neighbor: North Koreans in Kwŏn's Trilogy

In Kwŏn's novels, the monster is not as clear as it is in the propaganda images above. The Communist North Korean enemy that was portrayed as evil monsters in visual representations is portrayed as neighbors, family, and friends in Kwŏn's Korean War trilogy. Kwŏn's novels problematize the South Korean state's anticommunist master narrative by humanizing the enemy, chronicling violence and atrocities committed by multiple perpetrators, and calling attention to the global Cold War structure.

One way in which Kwŏn depicts the enemy monster as human is by singling out individuals, and this separates individuals from the mass that is singularly identified as the "Other." In *Mongsil ŏnni*, protagonist Mongsil's encounters with individual North Korean soldiers challenge the propagandized image of North Korean soldiers as monsters. By this point in the story, Mongsil has been separated from her birth mother; her father has been conscripted into the South Korean army; her stepmother has died giving birth to her half-sister Nannam; and the North Korean side is occupying her village. When instructed to hoist the national flag, Mongsil finds a T'aegŭkki, the flag of South Korea, to put out in front of her house. Soon, a male soldier from the North Korean army runs up to her house and informs her that she needs to hoist the Inmin'gi, the flag of North Korea, alerting her that putting out the "wrong" flag, no matter which side has control of the village, can result in death. He also warns her not to tell anyone else about the fact that her father had been conscripted into the

South Korean army, which would also put her in danger. Rather than reporting her to the North Korean authorities, he shows empathy and helps her. Soon, they bid goodbye, and he tells them that he hopes to see Mongsil and Nannam again someday. When he leaves, Mongsil feels lonely: "The brief moment of human affection that the young North Korean soldier had shown her had created a sense of loneliness for Mongsil" (Kwŏn 2012b, 112; my trans.).[5] The precarious situation of the war is confusing, especially for the young protagonist. The person who is supposed to be the enemy of South Korea in the division system, a monster in the propaganda images, becomes a friend of the protagonist in this precarious circumstance.

Later that night, a group of female North Korean soldiers comes into Mongsil's neighborhood. One of the soldiers named Ch'oe Kŭmsun helps Mongsil by giving her food and keeping her company into the night. Mongsil asks Kŭmsun about the violence she has observed thus far in the war, and Kŭmsun explains as best she can. For young Mongsil, struggling to survive all alone with her infant half-sister in the midst of the war, this North Korean soldier feels like a mother figure. This contrasts with the depiction of the enemy as "scary," as depicted in the messages and images controlled by the state. Kŭmsun has to leave in the middle of the night, and her final words to Mongsil show how she cares for Mongsil's well-being: "I will leave some food at Janggol Grandma's house. Take good care of Nannam. And be strong. […] We might meet again one day, so please be well" (Kwŏn 2012b, 124; my trans.). Mongsil develops a sense of kinship and closeness with Kŭmsun. The narrative separates the individual from the group and gives a humanistic portrayal of and voice to the enemy. Through this portrayal of the Korean War that deviates from the anti-communist master narrative of the state, the enemy is individualized and given human characteristics and a voice. In portraying the enemy as individuals that Mongsil becomes friends with, Kwŏn challenges the construction of North Koreans as the monstrous Other.

Kwŏn's novels also raise the question of who the real monster is, or who the monsters are, in the war. Violence is committed by both sides of the war, which does not corroborate the propaganda images of the North Korean side as the monster. Mongsil witnesses both North Korean authorities and South Korean authorities killing innocent villagers for supporting the other side, in the precarious situation of the two sides taking turns occupying her village. To her question of which side is "good" and which side is "bad," Kŭmsun responds, "Mongsil, the truth is, they are all bad, and they are all good" (Kwŏn 2012b, 122;

---

[5] All translations of the excerpts from the three novels and other Korean sources are mine unless otherwise noted.

my trans.). She goes on to explain, "Among the South Korean Army, there are bad soldiers, and there are good soldiers. And it's the same with the North Korean Army, there are bad people, and there are good people" (ibid.; my trans.). In this answer and through Mongsil's experiences with North Korean soldiers, the binary that is expressed by each that their side is the only good side and the other side is perpetually bad is dismantled.

Both sides of the war committing violence are also observed by the children in *Ch'ogajibi ittŏn maul*. The village in the novel is located in the southeastern corner of the peninsula, a peaceful rural village where everyone knows one another and all the children are friends and classmates. When the war breaks out, some of the families in the village pack up and leave town, fleeing the incoming North Korean invasion. When the South Korean side starts to push back and regains control of the village, those who survived the refugee life on the road return home. Disputes regarding the invaders occur between the villagers who stayed and those who fled and returned. The children get into arguments as well. In an argument, Pokshik says to his friend Yujun, "I hate the Soviet tanks, too; but I also hate the American airplanes. It was the American airplanes that destroyed our school. You said it's okay for the American airplanes to destroy all of our lands as long as you survive, right? That's what you said, right?!" (Kwŏn 2016, 154; my trans.). In *Chŏmdŭgine*, Kwŏn shows how war and ideology turn people against each other, even friends and families. In the village in which Chŏmdŭk's family settles when they return to Korea from Manchuria, a few young men who sympathize with the communists leave their families and go to live in the mountains in communist guerrilla groups even before the full outbreak of the Korean War in June 1950; at the same time, other young men go join the "punitive expedition" to capture the communist guerrillas. This happens to Chŏmdŭk's older cousin Sŭngho and his friends: "Sŭngho's friends Hot'ae and Tongsu joined the punitive forces. They've gone out to catch Sŭngho. Friends from the same village are now enemies" (Kwŏn 2012a, 121; my trans.). Such tragedy also happens between family members: "That also happened at the market. The younger brother was a Commie, and the older brother was a policeman, and they fought and fired shots at each other. Aren't they afraid of the heavens?" (ibid.; my trans.). The division and escalating conflict based on ideological differences turn friends and family members against each other, and this condition drives people to become monsters who shoot at their own kin. The monsters in the propaganda materials, the Communists, are family and friends living in the same village. At the same time, the creators and consumers of those propaganda images also committed monstrous actions during the war.

In *Ch'ogajibi ittŏn maul*, while the villagers have to flee their homes because of the North Korean invasion, all of their homes are destroyed by the bombings of the UN forces: "Except for the outhouse shed in Pujŏn's house, all seventeen houses in the village had been bombed. The airplanes of the UN forces dropped bombs after bombs on the tunnel where they believed the North Korean soldiers were hiding, but those bombing raids had completely devastated the innocent village" (Kwŏn 2016, 221; my trans.). *Chŏmdŭgine* also shows similar bombings by the South Korean side. After the full-scale war starts, the North Korean side invades Chŏmdŭk's village. In retaliation, the South Korean side, together with the US and UN forces, begin their air raids: "The combined forces of the South Korean side flew in, shaking the sky and the earth. The bombardments did not cease" (Kwŏn 2012a, 144; my trans.). Through such portrayals of US and UN forces bombing villages during the Korean War, Kwŏn's novels bring attention to the larger global Cold War structure in which the Korean division and war occurred. The innocent villagers were left vulnerable to multifaceted sources of violence, and Kwŏn's novels thus question the singularity of the "Other" as a monster purported in propaganda images produced in South Korea. There were many violent monsters committing atrocities.

Kwŏn's novels' portrayal of the violence of the US military is indicative of historically factual events. One such episode happens in *Chŏmdŭgine*, which reveals the brutality of the war against ordinary villagers. One day, in the middle of the war, everyone in Chŏmdŭk's village is told to wear white clothing and gather at the eastern riverbank instead of going out to the fields to harvest the crops. Although orders to gather to provide labor needed by the troops occupying the village were common, it was unusual that the villagers were told to dress in a particular way. The villagers found this aspect to be strange, but they "could only listen in silence, since the only way to survive during the war was to obey, whether it was the North Korean Army or the South Korean Army that was giving the orders" (Kwŏn 2012a, 173; my trans.). While Chŏmdŭk's sister Chŏmnye and P'ansun, their friend with whom they live, stay home because they do not have white skirts to wear, Chŏmdŭk, his mother, P'ansun's brother Chongdae, and P'ansun's grandmother put on their white clothes and go to the gathering place where over five hundred people had gathered. Being told that they would be listening to a speech, they wait around for the speaker. Some time passes without anything happening, and with no indication of a speaker arriving, people start to get restless, having already experienced the horrors of the war. Suddenly, they hear airplane sounds.

Their white wings shining under the sunlight, the airplane flew ahead of its sound. Flying right above the riverbank, it circled over the area where people were gathered. One plane, two planes, three planes, four planes—a total of four planes circled above the riverbank in the same motion as if they were showing off their tricks.

People's eyes circled around, following the circling airplanes. With thunderous sounds, the four airplanes flew down even lower, flying right above people's heads.

People were suddenly seized with fear. They covered their ears with their hands; those who were sitting crouched down even lower, lying on their stomachs; those who were standing hid their bodies in the grass field as if they were falling down. However, all of that was useless. The airplanes nosedived and began to pour down bombs on the group of people dressed in white.

In the midst of the sounds of all the skies and all the grounds shaking and breaking, people began to cry and shout. Fire rose up like clouds, and dust storms and rocks soared, turning the riverbank into hell in the blink of an eye. (Kwŏn 2012a, 176-177; my trans.)

Chŏmdŭk and his family clamor in confusion, falling over, being pushed over, and people try to escape, "but the airplanes clung on to the people with the determination of hunting dogs" (Kwŏn 2012a, 177; my trans.). The US warplanes begin dropping bombs on the villagers who had been told to gather "until all of the people dressed in white had collapsed and stopped moving" (Kwŏn 2012a, 179; my trans.). This episode in *Chŏmdŭgine* evokes historically factual incidents of massacres committed by the US military during the Korean War. The most widely known incident is the No Gun Ri massacre, in which US troops shot and killed South Korean civilians near a bridge in No Gun Ri.[6] In such mass killings, people are dehumanized—the murdered civilians are depicted as "a freshly plowed rice field" (Kwŏn 2012a, 180; my trans.). The war pushed all people into a dehumanized state, and both sides committed monstrous atrocities during the war.

Kwŏn's novels also show how war creates the potential for anyone to lose their sense of empathy and humanity, living in a state of vulnerability. Neighbors, friends, and family members become monsters during the war. In *Ch'ogajibi ittŏn*

---

[6] Asia Society Center for Global Education's page "Massacre at Nogun-ri" goes over the story of how AP uncovered the story, and the drama that ensued as some of their evidence showed to be false. Ultimately, the US military admitted to the killings of civilians near No Gun Ri in South Korea during the war (Holland, n.d.). Dong Choon Kim (2004) examines the No Gun Ri incident, along with other mass killings of civilians by the US and South Korean forces during the Korean War. Suhi Choi (2008) examines how the story of No Gun Ri has come to be forgotten again in the US media by silencing South Korean survivors' counter-narratives.

maul, the protagonist kids and their families come across an apple orchard near one of their refugee camps on the road while fleeing the war. As the attacks get closer to the area and people start to go hungry, people begin to lose their sense of rationality and steal all the apples from the orchard: "All of the apples that were shining in the sunlight getting plump just up to a moment ago, were all stolen by strangers. Nothing could be done about it" (Kwŏn 2016, 89; my trans.). In the midst of the war, life on the road as refugees, and the hunger that ensued, people lose their sense of ethics, turning into "beasts" and taking whatever food they can find, even if it means stealing: "This is what war is. People, all these people wrangling over food like beasts in order to survive…" (ibid.; my trans.). The conditions of the war turn people into monsters.

People, by choice or otherwise, also turn into images of animals in war. When the war breaks out, young men are conscripted into the South Korean army. In *Ch'ogajibi ittŏn maul*, Kŭmdong and his family witness a group of young men being rounded up and dragged onto a truck to be sent off to fight. The young men being loaded into a truck are compared to "chickens being loaded into a cart with their legs tied up to be dragged to the market" (Kwŏn 2016, 94; my trans.). In *Chŏmdŭgine*, Chŏmdŭk's older cousin Sŭngho, who joins the communist guerrillas, is eventually killed in a massacre of all the communists after they attack a US military base. When Sŭngho is caught and dragged away by the South Korean soldiers, "Chŏmdŭk remembered the sight of Sŭngho being bound by a rope and dragged away like a dog by the soldiers" (Kwŏn 2012a, 168; my trans.). In an episode in *Mongsil ŏnni*, crowds are gathered to watch the North Korean Army killing their prisoners. The North Korean side has control of Mongsil's village and its neighboring ones, and they imprison the individuals who had been in leadership positions in town when the South Korean side was in charge of it, including the chief of the town and the police constable. One day, as the sun was setting, the North Korean soldiers bring them out to execute them. Despite the pleas not to kill them, the executions get carried out. In the hues of the setting sun, everyone in the scene becomes monstrous: "The sunset became entirely blood-red, dyeing the faces of everyone there. With their scarlet red faces looking strange and bizarre like those of goblins, people resembled beasts" (Kwŏn 2012b, 114; my trans.). This imagery epitomizes how everyone becomes a monster in the midst of war.

The Real Monsters According to Kwŏn

In problematizing the South Korean state's anticommunist master narrative, Kwŏn's novels reflect the author's philosophy of nonalignment, peace, and nonviolence by pointing out the global Cold War structure as the real monster to the Korean people.[7] Kwŏn speaks through various characters throughout the three novels. In *Mongsil ŏnni*, to Mongsil's question about why the two sides are killing each other, Kŭmsun, the female North Korean soldier that Mongsil befriends, responds that both are good and both are bad:

> "All humans, even people meeting for the first time, can become good friends when they meet as human beings. These words might be a little difficult for you, but when people meet, and they are thinking about statuses or positions or profits, they can become bad. The South Korean army and the North Korean army, when they meet each other as soldiers, they are enemies, so they try to kill each other. But if they meet as human beings, they wouldn't be able to kill each other," explained Kŭmsun. (Kwŏn 2012b, 122; my trans.)

Kŭmsun's words seem to carry the author's own beliefs about war and violence, emphasizing the need to see the other as individual humans.

In *Ch'ogajibi ittŏn maul*, the children's school teacher explains that a war broke out between the two Koreas. He laments, "You may not understand yet, but I'm very sad that the same Korean people are at war with each other. Why did this happen? You must study hard and find out why this tragedy has happened" (Kwŏn 2016, 55; my trans.). Through the teacher's words, Kwŏn expresses his question of why Koreans are fighting against each other, their own people, in this civil war. Towards the end of the story, a new person moves into the village, and the children call him "Mr. Raccoon." Mr. Raccoon is from the northern part of the peninsula, but he moved down south when the war broke out and settled there. Even though he misses his hometown, he does not go back to the north. The children ask him why he is staying in South Korea, and the conversation turns into a question about ideologies:

> "And why do we have to quibble about if communism is good or capitalism is good, and why do we have to fight with guns and swords…"
>
> "So, what you're saying is capitalism isn't bad either?" asked Pokshik.

---

[7] Kwŏn's philosophy is most well-reflected in his poem "Aegukchaga ŏmnŭn sesang [A world without patriots]," in which he longs for a world without patriots and nationalists because such a world would mean a peaceful world where young people would not have to go to war to fight, and "cannons wouldn't be made / tanks wouldn't be made / nuclear weapons wouldn't be made" (Kwŏn 2000; my trans.).

"That's it. Capitalism or communism, each person can have good ideas for oneself and so everyone should have the freedom to make that their way of life," answered Mr. Raccoon.

"Then what's your ideology?" Pokshik prodded on.

"I don't have an ideology. If I had to choose, I'm a humanist."

"What's humanism?"

"It's where you value humans more than ideologies. It's not confining people to certain ideologies, but putting people above those ideologies. Simply put, humans come first, before capitalism, before communism." (Kwŏn 2016, 288-289; my trans.)

Kwŏn speaks through Mr. Raccoon's words, revealing his belief that ideological divides cause war and violence. For Kwŏn, these ideologies are the monsters.

Another situational monster that Kwŏn points to through the dialogues in the books is the continuing colonial condition of the Korean peninsula. At the beginning of *Chŏmdŭgine*, Chŏmdŭk's family was crossing the Amnok River (Yalu River), moving back to their homeland from Manchuria after Korea is liberated. When they are crossing the river, their father gets shot by a Soviet soldier who spots them and dies. The old lady who helps Chŏmdŭk, Chŏmnye, and their mother makes a comment about how Korea has not been liberated yet: "If we really were liberated, then why are the Soviets killing people? Now, the Soviets have taken over Korea in place of the Japanese. The Americans have taken over the south side. Only the owners have changed" (Kwŏn 2012a, 19; my trans.). Following Korea's liberation from Japanese colonial rule, the Korean peninsula was immediately divided at the thirty-eighth parallel through international political negotiations, with the USSR occupying the northern half of the peninsula and the US occupying the southern half. As such, gaining independence from Japan did not signify autonomy for Korea but rather neocolonial conditions under the Soviet Union and the US. Kuan-Hsing Chen argues that in the Cold War, "capitalist East Asia was pressured to avoid conflict within the anti-communist camp. Historical issues of Japanese colonialism in Taiwan and Korea could not be tackled because the Japanese, South Korean, and Taiwanese states were locked into the pro-American side; to address such historical issues would have entailed confronting internal contradictions within the capitalist bloc" (2010, 121). The end of the Japanese colonial period concurred with the onset of the Cold War, which obstructed the decolonization process and continued the colonial condition in South Korea. East Asia is thus still in "the shadow of colonialist and cold-war structures" because decolonization and the "de-cold-war process" are "two aspects of the same historical project" that have yet to be resolved (ibid., 123). Through his novels, Kwŏn points out the global Cold War structure that keeps Korea under a neocolonial system as a monster that causes the Korean people to suffer, challenging South Korea's master narrative of Communist North Korea as the singular monster.

Conclusion

This essay shows how Kwŏn Chŏng-saeng's Korean War trilogy is significant as a counter-narrative to the national master narrative that portrays the North Korean enemy as the monstrous Other. Propaganda leaflets during the war reveal the monster's characterization. After the Armistice in 1953, anticommunism became integral in the nation's education system, as seen in the textbooks, school curriculum, and other materials produced by the state for school-aged children. Children were made to be participants in the anticommunist endeavors, as exemplified by anti-communist posters and slogan contests. Children were further exposed to the dehumanization of North Koreans in animated films like "Ttori Changgun."

Within and against these state-led anti-communist initiatives and propaganda, children's literature often created room for the production of counter-narratives, as represented by Kwŏn's youth novels. *Mongsil ŏnni, Ch'ogajibi ittŏn maul,* and *Chŏmdŭgine* focus on the lived experiences of vulnerable individuals, particularly the poor villagers in rural South Korea, whose stories had not been allowed to be narrativized or legitimized within the state's anti-communist agenda. Kwŏn reveals the complicated and complex nature of wars, ultimately advocating for peace and a world without violence through his works. Showing both sides of the war committing atrocities against friends, families, and neighbors of the protagonists, these three youth novels challenge the propaganda images produced in South Korea in which the communist North Korean side is presented as the monster. Kwŏn points out that in war, there is no singular monster that perpetrates violence; there are multiple entities that kill, bomb, and destroy, and there are various victims of such violence. Furthermore, in a war, anyone can become a monster who commits or participates in violent incidents due to the circumstances. Kwŏn's Korean War trilogy illustrates that in the realities of the war, the "good" side and the "bad" side are not as clear as they are portrayed in the propaganda images.

Bibliography

Backer, Kristen Williams. 2007. *"Kultur-Terror:* The Composite Monster in Nazi Visual Propaganda." In *Monsters and the Monstrous: Myths and Metaphors of Enduring Evil,* edited by Niall Scott, 81-101. Amsterdam: Brill, 2007. Accessed August 3, 2022. https://search.ebscohost.com/login.aspx?direct=true&db=e0 25xna&AN=211909&site=ehost-live.

Changbi Publishers. n.d. "Chŏmdŭgine." Accessed August 30, 2022. https://w ww. changbi.com/BookDetail?bookid=2199.

Chen, Kuan-Hsing. 2010. *Asia as Method: Toward Deimperialization.* Durham and London: Duke University Press.

Choi, Suhi. 2008. "Silencing Survivors' Narratives: Why Are We *Again* Forgetting the No Gun Ri Story?" *Rhetoric and Public Affairs* 11, no. 3 (Fall): 367-388. https://www.jstor.org/stable/41940374.

Cohen, Jeffrey Jerome. 2020. "Monster Culture (Seven Theses)." In *The Monster Theory Reader,* edited by Jeffrey Andrew Weinstock, 37-56. Minneapolis: University of Minnesota Press.

Dong-a Kwanggo, Inc. 1978. "Ttori Changgun Che 3 Ttanggulp'yŏn [General Ttori: The Third Tunnel]." Retrieved from the National Museum of Korean Contemporary History digital archives. Accessed August 3, 2022. http://arc hive.much.go.kr/archive/nrms/view.do?idnbr=PS01002025001-005200-00000.

Holland, Elisa Joy. n.d. "Massacre at Nogun-ri." Asia Society. Accessed August 18, 2022. https://asiasociety.org/education/massacre-nogun-ri.

Hughes, Theodore. 2012. *Literature and Film in Cold war South Korea: Freedom's Frontier.* New York: Columbia University Press.

Jang, Yeon-Yi [Chang Yŏn-I]. 2009. "A Study for Expressing the Image of Anticommunistic Ideology Reflected in <Ttori Jangun>." *Cartoon and Animation Studies,* no. 15: 109-122.

Kim, Dong Choon. 2004. "Forgotten war, forgotten massacres—the Korean War (1950-1953) as licensed mass killings." *Journal of Genocide Research* 6, no. 4 (December): 523-544. Accessed August 18, 2022. DOI: 10.1080/1462 3520420003 20592.

Kim, Jeung-Yeun [Kim Chŏng-yŏn] and Jae-Woong Kim [Kim Chae-ung]. 2007. "Effect and Acculturation of Korean Animation by Policy of Korean Culture." *Jour. of KoCon.a* 7, no. 12: 55-65.

Kim, Sung-Jin [Kim Sŏng-chin]. 2008. "Adong ch'ŏngsonyŏn munhakŭi chŏngjŏn'gwa Kwŏn Chŏng-saengŭi 'hanguk chŏnjaeng 3pujak [The Canons of Korean Children's and Young Adults' Literature and Kwon Jeong-saeng's 'Trilogy of the Korean War'].'" *Munhakgyoyukhak* 25: 487-512.

Kwŏn, Chŏng-saeng. 2000. "Aegukchaga ŏmnŭn sesang [A world without patriots]." *Noksaekp'yŏngnon* [Green View], no. 55.

Kwŏn, Chŏng-saeng. 2012a. *Chŏmdŭgine* [Chŏmdŭk's family]. 2nd ed. P'aju: Changbi Publishers. First published 1990.

Kwŏn, Chŏng-saeng. 2012b. *Mongsil ŏnni* [My Sister Mongsil]. 4th ed. P'aju: Changbi Publishers. First published 1984.

Kwŏn, Chŏng-saeng. 2016. *Ch'ogajibi ittŏn maul* [The village with thatched houses]. Seoul: Bundo Publishers. First published 1985.

Lee, Namhee. 2002. "Anticommunism, North Korea, and Human Rights in South Korea: 'Orientalist' Discourse and Construction of South Korean Identity." In *Truth Claims: Representation and Human Rights*, edited by Mark Philip Bradley and Patrice Petro, 43-71. New Brunswick: Rutgers University Press.

Lee, Namhee. 2007. *The Making of Minjung: Democracy and the Politics of Representation in South Korea*. Ithaca: Cornell University Press.

Ministry of Public Information. 1966. "Pongnamiga marhanŭn aktok'an kongsandang [The Vicious Communist Party according to Pongnam]." Retrieved from the National Museum of Korean Contemporary History digital archives. Accessed August 3, 2022. http://archive.much.go.kr/archive/nr ms/view.do?idnbr=PS01002025008-004218-00000.

Moon, Seungsook. 2005. *Militarized Modernity and Gendered Citizenship in South Korea*. Durham: Duke University Press.

Paik, Nak-chung. 2011. *The Division System in Crisis: Essays on Contemporary Korea*. Edited by Bruce Cumings. Translated by Kim Myung-hwan, Sol June-Kyu, Song Seung-cheon, and Ryu Young-joo. Berkeley and Los Angeles: University of California Press.

Shin, Gi-Wook. 2006. *Ethnic Nationalism in Korea: Genealogy, Politics, and Legacy*. Stanford: Stanford University Press.

U.S. Army Special Operations Command History Office. 2020. "Psywar Leaflets from the Korean War: The J.B. Haynes Leaflet Collection, 1st Radio Broadcasting & Leaflet Group." Accessed September 6, 2022. https://arsof-history.org/articles/19dec_1st_rbl_leaflet_collection_page_1.html.

UNO Digital Humanities Projects. 2016. "Stop This Monster Propaganda Poster." Created c. 1941-1945 by Office for Emergency Management, Office of War Information, Domestic Operations Branch, and Bureau of Special Services. Accessed September 6, 2022. https://unodigitalhumanitiesprojects.omeka.ne t/items/show/32.

Vallée, Cécile. 2012. "Monsters and Clowns Incorporated: the Representations of Adolf Hitler in British and American WWII Propaganda Posters." *Revue LISA/LISA e-journal* 10, no. 1: 126-150. Accessed August 3, 2022. https://doi.org/10.4000/lisa.4880.

Yi, Myŏng-chu. 2021. "Tangshini poji mot'an han'gukchŏnjaeng: ②shimnijŏn… chŭngoŭi yusan [The Korean War That You Haven't Seen: 2. Psychological Warfare… Legacy of Hatred]." KCIJ-Newstapa, July 27, 2021. https://newsta pa.org/article/44Ata.

Zur, Dafna. 2009. "Whose War Were We Fighting? Constructing Memory and Managing Trauma in South Korean Children's Fiction." *International Research in Children's Literature* 2, no. 2 (December): 192-209. Accessed July 27, 2022. https://doi.org/10.3366/e1755619809000696.

Chapter 2

Weaponizing Monstrosity: Starz's *Black Sails* and the Power of Monstrous Narrative

Min-Chi Chen

Binghamton University, State University of New York

Abstract: Opening the television series with the declaration of pirates as *hostis humani generis* (enemies of all mankind) according to the laws of every civilized nation, Starz's *Black Sails* (2014-2017), a prequel to Robert Louis Stevenson's *Treasure Island*, and centering on piracy on New Providence Island, questions the traditional label for pirates as inhuman monsters in the early eighteenth century. The main characters in *Black Sails* embody the monsters that the British Empire defined to ensure the boundary between civilization and the uncivilized. By narrating the story from the perspective of the pirates, the television series not only reveals how the colonial narrative in the Golden Age of piracy shaped the concept of monsters but also portrays a variety of characters that understand the social construction of monstrosity, seizing control of the process of creating social meaning out of monstrosity through their bodies. *Black Sails* is thus more than a representation of the pirates as monstrous bodies; it exposes the narrative mechanism that defines monstrosity and depicts the possibilities of weaponizing monstrosity through the monstrous bodies once its audience understands the power of narrative.

Keywords: popular culture, television studies, media and film studies, cultural studies, monster studies

***

What is a monster? One of the paradoxes when analyzing human monsters onscreen is that, although the monster the viewers witnessed is both the manifestation of cultural stylization and a real-life figure that bears the cultural projection, the analysis of monsters often one-sidedly emphasizes monsters as cultural representation. For example, Robin Wood (2002) states that the monster's figure in horror films is "the dual concept of the repressed/the Other" (28), and Jeffrey Cohen (1996) emphasizes that the vampire's "monstrous body" is a cultural construct and projection (4). Both scholars reflect the perspective of monsters being a cultural or social phenomenon. While Marina Levina and

Diem-My T. Bui (2013) propose that monstrosity in the twenty-first century "has transcended its status as a metaphor" and serves "as a representation of change itself," their reading of monster and monstrosity omits the relationship between the representation and the visual figure presenting the cultural meaning (2).

The rupture between the figure and the figure of speech becomes the center of the biopolitical approach of monster studies. Analyzing the historical understanding of human monsters, Alexa Wright (2019) notices that the morphology of the body of modern monsters, such as serial killers, no longer visualizes their monstrosity. Although monster (the individual subject/object), monstrosity, and monstrousness are still a triad, it is the monstrous acts–the invisible behavior–that define the monster in contemporary society (Wright 2019, 4, 6-7). The concept of monster changes with the shift of defining monstrosity from monstrous body to monstrous act. As Andrea Torrano (2020) has argued, in modernity, the understanding of monsters is directly related to politics. In recent years, the monsters can signify either "the subjectivities that are constituted as monsters by the biopower" or "the capacity of some subjectivities to confront the biopower and create forms of life that reproduce neither the capitalist system nor gender and racial hierarchies" (134). In this sense, the distinction between different understandings of monsters–monster as a product of a mechanism and monster as a subjectivity that confronts the mechanism–lies in the approaches toward the figure that becomes the visualization of the monster. Given that the exact human figure can be defined as a monster by the power or resistance to the power depending on the perspectives, how the monster can be understood is more important than the human-monster figure. On the one hand, the changing perspectives free the human-monster on screen from being judged by morphology; on the other hand, they render the human-monster figure more vulnerable–for to be involved in the contemporary reading of monsters, one must not only understand the relationship between the monster and the power but aware of the narrative that shapes the figure into a monster. More often than not, the monsters on screen are monsters because they are defined by the narrative. There is no acknowledgment of the monsters' *raison d'etre,* neither from the narrative nor from the defined monsters.

I want to suggest that it is precisely the relationship between the power, the monster, and the narrative in making the monster that is highlighted by Starz's *Black Sails* (2014-2017). While no non-human monsters exist in the series, *Black Sails* constantly stresses how the British Empire culturally constructs criminal transgressors as monsters and questions the stereotypical understanding of pirates in the early eighteenth century. The narrative of the series, involving the historical, political, and epistemological perspectives of the storytelling on the monster, shows its understanding of the meaning of the monster on multiple levels. In the series, as in history, the British Empire uses the narrative of pirates as monsters to ensure the boundary between civilization and the uncivilized. Since the "monsters" presented in the story and on-screen are familiar with the mechanism of making monsters, they are able to confront the civilization that creates them. The way that the series overturns the audience's view on monstrous characters by changing narratives is a reminder that the colonial narrative in the Golden Age of Piracy created the concept of monsters through legitimate narration and perspectives about the pirates. At the same time, the audience's active participation in changing their perspective is as crucial as the official narrative in creating social meaning out of monstrosity through pirates' bodies. *Black Sails* is thus more than a representation of the pirate as a monstrous body: it exposes the narrative mechanism that defines monstrosity and highlights the possibilities to weaponize monstrosity through the monstrous bodies once the audience understands the power driven by visual narrative.

As a television series, Black Sails constantly prompts its audience to notice how its narrative works. The second episode of the first season presents a scene that seems irrelevant to any plot at the time. The quartermaster and bosun of Captain Flint witness two men arguing over the value of two paintings on the street of Nassau. One of them, the pirate captain Naft, is attempting to convince the appraiser that a copy of Dutch painter Adriaen Hanneman is the same as the original painting by pointing out that both works include "fruit," "tits," and "plant" (Steinberg and Levine 2015, 00:22:04-00:22:15). The appraiser responded with a painful look, claiming, "[to] suggest that the value of [the forgery] has any bearing on [Hanneman's work] simply strains the very bounds of reason" (00:22:26-00:22:40). The appraiser does not further explain the differences between the two paintings–with the poorly forged painting and Hannenman's work displayed side by side, the insistence of Captain Naft looks ridiculous for the appraiser and the audience–Flint's quartermaster and bosun. It is a scene that invites the audience of the series to join in the laughter. However, the insignificant scene becomes more meaningful when considering the connection between value and visual representation. The conversation between Captain Naft and the appraiser reflects that the two have divergent standards for the artwork. While the judgment of value is supposed to be based on the visuality of the paintings, the appraiser values Hannenman's work by something other than visual similarity and visual representation. In "What Is Wrong with a Forgery?" Alfred Lessing (1965) argues that when an artwork's historical context is considered as a part of the artwork's genuinity, the compared forgery loses its individuality (466-467). In this sense, although Captain Naft is ridiculed for his inability to tell the different values between the apparently fake and Hannenman's work, Naft is also correct: the two paintings can be "the same" if his standard of visual representation is the official judgment of value. Considering *Black Sails* is a television series prequel to Robert Louis Stevenson's *Treasure Island*, a representation of the pirates' fictional image in the Golden Age of Piracy, the short scene becomes self-referential.

Even though the series does not straightforwardly connect the pirates with monsters at the show's beginning, *Black Sails* begins by stating the stereotypical image of pirates from the perspective of colonial duality. The series starts with a declaration in words: "1715 West Indies...The laws of every civilized nation declare [the pirates] *hostis humani generis*—enemies of all mankind. In response, the pirates adhere to a doctrine of their own... war against the world" (Steinberg and Levine 2014, 00:00:11-00:00:35). The legal phrase *hostis humani generis*, originated from the admiralty law, signifies the special status of pirates as criminals in legal history. Looking into the legal perception of maritime piracy, Christopher Harding (2007) points out that pirates become a distinctive type of offender because maritime power came to a broad agreement that "all states were equally able, and equally obliged, to exercise jurisdiction, both to apprehend pirates and bring them to trial" (22). In other words, the term "enemies of all mankind" reflects the outlaw status of pirates. By participating in the act of piracy, the pirate becomes someone who is deprived of protection from their national identity, whom every maritime power can bring to justice anywhere. While the Latin term states the pirates as enemies of "all mankind," what they really become are the enemies of all "civilized nations." Here, the intertitle presents the very reason pirates become monsters: the dialectical relationship created by the civilized nation.

The cold opening of the pilot then displays the pirate's retaliation–their "war against the world" that fades out last in the intertitle. The series begins with the image of two vessels on the open sea, a seemingly boundless and lawless space. The scene quickly cuts to a closer look at the ships. The one more recognizable for the audience is flying Red Ensign with a Union Jack, a flag limited by law to privateers and privately owned vessels chartered by the Royal Navy, and a reminder that even on the open water, the empire and its law travels with its human agents.[1] Through the perspective of the merchant ship captain's telescope on the black sails of the other ship and the subordinate's report of the inevitability of escaping the pursuit, the meaning of "war against the world" in the intertitle comes to light. In the maritime legal order, European polities and jurists recognized the ship's law as a broadly similar configuration to the law of European sovereigns (Benton 2005, 704). In this setting, a vessel of a particular nation is a miniature of its society on the sea. Therefore, the pirate's attack on

---

[1] See Mary II, and William III, *By the King and Queen, a Proclamation, Concerning Colours to Be Worn on Board Ships* (London: printed by Charles Bill and the executrix of Thomas Newcomb deceas'd; printers to the King and Queens most excellent Majesties, 1694). During the Golden Age of piracy, there was more than one form of the Red Ensign flag. The English merchant vessels were entitled to fly a Red Ensign with a small St. George's Cross. Only vessels of the Royal Navy were entitled to use Red Ensign with a Union Jack.

the vessel declares war against "the world" in multiple ways. For the pirates, the vessel not merely signifies the "civilized" society on the open water. It is the British Empire, the system that defined "the world." Through the scene, the connection between pirates being declared as the enemies of "all mankind" and their doctrine of war against "the world" is visualized. In the world of *Black Sails*, the civilized nation *is* humankind and the world. As a result, to be a pirate, one loses the right to be considered a human being and their place in the civilized world.

The monstrous image of the pirates is, of course, the designed narrative of the series. As a part of the narrating device, the camera of the television series not only selects what is shown to the audience but rules how the story is presented (Allrath and Gymnich 2005, 13-14). The scenes involved in ship battles are fixated on the terror the merchant ship's crew experienced when under attack and continue to present the pirates as enemies of the civilized world until the end of the cold opening. From the point of view of the merchant ship crew, Captain Flint's crew brings chaos to the order and slaughters the sailors ruthlessly and cold-bloodedly. The howling and the sound of ritual from the invaders, accompanied by the usage of explosives on the ship, all support the declaration by the law of civilized nations–that the pirates are indeed enemies of all humankind. The chaos ceases suddenly when someone in Flint's crew stops his crewmate from killing the merchant ship captain on site. The masked character blocks the blow and tells the attacker that the assault "is done," then turns, revealing his face, and asks if the merchant captain agrees (Steinberg and Levine 2014, 00:06:32-00:06:46). Here, the narrative of the story has its first twist. Despite painting as the opposite of the civilized world, the fact that the pirates are able to drop their attack indicates that their monstrous slaughtering is not mindless and serves a purpose. The removal of the mask from the specific character becomes a visual reminder of the existence and the perspective of the narrative. The monstrosity that the audience witnessed until that point, just like the mask literally masks the face of the character, is the mask of something other than meaningless violence.

Following the removal of the mask is the entering of the title sequences. As Georg Stanitzek (2009) has argued, while the title sequence does not directly link to the plot, it sets the mood and the course of the plot (49). The elements in the title sequence, inspired by Pablo Genoves's photography of the architecture that represented European power being destroyed by water, are related to the series' background setting as well as its atmosphere. The style of Baroque and Rococo links the tableaux in the sequence to the eighteenth-century architecture, cathedrals, and palaces that once hosted power and authority. Knowing the series is set in the golden age of piracy with the pirates doomed to lose their battle with civilization, the Creative Directors and the Art Director arrange the opening and ending of title sequences with the image of dark water–an indication that the pirates' world and way of life will meet its dark ending. The images are also designed to show the duality between the icons of European power and pirates: "the youth of a maiden opposite a symbol of death, Europe vs. the 'exotic' colony cultures, land vs. sea, [and] the court vs. lawlessness… a hybrid world of old and new" (Landekic 2014). Strengthening the dualistic image of the pirate versus the civilized world and making it dubious whether the series stands with the pirates or the European-civilized power, the title sequence flips the narrative set by the cold opening again.

The ambiguity truthfully presents the historical image of pirates. Although the pirates were portrayed as particularly cruel, violent, and brutal creatures, it is an image that the Admiralty of England constructed in the eighteenth century. For example, in the seventeenth century, pirates were often referred to as buccaneers. Buccaneers were originally French hunters living on Hispaniola (modern-day Haiti). They turned into hunters of Spanish shipping after 1630 when Spain tried to drive the hunters away by wiping out the wild animals on Hispaniola and Tortuga. At the same time, seeing the buccaneer's behavior as a chance to break Spain's maritime monopoly, English and France commissioned buccaneers and privateers to harass Spain (Leeson 2009, 7-8). As the Admiralty stopped supporting buccaneers in the eighteenth century, pirates lost their legal support and public sympathy from the English government.

Even if the audience of *Black Sails* might not be familiar with the historical change of the meaning of pirates, the narrative of the series delivers it through the switch of perspectives. The scene of the aftermath of the hijack displays the life of pirates. In the previous scene, a sailor with African heritage who terrified the merchant ship crews to the point that he depletes their willpower to fight back is now shown playfully jump-scaring Flint's quartermaster and being chided as childish. Terrorizing and childish, the contrasting portrayal of the specific sailor's image in the eyes of the merchant ship crew and the pirate crew corroborates with the unmasked character's claim that the pirates have achieved their purpose. The monstrous violence and terrorizing images are indeed the means to force the captain to surrender the ship.

The violent behavior of the pirates is not the only stereotype that the series overturned. The narrative then focuses on the pirate who almost killed the merchant ship captain. He is preaching to the merchant ship crews, criticizing the tyranny of the captain and the meager wages, creating the impression of him being Captain Flint. However, when the plot shows Flint's quartermaster discussing the net income of their haul after injury payment with the accountant and the captain, the narrative shows that the notorious Captain Flint is the character who saved the life of the merchant ship captain and revealed his face to the audience. This particular captain who terrorizes the merchant sailors just by his name and banner is also on the verge of losing his captaincy in the upcoming vote because of the low profits the crews have earned in a row. Not in favor of his crew, Flint cannot even call off his crew to take out their anger on the merchant ship captain. The camera reverses the established impressions, showing not only that the fearsome pirate Captain Flint is more "civilized" and willing to communicate but also the different power structures between the pirate ship and the merchant ship. When the merchant ship captain realizes Flint cannot prevent his crew from torturing him, the captain accuses Flint of being a captain with "no control" over his crew (Steinberg and Levine 2014, 00:14:47-00:15:08). The disbelief of the merchant ship captain is rooted in the fact that the merchant ship operates under the law of European sovereigns. At sea, the merchant ship captains are authorities who hold semi-autonomy in judicial matters (Benton 2005, 704). As Peter Leeson (2009) pointed out, the pirates in the Golden Age of Piracy developed democracy and a system with institutionally separated power. Unlike the power hierarchy on merchant ships, which sustains the social hierarchy of the nation they belong to, the pirate ships operate under "one pirate, one vote" democracy (29). While the captain of a pirate ship is the one who maintains order, distributes payments, and imposes discipline on the ship, the pirate crew can depose the captain for reasons they see fit. Hence, between the merchant ship captain and the pirate ship captain Flint, the merchant ship captain is the one who has absolute control of his crew members. The complaint of the merchant ship captain calls the audience's attention to the order he has given since they engaged with Flint's crew. Not only did the merchant ship captain force his crew to fight back, but he also prevented his crew from taking shelter behind the barricade, leading them to be slaughtered. When compared to Captain Flint stopping his crew from murdering the merchant ship captain on sight, the scenes raise the question of which captain is crueler toward his crew. The fact that Flint is facing the consequence of losing his captaincy because of the poor profit proves what Flint's challenger has been preaching to the merchant ship crew to be true: crews of "enemy of all mankind" have more autonomy, political freedom, and economic freedom than the legitimate sailors.

The unmasking of Captain Flint hence marks the reveal of the complex layers of "pirate." The flip of perspectives at the very beginning of the pilot (all these scenes happen within fifteen minutes) is, on the one hand, a visual demonstration reminding the audience that the impression of the image of pirates depends on colonial duality. On the other hand, a more subtle memento indicates the relationship between the impression of pirates and the way the audience perceives them. The stress on the democratic system and the existence of injury payment on pirate ships immediately put "civilization" and "pirate," two meanings that are supposedly placed on opposite sides of dualism, at odds. For the modern audience watching *Black Sails*, the pirate's life experience is more progressive and advanced than the merchant ship sailor and fits more to the meaning of civilization nowadays. Through this gap between historical truth and stereotypical understanding of pirate's monstrosity, the series exposes the mechanism that shapes the audience's definition of monsters.

The shifting narrative that introduces the audience to different perspectives of the pirates in the pilot adds another meaning to the argument between Captain Naft and the appraiser. Just as Hanneman's painting and its forgery are compared and judged for their authenticity, the creators of *Black Sails* are aware that the image of pirates on the screen will be judged for its authenticity. However, since Captain Naft is derided for his inability to distinguish the two paintings, the series poses a dilemma for the audience, whether they can tell the difference between the forgery and the authentic image of pirates. As I have demonstrated previously, some images of the pirates portrayed in *Black Sails* are based on historical truth. Some characters, such as Captain Flint and his bosun Billy Bones, are the fictional creation of Stevenson, and others, like Charles Vane and Jack Rackham, are the fictionalized version of historical pirates. If, as the appraiser and the audience of the scene believed, the authenticity of the image roots in the historical context that created it, then the changing narrative that overturns the audience's understanding of the pirates by interweaving history and fiction is a challenge to the monstrous image of pirates in history told by the Admiralty.

Black Sails does not simply show the civilization's monster as a construct and a projection through its narrative. It also engages in how civilization creates its monster by its character design. Captain Flint is one of the first characters who call out how the British Empire established its legitimacy through the pirates' monstrosity. The home base of the pirates in the series is New Providence's Nassau in 1715, which was temporary without an English governor but under the threat of the British Empire taking back control. After an early hostile encounter with the British Navy in episode "I," Flint blatantly warns his bosun Billy Bones that when the king declares them as pirates, "he means to make [them monsters], for that's the only way his God-fearing, taxpaying subjects can make sense" of the pirates.[2] Moreover, the "civilization" is waging a war, aiming to "exterminate" the pirates (Steinberg and Levine 2014, 00:52:33-00:52:51). On one level, Flint's speech resonates with the historical transformation of pirates becoming enemies of all humankind. Tracing the historical and political usage of pirates, Douglas Burgess Jr. (2009) notes that the two Henry Every trials in the fall of 1696 marked the shift of the crown's anti-piracy policy as well as the usage of media manipulation, documenting England's attempt to create "a dominant historical narrative on piracy" (894). On the records, the Board of Trade and the Admiralty attempted to cast the infamous pirate captain Every

---

[2] *Black Sails*, "I," 00:52:33-00:52:51.

as a traitor to England to deny the Empire's key trading partner Great Mughal's accusation that England was sponsoring pirates (894). Interestingly, *Black Sails* also introduces the history of piracy of Nassau with Every. The second season reveals that Captain Flint was once a naval officer and the liaison from the Admiralty for Thomas Hamilton, the son of the Lord Proprietor of the Bahamas, whose task was to regain the English governance of Nassau. In episode "IX," Lord Hamilton introduced Nassau's history to Flint, saying it "started with a man named Henry Avery" (Steinberg and Levine 2015, 00:16:50-00:17:10). The explanation of Nassau's piracy, set in 1705 in the series, indicates that in *Black Sails*, England's effort of dominating the historical narrative on piracy since the Every trials in 1696 have paid off.

On another level, Flint's acknowledgment of the binary meaning of civilization and monstrosity created by the British Empire in the pilot hints at how much Flint understands the policy and media manipulation of the empire. In the flashback of episode "IX," Flint–who was naval lieutenant James McGraw in 1705–brings Thomas Hamilton to Execution Dock to explain the reason pirates flourished in New Providence. By directing Hamilton's attention to the crowd cheering for the pirate's execution, Flint tells him that "civilization needs its monsters," warning Thomas that one of the reasons that the government chooses to deal with piracy by public execution is because they are well aware of the consequences when the pirates are no longer the enemies of the government (Steinberg and Levine 2015, 00:25:24-00:26:38). It is a scene showing Flint already knows that the British Empire is using pirates' monstrous image to maintain power and authority even when he was still an officer of the Royal Navy. Flint's analysis of the relationship between the pirates and the government echoes Burgess' analysis of how Every's assault developed into the branding of pirates as enemies of all humankind. Historically, Every attacked the ship that belonged to the Great Mughal of India. The Khan responded to the assault by imprisoning men from the East India Company and threatening to attack the English city of Bombay. The East India Company and the English government promised their full support to execute Every and his crew to stop the attack. However, Every had left the jurisdiction of the East India Company and sought safety in the American colonies by then, turning piracy into a national and imperial problem (Burgess Jr. 2009, 890-892). The influence of Every's trial lasted more than 30 years and determined the fate of pirate captain William Kidd in 1701. Kidd captured two merchant ships in the Indian Ocean, one of them leased by a high official of the Mughal court, which led to his execution for murder and piracy. As the historian Benton pointed out, Kidd's execution highlights the official policy toward piracy at the beginning of the eighteenth century. Kidd started his career as a privateer and held the commission of the English government, which permitted him to capture French merchant ships when he captured the two merchant ships. While the ship leased by the official of the Mughal court was registered as a French vessel, and its captain presented French nationality to Kidd during Kidd's assault, Kidd was still convicted and sentenced to death by the English government. The conviction of Kidd's piracy is, therefore, sending a signal to the Great Mughal, a political and official response to Every's attack (Benton 2005, 707-711). Set in 1705, four years after Kidd's trial, the interpretation of the pirate's execution from Flint in *Black Sails* acknowledges the history of piracy and the political usage of pirates as monsters.

Flint, who once played a part in the empire, excels at controlling the narrative that creates monsters in the story. In the first season, Flint reclaims his captaincy by accusing the challenger of stealing information that will make the crew rich and then justifies killing the challenger by planting an empty page on the dead body. In the second season, Flint tricks another former crew member who took over his captaincy into attacking a merchant ship and forces that character into a situation where he has to decide to kill every sailor aboard. Because that character cannot carry out the act, Flint takes over the command to order the kill and regains his captaincy. In both cases, Flint reseizes his power as captain by reshaping whom the narrative deems as monsters, turning his opponents into those responsible for the danger his crews face.

On the one hand, Flint's maneuver is the tactic that he, as a naval officer, learned from the empire; on the other hand, it is the tactic that the empire used on him. The second season reveals the reason Flint becomes a pirate. Thomas Hamilton eventually persuaded Flint/McGraw that the piracy in Nassau should be solved not by hanging the pirates but by pardoning all of them and turning them into labor workers. The idea of transforming the monsters into workers was too politically dangerous and controversial, leading both Hamilton and Flint to be persecuted: Hamilton being pronounced mad and sent to the Bethlem Royal Hospital, and Flint being discharged based on his sexual relationship with Hamilton. When forced to choose between leaving London or facing the gallows, Flint chooses to become Nassau's pirate captain, James Flint, a monster that fits the punishment that the empire used to threaten him and the very problem that Hamilton's proposal could have solved. In episode "VII," when Miranda Hamilton, Thomas Hamilton's wife who became an outcast of London society with Flint, tries to convince Flint to accept England's pardon and make peace with England ten years after their exile, Flint replies, "[England] took everything from us, and then they called me a monster. The moment I sign that pardon, the moment [that] I ask for one, I proclaim to the world that they were right" (Steinberg and Levine 2014, 00:36:59-00:37:52). Here, similar to the pirate issue in Nassau, which begins with the legal trials turning government-commissioned pirates into traitors of England, Flint's reluctance to stop being a pirate in Nassau is also rooted in the legal narrative. While Miranda sees pardon as an official warrant of remission of penalty, Flint understands it as an official narrative that makes him a monster. In this sense, his refusal to accept the pardon is a refusal to fall into the official narrative.

Strikingly, even though Flint becomes a victim under the empire's maneuver, he continues replicating how the empire builds its narrative. His skillful operation of using the image of monsters in the first two seasons aims mainly to benefit himself. It helps him implant fear and hatred in his crew to manipulate their votes and choices more easily. The way Flint compiled stories is no different from the English government he hated and a remark that the piracy practice originated from the sponsor by the crown. It is after the finale of the second season, when Flint no longer believes in reconciliation with the empire, that he starts targeting the subjects of the British Empire as his audience and brings out the full potential of the monstrous narrative, turning monsters into active means to resist colonial power. Flint is captured and trialed in the Carolina Colony under the order of the Governor at the end of the second season. In episode "XVIII," his trial marks a turning point in the series where the characters stop passively being read as monsters and actively live as monsters. The authority asks Flint to respond to the allegations of his crime before announcing the sentence. Flint replies: "Everyone is a monster to someone. Since you are so convinced that I am yours. I will be it" (Steinberg and Levine 2015, 00:23:51-00:24:02). When he manages to escape his execution, he executes his claim by gutting the Governor and burning the whole town to the ground. The following season's opening "XIX," shows Flint and his crew deliberately launching attacks at colonial towns where their magistrates hanged the pirates, manifesting the monstrous image of pirates depicted by the British Empire (Steinberg and Levine 2016, 00:08:55-00:12:39). Through the response of the magistrate Flint interrogated, the series reveals Flint's aim: to terrorize the magistrates into giving up on enforcing capital sentences on the pirates. It is similar to how, in the Elizabethan era, English state-sponsored piracy was executed– "a means of employing force and terror to achieve political ends"– but now targeting the exact power that turned piracy into political means in the first place (Burgess Jr. 2006, 303).

One of the methods that the pirates in *Black Sails* use to weave their monstrous image into a political tool that challenges the empire's narrative is to carry the empire's logic to its extreme, especially through the plot related to capital punishment. As Foucault points out in his analysis of the economy of punitive power in the seventeenth and eighteenth centuries, public torture and execution became a spectacle because of the relationship between crime and punishment. Punishment developed the characteristic of terror to demonstrate the sovereign's power, and the terror created by punishment fulfills three functions: a reminder of crime as a horrendous act, a display of the sovereign's splendid and invincible power, and deterrence for future crime (Foucault 2003, 82-84). The public execution of pirates in the seventeenth century aims to achieve similar goals.

Historically, each process of the pirate's execution was designed to manifest the government's power in London. The public execution of pirates had long been a spectacle in London. Unlike other criminals' executions, the pirate's hanging happened at Execution Duck, a specific location that marks the Admiralty's jurisdiction over crimes on the sea. The procedure and staging of hanging pirates were also significant. Before their hanging, the pirates were transported to the execution location in an extended route, aiming to humiliate the prisoners publicly. The stage setting at low tide, within the tidemark, intends to show that the pirate's crimes had been committed within the Admiralty's jurisdiction (Lincoln 2016, 35). The sovereign power dictates the meaning created by the pirate's bodies even after their death. The bodies were left at the low water mark until the tides overflowed them, symbolically cleansing the sins of the pirates three times (Stow 1908, 375; Lincoln 2016, 37). In some cases, such as William Kidd, the remains were gibbeted, painted with tar for preservation, wrapped in iron, and displayed on the shore of Thames where "visible to passing shipping for an hour or more" for over twenty years (Lincoln 2016, 37-38). In other cases, the hangman sold the corpses to surgeons for dissection, and the bodies ended up being dissected in front of those who crowded in the sessions hall for the county of Middlesex (Lincoln 2016, 37). In these ways, even if some pirates refuse to repent while alive, their remains on display are still tools that the official narrative can use against them.

In *Black Sails*, the hanging has been foreshadowing the fate of characters since Flint/McGraw showed Thomas the execution scene at Execution Dock in season two. In season three, the series portrays the pirate captain Charles Vane, one of the main characters, being executed by hanging. Just as the historical pirate's execution is elaborately staged, Vane's hanging in the series is meant to carry layers of meaning. Noticeably, the execution scene of Vane in episode "XXVII" begins with cross-cuts between the clergyman urging Vane to repent and Vane being driven in the cart to the scaffold. The last journey of Vane to the scaffold, designed to humiliate him publicly, is shown to the audience while the clergyman's voice-over explains Vane's execution process for him (00:41:55-00:43:54). Through the separation of audio from the visual, the narrator from the person truly experiencing the sentence, the series highlights the power dynamics of the colonial government/pirate relationship. The admonition of the clergyman taking over the narrative of Vane's experience and feeling on his way to the execution transforms Vane's experience into a visual representation of the terror that the official intended to plant in the condemned mind. The voice-over also highlights the power of the official narrative–the power that dictates the meaning of what the crowd and the audience of *Black Sails* received.

Vane's body on display in "XXVII" becomes a tool the official narrative uses against him when he refuses to repent. The preaching from the court official to the crowd continues to pave the official narrative for Vane's execution. In the eyes of the empire, men like Vane: "are not men at all, but beasts [...] As long as those men roam free...fear will abound" in society. As a result, Vane's execution "marks the silencing of the most disruptive of those voices and a step towards the return of civilization in Nassau" (00:43:36-00:46:15). In the official narrative, the crowd is first reminded of Vane's dreadful crime and his status as non-human, then their faith in the sovereign power. Yet, this announcement delivered by the official, opposite to the scene where the clergyman dominates the narration of Vane's journey to the gallows, is rendered as the background voice of the pirates' plotting for Vane's escape on screen. The series subtly flips the narrative from the authority to the sentenced pirate through the rearrangement of audio and visual portions in the narrative. Noteworthily, how Vane exercises his last words shows the character's self-awareness of the "official function" of his death. Instead of targeting the authority, Vane's addressee is the crowd of Nassau, a lot of them former pirates who accepted pardons under the Act of Grace. Vane's last speech is a warning as well as a denunciation of the official narrative: "[The officials] brought me here today because...they know that my voice, a voice that refuses to be enslaved, once lived in you. ...They brought me here today to show you death and use it to frighten you into ignoring that voice" (00:16:51-00:47:25). Vane repeats the words such as "fear" and "voice" that the official just used to address him. However, unlike the official's announcement, which emphasizes Vane's otherness to the crowd, Vane stresses his sameness. "We are many. They are few," Vane reminds the former pirates, "They can't hang us all" (00:47:28-00:47:51). As Foucault (1977) has argued in *Discipline and Punish*, there is always a risk that the public execution becomes a political danger because while the ritual aims to show the horror of the crime and the invincibility of power, the crowd witnessing the execution is the one that feels closest to the condemned and feels most threatened (63). The series displays the agitated crowd turning silent during Vane's speech, showing that Vane has successfully called for the solidarity of the pirates.

Vane's last speech transforms his execution into a manifestation of the official's aim to make him an example. The hanging of Vane, like the historical hanging of pirates, is carried out with a shortened rope, slowly choking him from asphyxiation. The specific hanging process is nicknamed "the Marshal's dance" because of the uncontrollable jerk of the limbs when the pirate struggles on the rope, sometimes taking as long as half an hour (Lincoln 2016, 37). While the dangling body is usually a visual representation of the political aim to repress the dissidents, Vane's struggling body evokes sympathy in the crowd, turning the people in Nassau against the execution and the exhibition of power. Considering that Vane actively informs other pirates to let him be executed, Vane shows through his death scene not only his acknowledgment of the meaning of being a monster from the authority's perspective but also the metaphorical meaning that a monster can carry. In his last counterattack, Vane targets the narrative that creates the monsters, the one that produces knowledge and meaning for punishment and uses the torture of his body to expose exactly how the colonial power produces their knowledge.

The pirates in *Black Sails* thus not only resist playing a part in the imperial narrative but also create new meaning through the same way the empire built its official narrative. The series constantly reminds its audience that the characters' fight with the empire lies within the plot and the narratives. It even makes fun of the "official" narrative through Captain Naft's conversation with the appraiser in front of Hanneman's forgery in episode "II." In the scene, the appraiser tells Captain Naft that it is unreasonable to think the forgery and Hanneman's work have the same value (00:22:26-00:22:40). In *Black Sails*, "reason" is constantly highlighted as civilization's universal standard. Reason deems one who cannot recognize the value of the original work to be ridiculed without further explanation. It is the word Flint chose to describe his willingness to seek reconciliation with the Governor of the Carolina Colony in episode "XVIII"–his belief that "reason" could be a bridge between both parties (00:23:36-00:23:50). As the maneuver of the empire becomes more apparent in the later seasons, the word "reason" sometimes refers to both the universal standard and the concept of reason in the Enlightenment. The most direct connection is shown in Flint's final speech in the series' last episode "XXXVIII," where he points out how the logic of the empire works: "They paint the world full of shadows, and then tell their children to stay close to the light–their light, their reasons, [and] their judgments–because in the darkness, there be dragons" (00:40:06-00:40:25). Flint's speech, together with the scene where the clergyman urges Vane to repent his sins right before Vane's execution, crystallizes the relationship between reason, the Enlightenment, and imperial power. The clergyman, a literary agent of British imperialism whose voice dominates the meaning of Vane's execution, sits under the only light source in the cell when Vane, the monstrous pirate, is chained in the darkness. Flint's usage of light, reasons, and judgments, together with the historical time that the series set in, points to the rhetoric of the "light of reason" in the Enlightenment. "There be dragons" refers to both the warning of unknown danger on the medieval map and the analogy of the history of Western civilization, which marks anything that is outside of their definition as monsters. Flint's laments of the fate of pirates, that they will be "defined by [the empire's] histories, distorted to fit into their narrative, until all that is left…are the monsters in the stories they tell their children," continues to call the empire out on their making of the official narrative (00:42:55-00:43:25). The speech acknowledges the Enlightenment-influenced imperial narrative that considered pirates as monstrous bodies and critiques the official narrative, questioning the *raison d'etre* of monsters.

The argument between Captain Naft and the appraiser, the last speech of Flint, and Captain Jack Rackham's conclusion of the story of Black Sails in "XXXVIII" remind the audience of the importance of perspectives. As the fictionalized Rackham tells Mark Read, another fictionalized pirate of the Golden Age of Piracy: "A story is true; a story is untrue. As time extends, it matters less and less. The stories we want to believe...Those are the ones that survive, despite upheaval and transition and progress. Those are the stories that shape history" (01:03:06-01:03:46). The series challenges the understanding of history and historical agency by arranging for Rackham, a fictional character based on a historical figure, to tell the end of the pirate's monstrous story. It asks the audience to reconsider the story of pirates, not with the value of "truth" or "reason"–the standard built in the Enlightenment and tied to imperial history– but with a perspective different from the standard. For it is both the narrative and audience, the way the story is told and the people who understand it, that define what a monster is.

Bibliography

Allrath, Gaby, and Marion Gymnich. 2005. *Narrative Strategies in Television Series*. New York: Palgrave Macmillan.

Benton, Lauren. 2005. "Legal Spaces of Empire: Piracy and the Origins of Ocean Regionalism." *Comparative Studies in Society and History* 47 (4): 700–24. http://www.jstor.org/stable/3879340.

Burgess Jr., Douglas R. 2006. "Hostis Humani Generi: Piracy, Terrorism and a New International Law." *University of Miami International and Comparative Law Review* 13 (2): 293–341. http://repository.law.miami.edu/umiclr/vol13is s2/2.

Burgess Jr., Douglas R. 2009. "Piracy in the Public Sphere: The Henry Every Trials and the Battle for Meaning in Seventeenth-Century Print Culture." *Journal of British Studies* 48 (4): 887–913. http://www.jstor.org/stable/27752 637.

Cohen, Jeffrey Jerome. 1996. *Monster Theory: Reading Culture*. Minneapolis: University of Minnesota Press.

Foucault, Michel. 1997. *Discipline & Punish: The Birth of the Prison*. New York: Vintage Books.

Foucault, Michel. 2003. *Abnormal: Lectures at the Collège de France, 1974-1975*. London: Verso.

Harding, Christopher. 2007. "'Hostis Humani Generis' –The Pirate as Outlaw in the Early Modern Law of the Sea." *Pirates? The Politics of Plunder, 1550–1650*, edited by Claire Jowitt, 20–38. New York: Palgrave Macmillan.

Landekic, Lola. 2014. "Black Sails (2014)." *Art of the Title*. Art of the Title, LLC. January 28, 2014. https://www.artofthetitle.com/title/black-sails/.

Leeson, Peter T. 2009. *The Invisible Hook: The Hidden Economics of Pirates*. Princeton: Princeton University Press.

Lessing, Alfred. 1965. "What Is Wrong with a Forgery?" *The Journal of Aesthetics and Art Criticism* 23 (4): 461–71. https://doi.org/10.2307/427668.

Levina, Marina, and Diem-My T. Bui. 2013. *Monster Culture in the 21st Century: A Reader*. New York: Bloomsbury Academic.

Lincoln, Margarette. 2016. *British Pirates and Society, 1680-1730*. London: Routledge.

Stanitzek, Georg. 2009. "Reading the Title Sequence (Vorspann, Générique)." *Cinema Journal* 48 (4): 44–58. https://doi.org/10.1353/cj.0.0142.

Steinberg, Jonathan E. and Robert Levine, creators. 2014. *Black Sails*. Season 1, episode 1, "I." Aired January 25, 2014. https://www.amazon.com/Black-Sails-Season-1/dp/B00HWIC1LO.

Steinberg, Jonathan E. and Robert Levine, creators. 2014. *Black Sails*. Season 1, episode 2, "II." Aired February 1, 2014. https://www.amazon.com/Black-Sails-Season-1/dp/B00HWIC1LO.

Steinberg, Jonathan E. and Robert Levine, creators. 2014. *Black Sails*. Season 1, episode 7, "VII." Aired March 8, 2014. https://www.amazon.com/Black-Sails-Season-1/dp/B00HWIC1LO.

Steinberg, Jonathan E. and Robert Levine, creators. 2015. *Black Sails*. Season 2, episode 1, "IX." Aired January 25, 2015. https://www.amazon.com/IX/dp/B00VE6W5FW.

Steinberg, Jonathan E. and Robert Levine, creators. 2015. *Black Sails*. Season 2, episode 10, "XVIII." Aired March 28, 2015. https://www.amazon.com/IX/dp/B0 0VE6W5FW.

Steinberg, Jonathan E. and Robert Levine, creators. 2016. *Black Sails*. Season 3, episode 1, "XIX." Aired January 23, 2016. https://www.amazon.com/XIX/dp/B018T4U6JI.

Steinberg, Jonathan E. and Robert Levine, creators. 2016. *Black Sails*. Season 3, episode 9, "XXVII." Aired March 19, 2016. https://www.amazon.com/XIX/dp/B018T4U6JI.

Steinberg, Jonathan E. and Robert Levine, creators. 2017. *Black Sails*. Season 4, episode 10, "XXXVIII." Aired April 2, 2017. https://www.amazon.com/XXIX/dp/B01N2HVG5G.

Stow, John. 1908. *The Survey of London*. Project Gutenberg. https://www.gutenberg.org/files/42959/42959-h/42959-h.htm.

Torrano, María Andrea. 2020. "Politics over Monstrosity and Politics of Monstrosity. The Difference between Negative and Positive Consideration about Monsters." In *Monsters, Monstrosities, and the Monstrous in Culture and Society*, edited by Diego Compagna and Stetanie Steinhart, 131–55. Delaware: Vernon Press.

Wood, Robin. 2002. "The American Nightmare." *Horror, The Film Reader*, edited by Mark Jancovich, 25–32. New York: Routledge.

Wright, Alexa. 2019. *Monstrosity: The Human Monster in Visual Culture*. First edition. London, England: I.B. Tauris.

Chapter 3

The Move to Innocence: Reframing Monstrosity in Colin Trevorrow's *Jurassic World*

Aarzoo Singh

University of Winnipeg

Angie Fazekas

University of Toronto

Abstract: Media franchises often reinforce narratives of monstrosity based in cultural, racial, and other differences. As Jeffrey Jerome Cohen (1996) tells us, "The monster is difference made flesh, come to dwell among us" (7). Like many action-adventure films, Colin Trevorrow's *Jurassic World* (2015) trilogy follows a traditional Hollywood hero vs. monster narrative. At the center are our all-white, able-bodied, morally sound heroes, who simultaneously fight monstrous dinosaurs and the monstrous humans that created them. Trevorrow's finale of the *Jurassic World* trilogy reads almost as a checkmark response to critiques of the earlier films' reliance on heroic narratives of heteronormative whiteness. Our new heroes are mainly people of color who aid the original group of white saviors. Here we see the attempt to shift traditional narratives of monstrosity that get attached to racialized and queer bodies in Hollywood. In this paper, we think through this reframing with what Barbara Heron calls a "race to innocence," wherein heteronormative whiteness is highly invested in images of itself as good and ethical, leading to a denial of its complicity in racial subordination. These strategies or positionings attempt to assuage guilt or responsibility from narratives of monstrosity without changing the main frameworks that underpin their construction. That is, what we find is an "insert" to the "solution" of the problem of race as monstrous without real structural change. Furthermore, we see the plight of heternormativity being carried out, with the film returning to an ending that is predicated on the survival of the white nuclear family and thus precluding any attempt to reframe monstrosity. Ultimately, we argue that this foreclosure is emblematic of the possibility of monster narratives - that they refuse tidy solutions and narratives.

Instead, we explore what possibilities might reveal themselves if we reimagine the monstrous bodies of *Jurassic World* as located within white heteronormativity instead of threatening it.

Keywords: monstrous bodies, heteronormativity, whiteness, racialized bodies

***

In what is perhaps the most iconic scene in Steven Spielberg's original *Jurassic Park* (1993) film, Tim, a young boy, watches as ripples repeatedly form in a water glass, heralding the approach of a giant Tyrannosaurus and the beginning of a chaotic rampage that would end up destroying the titular park and many of its residents. Throughout the remainder of the film, Tim and his sister, Lex, are continually threatened by the escaped dinosaurs while the adult protagonists attempt to protect them and find a way off the island. In what would become a recurring theme in the *Jurassic Park* (1993-2001) and *Jurassic World* (2015-2022) film series, the movie ends with our heroes flying away from the chaos in a helicopter, Tim and Lex safely held in the embrace of the man who had become their father figure and protector.[1] *Jurassic Park*, and each of its five sequels, ends with the restoration of the (almost-always) white nuclear family.[2] The main conflict of each film centers on a threat to the white nuclear family and the restoration of said family as the ultimate happy ending. In so doing, the movies reveal an ongoing investment in heteronormative whiteness. The most recent entry in the *Jurassic Park* film series, Colin Trevorrow's *Jurassic World: Dominion* (2022), attempts to break with the previous films' reliance on white heroes and the white family by introducing us to a new roster of racialized heroes. However, as we argue, these characters act as performative additions that do not threaten the sanctity of the white nuclear family as the definitive location of the happy ending.

We contend that the narrative of the *Jurassic World* trilogy presents monstrosity as predicated on fears of advancing science and the ethics of manipulating genomes for profit. As such, an argument can be made that capitalism is the undeniable monster of the films. However, the movies continually fail to reckon with capitalism's investment in whiteness as fundamental to its operation, choosing instead to critique the dangers of uncontrolled scientific advancement while repeatedly investing in the safety and sanctity of the white nuclear family.

---

[1] The Jurassic Park series consists of the films Jurassic Park, The Lost World: Jurassic Park, and Jurassic Park 3 while the Jurassic World series consists of Jurassic World, Jurassic World: Fallen Kingdom, and Jurassic World: Dominion. For simplicity's sake, the entire series will be referred to as the Jurassic Park series for the remainder of this paper.

[2] In The Lost World: Jurassic Park, the threatened child is a Black girl while her biological father and pseudo-mother figure in the film are both white.

Trevorrow's *Jurassic World: Dominion* is an example of a "race to innocence" (Fellows and Razack 1998, 335) in its attempt to rewrite the previous films' reliance on whiteness through the conjuring of a new slate of heroic racialized characters. We use the concept of the "race to innocence" in reference to Mary Louise Fellows and Sherene Razack (1998) as they take up this idea in their work on the failures of feminist political solidarity when women fail to interrogate their own complicity in oppressive structures and subordination of other women's lives. They contend "when we view ourselves as innocent, we cannot confront the hierarchies that operate among us" (335). In this paper, we extend this idea into the realms of race, difference, and heteronormativity as it functions within *Jurassic World*. Moreso, we explore how this race to innocence solicits additive narratives of "redemption" from their past film's white-hetero-centered focus. This framework operates by distancing itself from heteronormative systems of white domination through the denial of its complicity in racial subordination. Ultimately, this formula fundamentally fails as the survival and reaffirmation of the white nuclear family work as the film's moral throughline, confirming its stakes in white heteronormativity.

Monster Theory and the Monstrosity of Capitalism

Each of the first four films in the *Jurassic Park* series operates on a similar basic formula. It functions as follows: the protagonists of the film, at least one white man and one white woman, along with one or more children (always white, with the exception of Kelly Malcolm [Vanessa Lee Chester] from *The Lost World*), travel to either Isla Nublar (the site of the original Jurassic Park) or Isla Sorna (Site B, where the dinosaurs were raised before being moved to the park) where, after intervention from the antagonists, disaster occurs and they are threatened by escaped or rampaging dinosaurs. The adult protagonists must protect the children while attempting to find a means of escape from the island. The fifth film in the series, *Jurassic World: Fallen Kingdom* (2018), slightly alters this formula in that the adult protagonists do not meet the child in need of protection until they have returned to the mainland along with a group of dinosaurs who are to be auctioned off by the film's antagonists. Nevertheless, all five films end with the adult and child protagonists safely reunited in a return to a version of the white nuclear family.

At first glance, *Jurassic World: Dominion*, the culminating film in Colin Trevorrow's *Jurassic World* trilogy, makes several sweeping changes to the formula audiences have come to expect from the film series. Dinosaurs, rather than remaining contained on a small Caribbean island, have spread across the world, threatening the safety of humanity wherever they roam. Monsters, it would seem, have come to live among us. Our group of heroes must reckon with the dinosaurs as well as a swarm of genetically modified locusts who destroy the facility in which they were taking shelter. Yet, as with the first five films, the dinosaurs and the locusts are only part of the film's narrative of monstrosity. So, how does monstrosity work in the films, and how does this connect to the continued reinstantiation of the nuclear family? To understand this, we now turn to monster theory to unpack the role of the monster in the film.

In his influential *Monster Theory*, Jeffrey Jerome Cohen (1996) offers a series of theses that unpack the cultural role of monsters and monstrosities. He tells us that the popularity of particular monsters offers a glimpse into the preoccupations, fears, and anxieties of a culture at a specific moment in time. For example, vampiric folklore and mythology often gain popularity in times of plague and pestilence, distilling fears of a contagious pathogen into a figure that spreads its monstrosity through blood. In the case of *Jurassic Park*, the monstrous dinosaurs represent a fear of science run amok. As Dr. Ian Malcolm (Jeff Goldblum) cautions in the original *Jurassic Park*: "Your scientists were so preoccupied with whether they could, they didn't stop to think if they should" (Spielberg 1993, 35:13). Written during a time period during which fears of genetically-modified food and cloning technology were ubiquitous, the films offer a cautionary tale – unrestricted scientific innovation, particularly that which disrupts the natural order, is a disaster waiting to happen.

In the two most recent films, *Jurassic World: Fallen Kingdom* (2018) and *Jurassic World: Dominion* (2022), these fears are taken to new heights with the introduction of human cloning in the form of Maisie Lockwood (Isabella Sermon), a young girl cloned from her deceased mother. Coming off the haunches of the COVID-19 pandemic, in a moment when conspiracy theories posit that vaccines and 5G cellular networks are an attempt to modify the natural order of humanity and make *us* into monsters, the addition of human clones to the *Jurassic Park* series reads as a distillation of these fears and conspiracies. Yet, simultaneously, as Cohen (1996) cautions, "the monster always escapes" (6), pushing past its initial cultural context and reinventing itself in new and different ways as societal fears and anxieties evolve. The figure of the zombie, for example, once a manifestation of the pain and suffering of transatlantic slavery, has since been co-opted and appropriated to represent xenophobic fears of the Other. Reading popular culture through the lens of the monster, therefore, provides not only striking insight into cultural fears and preoccupations but also the ways in which monstrosity resists easy categorization. Rather, as Cohen (1996) tells us, "[monsters] can be pushed to the farthest margins, hidden away at the edges of the world and in the forbidden recesses of our mind, but they always return" (20). The monster, in this way, cannot be defeated. The monster is always amongst us or *is* us, thus absconding a definitive form.

The *Jurassic Park* (1993-2022) film series demonstrates the monster's ability to escape boundaries in ways both literal and figural. The first five films in the series begin with the monsters – in this case, the human-created dinosaurs – safely locked away in enclosures and/or on islands. Over the course of each film, the dinosaurs break out of containment to wreak havoc and threaten our heroes. While the trailers and marketing continue to present the rampaging dinosaurs as sources of monstrosity and fear, the films also force a reckoning with the wider societal and cultural forces that gave rise to the dinosaurs in the first place. When monsters return, as they do in each subsequent *Jurassic Park* film, they bring a deeper understanding of who we are as humans. Cohen (1996) elucidates this:

> [T]hey bring not just a fuller knowledge of our place in history and the history of knowing our place, but they bear self-knowledge, human knowledge. These monsters ask us how we perceive the world, and how we have misrepresented what we have attempted to place. They ask us to reevaluate our cultural assumptions about race, gender, our perception of difference, our tolerance toward its expression. They ask us why we have created them. (20)

The very creation or positing of monsters in our stories about ourselves forces us to confront the particular investments, fears, or preoccupations that brought about their creation in the first place. In other words, monsters are an operative tool in understanding what we value and, perhaps more importantly, what we do not. They reveal the liminal, changeable nature of human belonging as well as the forces that shore up the definition of what it means to be human. In the case of the dinosaurs of *Jurassic Park*, their creation and repetitive return demonstrate not only the economic forces that underlie their existence but inadvertently shine a spotlight on the motives and monstrous intentions of their makers.

Monsters in the narrative of the *Jurassic World* trilogy take on two forms: the actual monstrous creatures of the dinosaurs and the monstrous people who created them. The films attempt to trouble the idea of monstrosity beyond its mythical implications. It has us, as the audience, asking questions about monstrosity: yes, there are murderous dinosaurs – monsters – who kill people, but as wild carnivorous animals, is it not in their nature to do this? What of the "civilized" humans who brought these creatures into existence into a context that sets up this consequence? Isn't the real monster capitalism, as plutocratic ventures are ultimately the driving force behind the resurrection of the monsters? Who or what is to blame for the violence? It is the rapacious greed incurred by capitalism's promise of infinite profits that is where monstrosity truly resides in *Jurassic Park*. As Cohen (1996) argues, "[what] is monstrous about [John Hammond][3] is that he believes that Jurassic Park can combine science, law, and commerce at the point where each is fused by its own greed with an inexhaustible prospect of profit and power" (296). Capitalist ideology promises that with the right idea, everything, especially the natural world, can be transformed into a source of profit. *Jurassic Park* simply takes this premise to its extreme in its use of extinct animals as sources of profit – here, even death itself is not a barrier to the infinitely increasing profits promised by capitalist innovation.

While reading capitalism as the true monster of *Jurassic Park* is not a new idea, we find that monstrosity in the *Jurassic Park* film series has yet another level of operation – one that draws our attention not only to the plot but also to the process and creation of each film. As we argued earlier, the *Jurassic Park* film series follows a traditional Hollywood action-adventure blueprint where a group of heroic protagonists battle dangerous monsters. At the center of this narrative are our all-white, able-bodied, morally sound heroes, who are simultaneously on the side of the innocent dinosaurs and victimized humans. They are obviously the ones to save the world. This formula, which recurs in four of the first five films in the franchise, has been met with repeated criticism from fans (Ramirez 2014; Jones 2015) for its centering on whiteness as the ultimate location of heroism.

Monique Jones (2015) argues that while the first *Jurassic World* film introduces us to a more multicultural cast than ever existed in the earlier *Jurassic Park* trilogy, by the time the movie ends, "you're nearly back to an all-white cast, mostly because the most important people in the film are the leads (who are, of course, cast as 'default' white actors)" (n.p.). Particularly in regards to the *Jurassic World* trilogy, written and produced in a time when conversations about race in Hollywood were gaining traction, fans began to question why the franchise continued to rely on this predictable and outdated white heteronormative formula. After all, when we imagine only whiteness as heroic, everyone and everything else, including the racialized Other, must either be irrelevant or become monstrous themselves. It is here we see the film's attempt to erase the overwhelming whiteness of the previous five films by "racing to innocence" through the declarative addition of racialized characters without ever substantially engaging those characters or the implications of their presence.

Creating the Monstrous Other and the Race to Innocence

Examining *Jurassic World* through the lens of a "race to innocence" reveals a sanitizing of its own complicity in the oppressive structures of white

---

[3] John Hammond, played by Richard Attenborough, is the creator and founder of the original *Jurassic Park* theme park.

heteronormativity through its utilization of racialized Others as tools of absolution. These manipulative forms of consumption allow the final narrative of the trilogy to lean into the belief that it is rebelling against white supremacist culture, but, as bell hooks tells us, capitalism encourages white consumers to feel an imagined intimacy with racial otherness via exotic or primitive fantasies, which in fact reinforce the status quo (hooks 1992, 22). In other words, capitalism's reliance on the apparatus of whiteness compromises the film's attempt to escape the conversation on race. Through this final film, we look at the "race to innocence" as it shapes the ways in which constructions of monsters and monstrous bodies operate in this narrative through its predication of the normative subject.

The films work hard to free themselves from their investment in heteronormative whiteness–or the "production of the ordinary" (Ahmed 2004, 118). That is the ordinary white subject–the normative subject–itself is a fantasy, but emotions of fear work to bring that fantasy to life by constituting the "ordinary as in crisis" (118). All the *Jurassic Park* films operate on this premise, on a predicated threat of the ordinary subject's demise–regardless of whether that threat was brought about by their own doing. This is where we see a continual return to the story's reliance on saving white children. After all, the maintenance of existing conditions in the normative subject lies at the core of the model of the nuclear family. And it is the normative, white, nuclear family that is ultimately saved at the end of the series – it was what needed to be rescued and protected from the monsters (whether it be people or the actual dinosaurs). In this, the film undermines its attempt to assuage itself from guilt or responsibility of these narratives through its "race to innocence."

Up until the last film in the *Jurassic World* trilogy, *Dominion*, the ordinary white person, or our heroes, was already posited as under threat by imagined Others, dinosaurs and otherwise. The ordinary or normative subject was continually reproduced as the "injured party: the one 'hurt' or even damaged by the 'invasion' of others" (Ahmed 2004, 118). This framework reveals the ways in which constructing and protecting the ordinary or normative subject must call a body of Otherness into its relation. From this, bodies of Others are transformed into "the hated," the "monstrous," "those to be feared" through a discourse of pain. Sara Ahmed (2004) explains that Othered bodies are assumed to "cause" injury to the ordinary white subject "such that their proximity is read as the origin of bad feeling" (118). That is the feelings around monstrosity, which get attached to Othered bodies, are subjected to processes of identification, which determines their place within hegemonic thinking. Otherness as identity becomes static, unmoving, and unchanging–it is dependent on "fixity" for its construction (Bhabha 1994, 64). And this is something we see in media representations of racialized characters – an eager cultivation of monstrous imaging that keeps certain bodies categorized in static, unevolving roles.

A helpful way to think about the processes of Othering is through Homi Bhabha's (1994) breakdown of processes of identification of the Other. This process is threefold; 1. To exist is to be called into being in relation to an Otherness–that is, Otherness cannot exist without the backdrop of what is constituted as "normal" or "ordinary," thus one must "place the object" for its identification; 2. This space of identification is a space of splitting; 3. The question of identity is never the affirmation of a pre-given identity—it is always the production of an image of identity, therefore, the subject speaks and is seen from where it is *not* (64). Monstrosity is presented as other than the white ordinary subject, thus, the Other becomes monstrous. From this, we can contend that monstrosity is assigned to Othered bodies as a way of protecting the ordinary subject. And this process is anxiously repeated throughout the *Jurassic World* trilogy, until its final installment, when we see a sudden shift in who the film constitutes as its heroes or its ordinary subjects. That is, all of a sudden, the Other becomes useful to the films' attempt at its "race to innocence."

Within current debates about race and differences in popular culture, we can find a rise in the idea that there is "pleasure" to be found in acknowledging and even celebrating racial differences (hooks 1992, 22). This is to say, it is fashionable to be "woke" to be alert to racial differences in our current political moment. hooks (1992) elucidates this idea and states, "[t]he commodification of Otherness has been so successful because it is offered as a new delight, more intense, more satisfying than normal ways of doing and feeling. Within commodity culture, ethnicity becomes spice, seasoning that can liven up the dull dish that is mainstream white culture" (21). In *Jurassic World: Dominion*, a stark utilization of the consumption of the Other operates through a modality of benignity. There is almost a feigned benevolence in the ways in which the film shifts stereotypes of the Other *slightly* to the left to claim its innocence within these conversations.

A blinding example featured in *Dominion*: dinosaurs are being sold in "underground dino markets" in Malta; fashioned as almost cliché in its Orientalist depiction of the souk bazaars of the Middle East–chaotic stalls stacked with goods made of dinosaur skin, dinosaur meat bubbling on rotisserie spits, exotic dinosaurs caged and displayed, shady characters cloaked and masked lurking in every corner, even a "dino-fighting" pit for the pleasure of customers. The score weaves in vaguely African and Arabic music, signaling to the audience where, indeed, this scene should be associated. We see one of our heroes, Claire, a white woman, move through this space while sticking out like a sore thumb. Her ordinariness strikes a stark contrast to the seedy scene she finds herself in – even being asked, "You lost?" (Trevorrow 2022, 49:19) by another character as an emphasis of her whiteness being at odds with the inherent criminality of such a space. It is also one of the few scenes of the film where we see the most people of color congregated into one space.

In situating this market within Europe rather than the Middle East, we see the film's rush to innocence. An attempt to alleviate the film from its ties to various systems of domination comes through clearly. And from this safe distance of any named foreign and exotic place is where the film's exploration of racial difference is found – one that pre-excuses itself from recycling the tired tropes about spaces of Otherness as being inherently criminal and sinister. Here, we see the positioning of monstrosity as it attaches itself to particular bodies within this story. And once discourses of racial, ethnic, and cultural difference have been commodified into the film's content, the Other is "eaten, consumed, and forgotten" (hooks 1992, 39). In other words, when the Other no longer serves the purpose of enhancing the "white palate," it is discarded (39).

The other scene where we see most people of color congregated into one space comes in sharp contrast to the Malta market scene, yet still somehow makes monsters out of them. The scene takes place in a lecture hall in which Dr. Ian Malcolm addresses a room of budding intellectuals on the "ethics of genetic power" at the BioSyn campus. The students in this room are employees of BioSyn who are posited as well-meaning in their idealism in the development of genetic power in unlocking the potential within the study of genomes but ignorant of BioSyn's immoral engineering of prehistoric creatures. Dr. Malcolm's lecture essentially tries to warn them about the consequences of manipulating nature for capitalist interest; a 'you are the future, handle it wisely' type of speech. We see a room of hopeful young people who represent exactly this, the future–filled with a sea of heterogeneous bodies. Framed closeups of a range of checklist "diverse" young faces appear throughout – an Asian girl with glasses, a Black woman with an afro, a studious-looking Asian man, and a young Black man, all rapturously captured by Dr. Malcolm's oration. Again, hooks' (1992) words resonate: "ethnicity becomes spice, seasoning that can liven up the dull dish that is mainstream white culture" (21). The film signals to us exactly this, there may not have been diversity in its past, but here it is in its future. Even if this is the final installment of the franchise and this is the extent to which we will see this diversity, it is being nodded to here, just enough of the "spice" sprinkled in for us to savor. And yet, monstrosity fails to escape these young hopefuls.

The room is full of people deemed the "best and brightest," yet they do not know that their company creates monsters in their work. In a way, making them monsters themselves for *their* complicity in the environmental crisis caused by the prehistoric creatures, even if done so through ignorance. But we never really come to know much about the monstrous hopefuls beyond this scene. All supplemental characters of color within the film function on their ability to further the cause of protecting the white nuclear family with no further development to their character.

Dominion further attempts to rectify the overwhelming whiteness of the earlier films by adding several racialized characters in prominent roles. The key word here is that it is additive – these characters play an important role in the plot of the film but are given little backstory or connection to other characters in the franchise. Indeed, in spite of the addition of several racialized characters, the bulk of the emotional impact of the film still rests on the shoulders of the white nuclear family as well as the supposed monsters, the dinosaurs. The new characters of color are given relatively sparse backstories and exist mainly to assist and support the primary trio Owen Grady (Chris Pratt), Claire Dearing (Bryce Dallas Howard), and Maisie Lockwood (Isabella Sermon).

Take the character of BioSyn pilot Kayla Watts (DeWanda Wise) as an example. What we know about her is that she is a former Air Force pilot, after which she began flying illegal cargo in and out of Mombasa. It was here she was noticed by BioSyn when they employed her to fly and sell their own illegal products (the dinosaurs) to be used in the underground market in Malta. Her backstory gives us minimal information but just enough for us to associate criminality with her Blackness. Kayla's character follows the trope of a 'criminal with a conscience,' and it is only when she risks her own survival to save and reunite the white nuclear family that she is redeemed from her criminality.

She is initially unwilling to help Claire and Owen rescue their adopted daughter but eventually agrees to fly them to BioSyn's dinosaur reserve, where they find the kidnapped Maisie. But even in her redemption, which is meant to absorb her into the group of white heroes, she still stands on the periphery of their unit, her value to them being her ability to fly them out of the perils of the island. In a scene where the clone child Maisie is reunited with her adoptive mother Claire, she warmly thanks Ellie Sattler (Laura Dern) for her role in bringing her child to her as Kayla watches from the side. Kayla did not get a heart-filled gesture of gratitude from Claire for her role in helping her in the same way. All emotions of tenderness fail to touch Kayla's character in that moment, as she quickly warns the group to keep moving as the dinosaurs approach. The audience is never given any real opportunity to emotionally connect with Kayla despite her vital role in saving the saviors. Kayla is rewarded at the end with a new plane, but no real human connection–her value is still reduced to her labor.

We see this formula repeated with most of the other main characters of color. Dr. Henry Wu (BD Wong), who is a biochemist and chief geneticist of BioSyn, is responsible for the cloning programs at Jurassic Park and Jurassic World. He is portrayed as having little concern for the prehistoric creatures he brought back to life or the devastating effects that creating genetically modified hybrids would have on the world. But at the very end of *Dominion*, as the BioSyn sanctuary falls, he rushes to our heroes and exclaims that he can fix the ecological disaster he created. He explains that by studying the genetically altered clone child Maisie – who was created by her "mother" (or her own self) but genetically altered to not suffer the same terminal illness she did – he would be able to reverse the biologically modified state of the prehistoric forms he created. His redemption is also based on his labor, on protecting the future of these white heroes and the nuclear family at its center. They need him therefore, he is allowed to survive. Again, this blueprint is used for another added character of color, Ramsay Cole (Mamoudou Athie). He is presented as the head of communications of BioSyn but is secretly a whistleblower who warns Dr. Malcolm of BioSyn's illegal activities and helps our white heroes escape BioSyn's sanctuary as it is destroyed. All of these characters are operative tools in the story of protecting the white family from demise with no real character schemes or development.

The dinosaurs, alternatively, are given much more nuanced emotional arcs than the characters of color – with backstories extending, in one case, up to 65 million years. Two dinosaurs in particular, the velociraptor, Blue, and the Tyrannosaurus, Rexy, have extensive backstories and ongoing emotional relationships with our human protagonists.[4] Blue, who was raised by Owen Grady at Jurassic World before its destruction, has become a mother by the time of *Dominion*. In the film, the villains kidnap her child, a moment that is paralleled with the kidnapping of Maisie, Owen and Claire's adopted daughter. The happy ending wherein Owen, Claire, and Maisie are reunited is again mirrored by the reunion of Blue and her child. Additionally, the film follows Rexy, a Tyrannosaurus who was first introduced in the original *Jurassic Park* (1993). In the original (since-deleted) opening scene of *Dominion*, we return 65 million years into the past to witness the life and death of the Tyrannosaurus, who would eventually be cloned as Rexy. In the climactic fight sequence, Rexy is nearly killed in a manner that calls back to that opening scene, before eventually persevering and continuing to live freely in a newly formed dinosaur reserve.

What is particularly striking about the storylines of Blue and Rexy, is how much more emotional weight and impact is put onto the supposed "monsters" of the movie as compared to the new slate of racialized characters. Consequently, the dinosaurs in the film read as significantly more sympathetic to the audience. Particularly given the previous films' reliance on the trope of white heroism, this narrative imbalance seemingly locates the dinosaurs as central characters while continuing to place racialized characters in the position of the Other despite the film's "race to innocence" in its attempt to maintain mainstream white normative culture.

---

[4] Rexy is the fan-given name for the Tyrannosaurus who appears in every film other than *The Lost World: Jurassic Park* and *Jurassic Park 3*.

Returning to Cohen's (1996) assertion that monsters "bring not just a fuller knowledge of our place in history and the history of knowing our place, but they bear self-knowledge, human knowledge" (20) reveals the impact of the uneven distribution of empathy in the film. Rexy and Blue are given traits and storylines that make them sympathetic and likable to the audience. They each have storylines stretching over several films and prompt significant, continuing audience engagement. The Jurassic Park Wiki, for example, contains substantial, multi-page entries detailing the histories of both Rexy and Blue, while the entry for Kayla Watts spans only a few paragraphs ("Jurassic Park Wiki"). Rexy's storyline over the course of the film series has her repeatedly triumphing over other, more dangerous, dinosaurs and, in the process, saving our heroes. Blue has a significant, ongoing familial relationship with Owen Grady and his adopted daughter, Maisie. As such, the audience is primed to recognize these humanizing traits and sympathize with the dinosaurs.

Conversely, the racialized characters of *Dominion* seemingly exist only to serve a function in the plot that still revolves around the survival of the white nuclear family. Beyond their narrative function, these characters have no familial ties or substantial relationships and are thus not positioned to be relatable or sympathetic to the audience in the same way as the dinosaurs. As such, despite its attempts to "race to innocence," the film ultimately ends up positioning the dinosaurs as more 'human' than the actual human characters of color. In so doing, the film reaffirms that full access to human belonging is only the purview of whiteness – even prehistoric monsters get more access to humanity than the racialized Other. Indeed, other than the main nuclear family formation and the heroes returning from earlier films (Laura Dern as Dr. Ellie Sattler, Sam Neill as Dr. Alan Grant, and Jeff Goldblum as Dr. Ian Malcolm), the velociraptor Blue receives the most detailed and sympathetic treatment of any character in the film, through her experience of motherhood, loss, and reunion.

Reproducing and Rescuing the White Nuclear Family

While one of the main emotional throughlines in the original *Jurassic Park* was Dr. Alan Grant's journey towards the role of father figure to Lex and Tim, *Jurassic World: Dominion* shows a similar emotional investment in motherhood and the sanctity of the nuclear family. Motherhood, and specifically white motherhood, continues to play a significant ideological role in reinforcing racial boundaries and the 'ordinary subject.' As Mary-Louise Adams (1997) argues, much societal preoccupation with protecting the nuclear family is bound up in the desire to protect the future of the white nation. As mothers quite literally reproduce the nation, idealizing white motherhood is used as a tool to protect and strengthen the future of the white nation.

Our main family formation throughout the film may have a non-normative beginning but ultimately serves to reaffirm the nuclear family as the bedrock of a peaceful society. The *Jurassic World* trilogy begins with the soon-to-be parents, Owen Grady and Claire Dearing, working at the Jurassic World theme park and navigating a contentious relationship. Over the course of the first two films, Owen and Claire gravitate towards each other, eventually developing a lasting romantic relationship. However, this relationship is only solidified after their rescue and subsequent pseudo-adoption of Maisie Lockwood, the young human clone. Owen and Claire's attempts to rescue Maisie throughout *Fallen Kingdom* and *Dominion* become the basis of their reunion and partnership. While all three characters are initially presented as outcasts – Owen for his relationship with the velociraptors, Claire for her over-investment in her work, and Maisie for her status as a clone – they come together to become emblematic of the sanctified white nuclear family. *Dominion* begins with all three living off-the-grid in an attempt to keep Maisie away from BioSyn, who wants to use her to continue their experiments in genetics and cloning. And, of course, we should not forget that BioSyn is an organization whose "best and brightest" are presented as young, hopeful people of color – their monstrosity is posited as threatening to the survival of the family unit. Right off the bat, the audience is guided towards sympathy for the characters that make up this precarious familial formation – a sympathy that is only reinforced and strengthened by the emotions Owen and Claire show when Maisie is kidnapped.

Indeed, Claire, who in the first *Jurassic World* film was uncomfortable with children and devoted almost exclusively to her job, is now positioned firmly in the role of mother, mirroring the experiences of the velociraptor Blue. Claire's primary role as mother is repeatedly reinforced throughout the film as she and Owen attempt to rescue their adopted daughter. Even when navigating the dangerous 'dino markets' in Malta, Claire's emotions are never far from the surface as she uses her role as mother to beg for help from the pilot, Kayla Watts. Later in the film, Owen explicitly confirms that Claire's most important role in the narrative has become that of the mother when he tells her, "You're the one who's got to go to get her [Maisie]. You're her mom. You're her only shot" (Treverrow 2022, 1:17:28). Owen says to Claire as their plane, piloted by Kayla, plummets to the ground in their attempts to enter the BioSyn sanctuary. In a moment where all were to perish except for one (because there is only one parachute), Owen makes the executive decision that Claire's life is more worthy than Kayla's because of her position as a mother. This further reifies that Kayla's only purpose in this narrative is to assist in reuniting their family unit.

Claire, who entered the *Jurassic Park* film series in the role of an executive before becoming a dinosaur rights activist, is now firmly identified by her role in the white nuclear family. She is a mom, and her primary function is to protect and rescue her adopted offspring.

Particularly given the role white motherhood serves in shoring up racial boundaries and the white nation (Adams 1997), Claire's evolution from coldhearted executive to loving mother throughout the trilogy works to reinstate the white nuclear family as 'ordinary subjects' in need of protection and deserving of a happy ending. Take the child Maisie, for example. Maise's 'real' mother is the woman from whom she was cloned, therefore making Maisie technically motherless, or in another way, her own mother. Maisie, as the center of our white nuclear family unit, becomes the ultimate child and mother combined – she thus must be protected. And so even though Maisie is a clone and can be read as monstrous herself, she is safely recuperated into the folds of the nuclear family, where she fits neatly into the parameters of the ordinary subject.

The happy ending of *Jurassic World: Dominion* is predicated on the dual reunions of Blue and her offspring and the nuclear family of Owen, Claire, and Maisie. Despite its attempts to shake off the white-focused history of the previous *Jurassic Park* movies by "racing to innocence," the final line of the film sums up why this was always doomed to fail. In a video message, Maisie's 'real' mother (the woman from whom she was cloned), Charlotte (Elva Trill), tells the audience that in order for us all to survive, we must learn to "co-exist" (Treverrow 2022, 2:15:31). Rather than attempting to reckon with *Jurassic Park*'s continued investment in whiteness and the white family, the film thus ends with the sanctity of the nuclear family firmly intact and a vague platitude that serves only to continue to sideline the lives and experiences of the racialized Other. As such, if we look beyond the chaos and havoc wreaked by the dinosaurs, it becomes clear that the real monster looming over the *Jurassic Park* series is and has always been white *Dominion*.

Bibliography

Adams, Mary Louise. 1997. *The trouble with normal: Postwar youth and the making of heterosexuality*. Toronto: University of Toronto Press.

Ahmed, Sara. 2004. "Affective Economies." *Social Text*. 22(2): 117-139.

Bhabha, Homi K. 1994. *The location of culture*. London: Routledge.

Cohen, Jeffrey Jerome. 1996. *Monster Theory: Reading Culture*. Minneapolis: University of Minnesota Press.

Fellows, Mary Louise and Sherene Razack. 1998. "The Race to Innocence: Confronting Hierarchical Relations among Women." *Gender, Race & Justice* 1:335-352.

hooks, bell. 1992. *Black Looks: Race and Representation*. Boston: South End Press.

Johnstone, Joe, dir. 2001. *Jurassic Park III*. United States: Universal Pictures.

Jones, Monique. 2015. "Jurassic World? More Like Jurassic Whitewash." *The Tempest*. July 29. https://thetempest.co/2015/07/29/entertainment/jurassic-world-more-like-jurassic-whitewash.

Ramirez, Ramon. 2014. "*Jurassic Park* is Way More Racist Than You Remember." December 1. https://www.dailydot.com/unclick/jurassic-park-has-a-racism-problem.

Spielberg, Steven, dir. 1993. *Jurassic Park.* United States: Universal Pictures.

Spielberg, Steven, dir. 1997. *The Lost World: Jurassic Park.* United States: Universal Pictures.

Treverrow, Colin, dir. 2015. *Jurassic World.* United States: Universal Pictures.

Treverrow, Colin, dir. 2018. *Jurassic World: Fallen Kingdom.* United States: Universal Pictures.

Treverrow, Colin, dir. 2022. *Jurassic World: Dominion.* United States: Universal Pictures.

Chapter 4

Dark Zombiecologies: Trekking through the Transformative Zombie Forest

Joshua Nieubuurt

Old Dominion University

Abstract: The power of media artifacts has not been ignored by audiences in cinema and institutions. One popular example is the Center for Disease Control's (2021) "Zombie Preparedness" webpage, which aids in "reach[ing] and engag[ing] a wide variety of audiences on all hazards preparedness" through the use of the zombie form. Zombies are a relatively new monster in Western Culture. Zombies first found a level of cinematic popularity in the 20th century with the film *White Zombie* (1932). The inception of the zombie films and modern iterations have substantial differences, but at their core, maintain a unique shared trait. This trait is the ability to transmogrify the social anxieties of their time into the form of a monster. Through the use of media archaeology and a Franken-theory (including Timothy Morton's Dark Ecology and Corline Levine's notion of forms), this paper proposes that contemporary renditions of zombies are a form of eco-apocalyptic projection of human and non-human threats. In short, the zombie aesthetic's shape, form, and application are altered by the Postmodern anxieties of the individual and their collective roles in a global ecology. Zombies, coupled with artistic agency, hint at being a potential method in which to subvert the looming eco-apocalypse through entertainment and eco-literacy.

Keywords: Monstrosity, Zombies, non-human, eco-apocalypse, eco-literacy

***

In late December 1895, the Lumière brothers first tilled the field of what would later grow into a culture-building creature known as cinema. Two decades after those flickering December nights, monsters arrived and found a new cultural mode of conveyance outside the pages of literature and off the well-worn wooden stages of eras past. This new technology amplified cultural productions like never before and allowed for new methods of rhetorical transformation. Among the first was the 1915 film Der Golem: Wie er in die Welt kam (The Golem: How He Came into the World), which drew inspiration from the Jewish legend of the Golem. Mia Spiro writes, "the Golem is always an artificial humanoid, most often made of clay and brought to life through supernatural means" (Spiro 2013, 13). The golem was among the first monsters to seed the fertile soils of the cinematic realm. As it sprouted into a tree sapling, grew, and produced new seeds, other movie monsters began to spring up from this vibrant new landscape. Many of the first monsters on the silver screen hailed from the well-trod literary mythos. Films such as Nosferatu (1922) allowed audiences to view vampires up close and personally. Yet, a common trait of these films was their already established literary history and localization in the "old world" and ancient mythos. These stories sprouted from the roots of petrified trees across millennia but bore fresh cultural fruit through the technological miracle of film. As cinema began to stake a claim in the United States, these "old world" monsters continued to be re-represented, but along with them, a (mostly) "new world" monster germinated just below the surface. The zombie in its imbibition stage, absorbing the zeitgeist of the world above, would eventually give rise to a rhizomatic presence in the world of monsters and cinema.

The power of zombies and other media monsters is vast, and their combined influence haunts along the periphery of the daily experience. The monster, in whatever shape it manifests, often holds power over some of the most base and carnal instincts, allowing it to rustle through the seasonal leaves of popular culture at breakneck speed. The exhilaration felt by audiences experiencing media-based ghosts, vampires, aliens, etc., ebbs and flows. But, from among the legions of monsters, the zombie continues to re-animate itself to linger on among the dusty aged corpses of the other monsters. The zombie's forms are vast, their vigor inexhaustible, and their desire remains steadfast to devour their time's shared apprehensions and anxieties. They now rank among the most widely dispersed monsters in the ever-expanding cinematic production fields.

The Zombie form has cross-pollinated into a multitude of human experiences ranging from engaging audiences' imaginations on the screen or page to altering the typical dynamic of healthcare education through adaptation, and it has even given rise to new forms of social play. The zombie's vast range, usage, and materialization places it in a unique category for monsters. It is a monster that evolves and transforms along with its creators, their respective cultures, and their localized anxieties whilst still being bound to its malleable topoi. Arguably, these transformations have primarily taken place in cinema, but their sanguineous reach has clawed into other--more material--realms.

As of May 2020, Stacker.com aggregated a list to produce the "60 Best Zombie Movies of All Time," drawing from over 7900 zombie films from across the world ("60 Best Zombie Movies of All Time," 2020). One would be hard-pressed to find someone who has not crossed paths with the cinematic zombie at one time or another. The Centers for Disease Control's (2021) "Zombie Preparedness" webpage aids in "reach[ing] and engag[ing] a wide variety of audiences on all hazards preparedness" (Centers for Disease Control 2021). Through the use of the zombie form, an educational general health purpose is served in a fun and engaging way. Here, the zombie form is adapted as an educational medium for real-world preparedness, a far cry from on-screen exigencies. And the biggest little city in the world – Reno, Nevada – hosts the annual Zombie Crawl, which culminates in "15,000 zombies, 40+ bars, 150+ specials & one friggin' sweet night!" (Crawl Reno 2022). Thousands of participants don costumes and scramble through the streets for an evening of festive social play. Here, the zombie bridges the gap between the real and unreal; allowing folx to briefly depart from the daily struggle of existence in the form of the undead, only to be resurrected the following day (brain-splitting headache optional). These are just three examples, among many more, that pay homage to the zombie form and its malleability to be utilized for purposes far outside of its initial appearances in literature, on stage, and in cinema. Much like the now relatively codified tropes of zombie cinema, the plague of zombie usage did not occur overnight despite its status as a relatively new monster.

The zombie's cinematic genesis began in the early twentieth century with the film *White Zombie* (1932), which utilized a zombie form distinct from those found in the twenty-first century. Contemporary portrayals of zombies with their grizzly and gory tropes abound in popular media, both on screens and in print. The dissolution of the human into the monster has been an idea that has continued to titillate minds across the globe and across seas of time. However, the historical and cinematic roots of the zombie form are quite distinguishable from modern portrayals.

The journey of the zombie as a figure cross-pollinated from African mythos to the flesh-hungry embodied undead displays a unique trait uncommon among most portrayals of monsters. The unique facet that distinguishes the zombie above most, if not all, other monsters is the fluidity of its rhetorical transformation. This special trait gives people the ability to transmogrify the social anxieties (for education, play, entertainment, etc.) of their time into the form of a zombie. In other words, the ability of the zombie form to take on newer, broader, and more inclusive meanings is a superpower capitalized upon by people to encapsulate diverse, often divisive, meanings via the form of the zombie.

In their groundbreaking work *Still Life with Rhetoric*, Laurie Gries defines rhetorical transformation as "the process in which things become rhetorical in divergent, unpredictable ways as they circulate, transform, and catalyze change" (Gries 2015, 27). As this chapter will illustrate, the zombie has and continues to be altered and, in turn, alters the people, cultures, and times in which it appears. The multitude of cultural and artistic usages displays the continuity of rhetorical transformation as the zombie form engages with diverse minds and times. Gries further argues that "rhetorical transformation acknowledges that such rhetorical becoming is a spatiotemporal, distributed process that intensifies with each new actualization and with each new encounter" (Gries 2015, 28). The zombie's ability to be rebooted and retooled through time and to still be considered a "zombie" illustrates the incredibly broad potentialities of the monster.

Despite the rather placid nature (in terms of their usage and physical forms) of other monsters, the zombie continues to reiterate despite being bounded by rather codified artistic topoi. This chapter aims to illustrate the rhetorical transformation of the zombie form as a time capsule of societal anxieties at their given point in history. For metaphorical purposes, this time capsule may be best visualized in arboreal form. Each iteration of the zombie shares the genetic traits of past iterations, but it is unto itself a new cross-pollinated hybrid: owing its existence to both the past and the present. Their connection, although tethered to their time, is akin to a forest expanding its peckish reach over the course of nearly one hundred years, one new sapling at a time. This dark forest's growth is fueled by the social and ecological anxieties of a given epoch. These anxieties have been stripped, chopped, and used as a kindle to shine a brighter light on the "monsters" within and those still lingering in the shadows just out of sight, but certainly never out of mind.

To display the rhetorical transformation and to see its applications to unique cultural anxieties taking place at their respective kairotic moment of creation several theoretical tools will be wielded. First, the notion of rhetorical transformation and its situation within a new materialist lens will be fleshed out. Second, is the inclusion of ecocriticism by focusing on Timothy Morton's terms "nature," "mesh," and "the strange stranger" to display their importance for understanding the bedrock beneath many of the zombie form's iterations. Third, the zombie form itself will be considered along with several key iterative moments in its historical cinematic transformations. These key iterative moments will be capped primarily by two examples, *White Zombie* (1932) and *Army of the Dead* (2021), acting as the edges of the forest: a chance to see where the "old" forest growth began and where the "new" growth is expanding into.

This final trek through select portions of the zombie forest is by no means meant to be an exhaustive account of the zombie's rhetorical transformation. Rather, it is meant to function as a guided tour in and through catalyzing moments of social change. The zombie form is a mirror of humanity's collective anxieties, and this chapter is meant to illustrate the implications of rhetorical transformation relating to increased anxiety. Anxiety relating to the ecological, natural, and societal peril. So please, stay close, keep your limbs out of hungry mouths, and be prepared to view horrors in a new light.

Rhetorical Transformation and the Zombie Form

A walk through the ecological succession of the zombie forest illustrates the ways in which the meaning behind the forms has been applied. Each respective epoch's specters have grown to represent the anxieties of their emergence. As Peter Dendel postulates, zombies act as a "barometer of cultural anxiety" utilizing their unique form to perform these anxieties and play them out from the safety of a screen (Dendle 2007, 45). They are a chance for the audience to view the ill omens of their time, momentarily face them, and then move on with their lives. Each rhetorical transformation plants a new sapling, expanding the forest and the length of its shadow. These metaphorical trees have been shown to represent a wide range of anxieties, including the following: post-colonialism, consumerism, conformity, anti-war, capitalism, race dynamics, plagues and viral infections, among many others. What is lost among the ever-growing collection of theoretical lenses is a sense of the zombie form as a co-actant shambling alongside humanity. They are a visual spectacle and a thing that has the power to alter the actions of humans. This growing collection of "meanings" and co-agency hacks at the undergrowth of the forest to open a new trail. A path being cut and trod out by new materialism.

The significance of this lies in new materialism's ability to, as Laurie Gries (2015) writes, "display how things become rhetorically meaningful via the consequentiality they spark in the world" (3). In the realm of rhetoric, the focus then is not exclusively to draw parallels between metaphors and form, the ars gratia artis, or even the grander significance of veiled political messages, but rather the ways in which the non-human utilizes its bounded agency. Quite often, [co]agency has been exclusively framed with an anthropocentric mindset; hindering any other thing (be it creatures, critters, or objects) from wielding power. New materialism posits an alternative positionality, displaying power and agency as something not only wielded by homo sapiens with axes but things and critters as well.

Diana Coole and Samantha Frost (2010) note that displacing anthropocentric positionality is no small feat, "the challenge here is to give materiality its due while recognizing its plural dimensions and its complex, contingent modes of appearing" (27). Through the act of rhetorical transformation, each iteration of the zombie exhibits new and exciting consequentialities for people and things alike. However, it should be noted that these consequentialities are often far displaced from their origins. As each new sapling is planted, traces of its genetic legacy may lie recessive until a special kairotic moment calls them forth. New materialism highlights the exigence of things (including critters and monsters) in this process of becoming. Furthermore, it seeks to give these things their due in the tangled webs of existence. In a way, the zombie (a non-human) acting in the fictional and material world is a prime example of non-human agency altering the way both things and humans dwell. To that end, the long-lived corpse of Cartesian duality within the zombie genre must finally be laid to rest: Humans and zombies literally trod together: enmeshed in a greater assemblage of being.

Enmeshed Hybrids by *Nature*

In order to see how humans and zombies are enmeshed, there is an idea that must first be pinned down and devoured: The notion of "nature." The usage of nature here is not the Disneyfied iteration passed down from the Romantic period; idyllic, pristine mountains oversee lush green meadows in which cute furry animals frolic. Rather, it is an assemblage of "strange strangers" and *things* (in the Heideggerian sense) existing, entangling, and metamorphosing the reality in which they dwell: the mangling of the human, machine, animal, and material.

Timothy Morton (2010), lamenting upon the colloquial understanding of nature, deems such anthropocentric nostalgia as "an ideal image, a self-contained form suspended afar, shimmering and naked behind glass like an expensive painting" or "a cheap plastic knockoff" (Location 85). Nature is rather alive and in motion; constantly shifting and rearranging, a space with no specific locus. All the time, things appear to be simply coming or going. Looking at it from a new materialist perspective helps to understand that things are transforming within a greater ecology than a singular mind can fathom.

For the purpose of this text, Morton's notion of the "mesh" may help to illuminate a path through the zombie forest. Morton defines the "mesh" as "a complex situation or series of events in which a person [or being] is entangled" (Loc. 379). These entanglements certainly include cultural, historical, material, and ecological issues of the human world. There is no spatial or temporal center to the mesh, the entanglements are ambient in nature, and art is one way in which humans interact with each other and non-humans while in the midst of the mesh. [Co]Actants within this mesh then take on a unique role in and amongst each other: The role of the "strange stranger." Morton defines this term through the phenomenological experience of considering other beings. He writes, "Our encounter with other beings becomes profound. They are strange, even intrinsically strange. Getting to know them makes them stranger" (Loc. 211). The zombie form is an exemplary metaphor for this idea of the strange stranger: once human, now other. Once known to dwell with certain actions, it is now an Other with unforeseeable and unknowable paths to tread. The known within this form become encapsulated by the unknowns, leaving in its wake a grim reminder of the amorphous boundaries of what it means to be human.

The unique perspective of realizing the other being as a lifeform dwelling in the world, coupled with self-reflexivity, generates the potential for "strange" to occur. This notion of the strange stranger is "at the limit of our imagining" (Morton 2010, loc. 241). It is both that which resides in oneself as an individual, as a member of a species, and as one species among many. The entangling properties of dwelling within a world of beings place the existence of being outside of oneself into a category of other. Especially those closest to oneself (family, friends, and pets) may only become strangers upon a greater understanding of them as a being in the world. This is paramount in understanding and "seeing" the zombie as a manifestation of human anxieties and acting in the world of humans. The strange stranger helps to display the inherent debacles present in contemporary discourses on the implications of humanity's role(s) in potential [eco-]apocalypse; it both is and is not us as individuals creating potential [eco-]apocalypses. The human-made problems combine with exterior forces (i.e., trans-species disease, climate change, natural phenomenon, etc.) beyond anthropocentric ideas of control to permit the zombie as a locus for anxieties.

To return to the idea of nature, the zombie form and its rhetorical transformations aid in discovering, exploring, and iterating upon the potential threats found within the mesh. By reconsidering nature as the mesh, one is forced to remove the unalterable forms placed upon it as static material. Rather, it is an essential component of the transformational properties inherent among the strange strangers that dwell within it. Although fictional, the zombie does "exist" within human and non-human ecologies and brings forth powerful consequentialities for humans to either enjoy, enact, act upon, or perform.

The concept of "form" among monsters is also important to consider. Vampires are not vampires unless they take on the form of a bloodsucking monster (movie star faces optional); werewolves are not werewolves unless they are humans that transmogrify under a full moon (and have expensive clothing bills). But what form do zombies *do*? Certainly, tropes exist: they eat flesh, people generally become them through bites or infections; and the transformation dissolves one's ability to act according to pre-established societal norms: making them savage. Although, as displayed over the course of the twentieth and into the early twenty-first century, each of these tropes has been bent, broken, or even non-existent within forms of the zombie.

According to the work of Caroline Levine (2016), forms are "any arrangement of elements—any ordering, patterning, or shaping." Levine (2017) also notes that forms are not limited to the aesthetic realm but also the political and social. When applied to the zombie, the physical forms have been altered, as well as the more malleable political innards that seep out of their porous cadavers. Placing the zombie as a form entangled within the realm of new materialist theory allows for the displacement of anthropocentric [eco-]apocalypse onto a fictional–yet uncannily recognizable– strange stranger for the enjoyment of zombie fans the world over.

Hereafter, the terminology "Zombie form" will incorporate aspects of nature, strange strangers, and forms as an assemblage of transformational meaning-making. To better understand the rhetorical transformations evident in the zombie form, it is essential to trace and examine key moments in the iteration of the zombie form through its portrayals in cinema. The key moments of rhetorical transformation described here are some among legions of others. Despite the plethora of potential focal points, the ones here have been chosen as moments in which the recessive traits were called forth to address critical kairotic moments for people and things alike.

By definition, rhetorical transformation is unpredictable (Levine 2017). This unpredictability can often be illustrated through tracing the origins of words, phrases, concepts, and media artifacts as they travel and materialize through space and time. The etymology and history of the word and concepts of "zombie" may help illuminate some of the cross-pollination already mentioned. The histories of the zombie are well-tread and have been extensively researched through various lenses. With that in mind, the following section focuses briefly on African mythos and its relationship to rhetorical transformation.

African Mythos Fertilizing the Zombie Forest

Sarah Julie Lauro's (2015) groundbreaking work *The Transatlantic Zombie* focuses on displaying the relationship of the zombie to slavery and rebellion. For Lauro, "the zombie is not a figure of resurrection but only of living death, and insofar as the zombie metaphorizes both slavery and slave rebellion" (29). In establishing a solid case for their stance, Lauro traces the etymology, their proposed origin of zombies, and their relationship with the Transatlantic slave trade and Haitian Revolution.

Lauro's exhaustive look into the murky origins of the zombie itself exhibits the fundamental properties of rhetorical transformation. As Lauro writes, "with the zombie there is always a 'yet' or a 'but,' or a 'however' and a 'nonetheless'— the irresolution of the zombie's dialectic (not master/slave but slave/rebel- slave) continues to thwart attempts to read the figure as wholly resistive" (33). Although Lauro beautifully displays the paradigm sought by their lens, the concept of rhetorical transformation extends and invigorates the divergent powers the zombie possesses. Indeed, the lack of definitive sources as to the origin of "zombie" has left scholars scratching the soil, hoping to unearth the first mummified zombie corpse. As Lauro's research exhibits, it is likely that cross-pollination of African mythos was iterating long before zombies entered popular usage.

Lauro singles out the first kairotic moment of transformation to be the Haitian Revolution, noting that the seeds and fertilizer of the zombie hail from across the Atlantic Ocean. These essential parts have been attributed to "the Angolan Zombi, Congo's Nzambi or zambi, or the Vaudou lwa Damballah, called Li Gran Zombi in New Orleans, or even malicious ghosts like the duppy" among others, and help to trace the genetic lineage of the zombie in the myriad of forms it is found today (Lauro 2015, 33). It is of special note that these deep roots all contain a unique malleable property: the ability to transform or shapeshift in spiritual or corporal ways. Doris Garraway writes, "the zombi accrues meaning as a frightful entity in the colonial imagination, one that is believed to shapeshift, or metamorphose, in myriad ways" (Cited in Lauro 2015, 35-36). Much like the later transformation of living to dead to undead, the evolution of the zombie in cinema maintains and builds upon these rhetorical transformative properties.

White Zombie

Nearly forty years after the Lumière brothers first dazzled a small audience with their moving pictures, and an ocean away, the zombie form stepped out of mythos and was projected into cinematic lore. Victor Halperin's *White Zombie* (1932) gave audiences the first glimpse into the vacant eyes of a monster that continues to outlive most audience members of the time. Despite this being the first zombie-centered film, zombies and other magic-based monsters had already begun to plant their rhizomatic roots into the social consciousness through other artistic means.

Slightly before the production of White Zombie, American audiences were entranced with tales of mind control, monsters, and dark magic found in texts and stage plays (Pop 2014). To continue the arboreal metaphor, *White Zombie* was a seedling that sprouted under the perfect conditions to grow and reproduce new and exciting zombie forms through the medium of cinema. The rhetorical transformation out of pages and stages and onto the silver screen was a catalyzing moment for the zombie form. Despite the transition, *White Zombie* maintains the essential genetics of its aged ancestors, particularly in relation to location, zombie form, and metaphorical properties.

White Zombie (1932) takes place in an exotic locale of post-slavery Haiti. At the time of the film's appearance, Haiti had undergone an occupation by the United States. Lauro writes, "the zombie only comes into US cinema because of the American occupation of the sovereign republic of Haiti (1915– 34)" (4). This entanglement is exhibited within the film's locale as well as inter-character social dynamics. The master/servant binary and post-slavery mindset are still lingering as backdrops to the action. As Benedetta Rossi (2015) writes,

> The term post-slavery refers to historical and social circumstances
> identifiable in contexts where slavery was a fundamental social
> institution and its legal abolition was followed by resilient legacies of
> past hierarchy and abuse. (303)

Haiti as a setting allows the audience to see post-slavery from an outside
positionality. For the audience of the time, it was not the slavery found in the
US a few generations prior, but some form of it living elsewhere. A place
strange, exotic, and perhaps a bit "savage." Although thematically familiar to
audiences, this choice acts in line with Morton's strange-stranger. One knows
such worlds exist[ed], and by considering it even more deeply, the stranger and
more foreign the idea becomes. This, in turn, enables the zombie to play the
anthropomorphized role of their anxieties relating to slavery and the fear of
losing one's corporeal control to someone else's will.

Halperin's zombies and the rhetorical transformation from page to screen set
the stage for cinematic zombies to signify the anxieties of their time for wider
audiences. Referring to the initial portrayals of zombies, Doru Pop (2014) writes
that they are "basically humans at the mercy of their fellow men, which can be
put to mindless work for the benefit of others. They are representations of
slavery in the purest form" (120-121). The anxiety lingering in the social
consciousness from the form of slavery allows zombies to "mindlessly"
represent the juxtaposition of being alive whilst under the control of another.

In the film, people are made into zombies through a potion brewed by the
antagonist. This potion has a real-world history that was investigated by
Harvard Anthropologist Wade Davis in 1985. Davis writes, "Vodoun priests,
called bokors, possess a keen knowledge of natural drugs and sedatives and
have created a 'zombie powder'—called coup poudre—that renders its victims
clinically dead" (Davis and Laben 2017, 90). This powder allows for the
hypnotization and utilization of human bodies for the will of another; the total
loss of embodied power. This loss is encountered through the distilled usage of
the products harvested from nature, a natural ally to the devious ends of
humankind. Such forms of Zombies as utilitarian tools persisted throughout
early iterations of their use. The mesh represented within the film shows the
deep roots of both human and nonhuman entanglement and how each form
has power over one another; but neither holds the upper hand. The drugs
derived from the natural in the hands of humans used for malevolent deeds
lead to the downfall of the antagonist and the saving of the zombies' humanity.
The localized issue is solved by humankind, and life goes on as "normal."
Despite being "zombified," the female protagonist's physical form is mostly
unaltered, as are the other zombies throughout the film. The gory physical
transformation of the zombie had yet to take place, but the metaphorical
transformations had found a starting point.

The zombies of this film are not the decaying, flesh-hungry, gore-monstrosities of today. Their flesh, although perhaps bent and battered by the will of the film's antagonist, remains intact, their bodily motions and their capacities are akin to their non-mind-controlled state. At a skin-deep level, zombies here act as extensions of the antagonist.

Delving deep into the flesh and into the metaphorical anxieties they relate to has primarily been linked with post-slavery America. Although, a new branch of thought was also being applied: the growing understanding of post-industrial revolution alienation within the realm of labor. As Wonser and Boynes (2016), focusing on the zombie from a sociological lens, write, fear of the 'other,' apprehension about the loss of autonomy, and threats of totalitarian control and exploitation—motifs of enduring centrality to zombie films—all have been central concerns of the American experience (630). As seen in *White Zombie*, the real-world anxieties faced in the 1930s found a monster in which they could be displaced, viewed, examined, and cast into a form meant to entertain. When combined, these traits allow the zombie to embody such anxieties without the audience having to see themselves as the locus of these feelings, at least directly. Dwelling alongside post-abolition anxiety is the increased alienation felt by workers in the post-industrialization era.

Craig Finlay (2014) notes that early Marxist lenses used to categorize the zombie as a metaphor for the alienation of the worker and the monotony that comes along with such existences. Finlay writes, "Zombies of this sort are a better analogue for the factory worker, performing an unthinking, endless task at an assembly line" (135). An early scene in *White Zombie* film depicts zombies working in a sugar refinery, they shamble along in a mindless fashion, working at their task. Their bodies show slight signs of wear and tear, and at one point, a zombie even falls into the sugar cane grinding apparatus unnoticed by those working alongside him. Following this branch of thought, the depictions of zombies in *White Zombie* once again corporealize the anxieties faced by hardworking folx grinding out a living whilst amid the Great Depression. Many of whom were "ground up" in the wake of unfettered pursuits of profit by others; others that (in part) had some level of corporeal control over their embodied selves. Despite the challenges presented through this film's zombie form, there remains some sense of hope for overcoming such anxieties.

At the conclusion of the film, the female protagonist overcomes her mind control. The zombies and their master are cast over a cliff to their [real] death. The lead protagonists presumably return to their home country to live happily ever after. The natives, the wild jungles of Haiti, and the existence of zombies remain localized to a small island in the Caribbean. The film appears to state that the troubles of slavery and alienation can be extinguished and that a new world of freedom from such bonds exists elsewhere, specifically in the places where the film's audiences dwell. Here, the zombie exhibits the properties of the malevolent anxieties that can, should one try, overcome. Though, as later iterated by further zombie rhetorical transformations, such thoughts may have been a bit too optimistic.

White Zombie was the first sapling cast into the soil of the social consciousness. Its genealogy hints at a hybrid association with African and "old world" mythos: the heartwood that remains common to the initial zombie form's descendants. The seeds of which found fertile soil in the Americas. But as the sapling grew and its seedlings were thrust into the wind, new iterations of the zombie took root as newer saplings intermingled and created cross-pollinated hybrids. Eventually, their respective branches become enmeshed with others but still budding with the potential to bear the juicy anxiety-driven cultural and physical fruits of their given time and place. The following section can be envisioned as a quick jog through the ever-growing zombie forest. It is meant to swiftly display the rapid rhetorical transformations as the zombie form moved from its afforestation into new growth areas.

Cross-pollination, Rapid Iterations, and Transformation in Action

After *White Zombie*, other films sprouted alongside it, slowly iterating the zombie form. Films such as *King of the Zombies* (1941) and *Revenge of the Zombies* (1943) utilized the zombie form to highlight anxieties of both scientific advancement and Nazism. *Zombies of Mora Tau* (1957), displaced from the World War Two era, harnessed the power of consumer culture and adventure to speak to changing audience tastes. Despite being a rather small sapling in the zombie forest, Peter Dendle (2001) notes the importance of this film writing, "This awkward and talentless movie is nonetheless surprisingly prescient in zombie film history, anticipating a number of motifs that would reappear in later decades" (211-212). At the initial stages of its application and iterative processes, the zombie form maintained a slow but steady rhetorical transformation. Each iteration incorporates elements from its temporal position and its anxieties.

The zombie form maintained the soil of its first planting, holding onto conceptions of mind control, voodoo, or magic as the catalyst for raising the dead or imprisoning the mind. Such early films also borrowed heavily from other monster genres of the time. It was not until the late 1960s that the zombie sapling, which folx today would recognize, began its rapid growth and created its own distinguished and clearly transformative canopy.

The codification of the zombie as we know it to be in the twenty-first century is indebted to George A. Romero's 1968 film *Night of the Living Dead*. It is here where the physical traits of zombies not only begin to be altered more vibrantly, but their pith undergoes further rhetorical transformation, increasing the potential for divergent catalyzing change. As Wonser and Boyns (2016) note, *Night of the Living Dead* infused new vigor and vitality into the zombie genre, irrevocably altering its form and function as well as establishing the zombie as a symbolic representation of societal ills—a pattern that continues in present-day cinema (631). To put it more colloquially, this film allowed the zombie to crack open the skulls of audiences, devour their fears, and spread their viral cathartic powers to mass audiences through the genre of horror. Simultaneously, those rotting corpses of the audience would themselves transform into the fertilizer used in zombie movies generations after.

Night of the Living Dead (1968) and its younger sapling *Dawn of the Dead* (1979), brought new zombie forms to the screen. The image of [bluish] bloodied corpses yearning for flesh in much more visually descriptive and violent means was a dramatic transformation that resonated with audiences. Along with the physical changes, audiences and critics tore the bark from the tree to apply their own conceptions of what the zombies metaphorically represented.

Night of the Living Dead and *Dawn of the Dead* have been given a wide range of metaphorical applications, from visualizing race dynamics to criticizing consumerism and capitalism and anxieties faced in the middle of the Cold War and Vietnam eras.[1] The multiplicity of potential meanings taken by audiences, scholars, and critics shows how our metaphorical zombie forest burst through the horror genre canopy and into the vast forms it utilizes today.

As Romero's two films age, their influence can be felt decades displaced from their conception. The physical forms grow more grotesque and more *real*, and the social anxieties applied continue to branch off into new and divergent directions. Kyle Bishop (2009) notes, "As audiences have become more familiar with special effects and more accustomed to images of violence, cinematic depictions of zombies have had to become progressively more naturalistic and horrific" (19-20). The zombie form, in part, played a consequential role in how the material forms of horror films (including those outside the zombie genre) have been and continue to be altered. From the fascinatingly diverse range of special effects and extending into the way in which zombies move and interact with the non-anthropocentric realm: the realms of animals and things.

As the zombie entered the new millennium, new forms began to be applied to a post-9/11 world. Bishop (2009) declared a "Zombie Renaissance" that focused on the kairotic moments in which the zombie now dwelled. Bishop postulates that "the primary metaphor in the post-9/11 zombie world is terrorism" and the potential for fears relating to it to seep into one's daily life

---

[1] Remarkably, nearly all zombie sources used in this chapter reflect this general idea.

(19). Films during this period, such as *Land of the Dead* (2005), focus on the zombie event as a metaphor for border control (Bishop 2009, 24). A situation in which insulation from the outside is paramount to the survival of those inside the borders of society. Through such a process, the "monsters" outside those walls become less of a problem compared to the troubles made by the people within them. A message that certainly resonated with people facing the grander implications of 9/11, both at home and abroad. Although the dangers of fellow humans are present throughout the zombie genre, the greater implications of human activities on nature and the environment also began to ooze from the zombie form.

Finlay (2014) taking a Deep Ecology approach, finds modern zombies to be "the very embodiment of our own anthropocentric attitude toward the planet, which holds that we have a right destroy nature, exterminate other species and subjugate entire ecosystems in the name of supporting our own consumption habits and massive overpopulation" (131). The shift in focus displays a transformation from a mirror of externalized social anxieties and reveals the "monsters" that are behind the zombie are our own species. It also displays how conceptions of things and critters have joined into the grander assemblage of the zombie form's recursive powers.

Films such as *28 Days Later* (2002), *28 Weeks Later* (2007), the *Resident Evil (Biohazard)* franchise (2002-2016), and *World War Z* (2013) become intimately linked and morphed due to the multidirectional rhetorical transformations taking place within the genre and within the worlds they create. More and more real-world anxieties are placed onto the zombie, altering its forms to be more monstrous and the zombies' physical forms more duplicitous as the anxieties faced become more known and discerned to be global problems. Such films remove themselves from a localized problem (such as the one seen in *White Zombie*) and highlight the interconnected complexities of twenty-first-century existence: a problem for one area can quickly become a problem for everyone. This became evidently clear as the COVID-19 pandemic swept across the globe.

Wonser and Boynes (2016) note, "the zombie film is an important source of cultural critique, and provides a rich, sociological expression of the dynamics of identity and disease, contagion and pandemic, and the privileges that circumscribe health and social inequality" (650). As the issues faced by contemporary societies evolve, so do the fears surrounding them.

Although many zombie films focus on action, suspense, and/or horror as their go-to genre, zombies have and continue to infect the genre of comedy. Films such as *Shaun of the Dead* (2004), *Zombieland* (2009), *Zombie Land: Double Tap* (2019), and *The Dead Don't Die* (2019) utilize satire and humor as "symbolic and critical representations of the societies from which they emerge and as metaphorical illustrations of the culture's zeitgeist" harnessing the expressive powers of the zombie form (Wonser and Boynes 2016, 629). Although the performance mechanisms are slightly different, anthropocentric anxiety remains the key evoker of rhetorical meaning within comedic portrayals of zombies. They remain as important parts of the zombie forest, expanding its reach to those outside of horror fans and allowing for laughter to replace fear for a similar outcome. In the following section, the quick tour through the zombie forest will take a slight detour into how anthropocentricity has been evoked and reversed in one of the latest rhetorical transformations.

Army of the Dead: Reverse Roles

In the 89 years since *White Zombie* shambled across the silver screen, the zombie displays an increased understanding of the range and carnality of the human experience. Due to the efforts of creative minds, filmmakers, audiences, and the changing ecosystems of the anthropocentric world, the tropological forms of the zombie continue to cross-pollinate, evolve, and displace the anxieties of their time into the zombie form. The tropes that linger on among the now fallen and rotting trees of their progenitors of the early twentieth century include the increasingly grotesque form of the bodies of zombies, a [near] apocalyptic setting, and a sense of blandness akin to the "real world" (Bishop 2006). Zack Snyder's 2021 film *Army of the Dead* is one of the most recent cinematic visions to enter and alter the zombie's form, highlighting the essential cross-pollinations of the genre.

The film takes place in a quarantined Las Vegas in which a presumed military experiment with a taste for flesh and the viral ability to "turn" humans into zombies resides. Unlike *White Zombie*, Snyder's zombies have a monarchical form, language, and keen intelligence. Furthermore, the inclusion of animals as zombified dwellers also alters the nature-being forms displayed in many previous iterations (though they are occasionally depicted in films such as within the *Resident Evil* franchise). Here, the established trope of utilitarianism is localized to the human-dwellers (a narrative device propelling the plot), while the zombie has reversed the role and is relatively "free" within its decaying domain (a transformation in the master/servant binary). In short, the film at first appears to rely on the notion that humans are slaves to money (critiquing capitalism, consumerism, the military-industrial complex, and Internet culture), interlinking its branches throughout the zombie forest. Furthermore, the dynamics between human characters echo the notion that zombies are certainly obstacles, but the real trouble is anthropocentric [in]action.

This reflection of lingering fear also branches into the greater concerns of human-generated [eco-]apocalypse (via unethical human experimentation and nuclear weapons) or those of the zombie expansion (a viral plague). All the while, the zombie, as a new form in nature, finds a niche in which to dwell (the supplanting of the anthropocentric reality). The institutionalization of the zombie via monarchical structure lends itself to Levine's (2017) idea that "institutions preserve forms. Their repetitive rhythms over time afford stability" (Loc. 1430). The zombies of the film establish a hierarchical structure, shape, mold their ecosystem, and find themselves in direct competition for resources (colonialism). In short, these zombies are "us" and the depictions of "Other" simultaneously. They represent the spectrum of the human experience displayed throughout the rhetorical transformations of the zombie form thus far. The peripeteia is evident in the outcomes of both parties at the conclusion of the film.

As the stability of human forms is on the edge of collapse, the rise of the zombie's monarchy is seeing the beginnings of its establishment in a new ecological order; an order at the forethought of societies battling their own real fears of [eco]apocalypse. Again, the zombie form as an aesthetic creation continues to mirror contemporary conversations and anxieties of the time in which it has been produced. In the end, "Nature" continues, but humanity's role within its mesh is at stake. The film asks audiences to consider the boundaries of nature and the strange stranger alongside the issues faced by wandering into other areas of the zombie-form forest. The locations and entanglements of each being blur as the actions of humans, present and past, collide into real-world ramifications. This specific branch of the great zombie forest utilizes the topoi generated through nearly 100 years of zombie cinema, illustrating its genealogy, hinting at the possibilities of future iterations, and beautifully displaying the anxieties faced as we race deeper into the twenty-first century.

Transformations Outside of the Screen

Although this chapter focuses primarily on the cinematic zombie, their presence has become an ambient part of twenty-first-century life that needs to be briefly touched on to see the greater implications of their cinematic rhetorical transformations. According to a survey by YouGov (2017), 12% of respondents (N=2204) stated that they had a zombie survival plan. This bridging of reality and fantasy (albeit more than likely just a fun, imaginative activity) literally has moved the minds and bodies of people. This is also evident in the leisure activities of people around the world.

For decades, Zombies have also held a prominent role in the gaming industry. The *Resident Evil* gaming franchise has sold over 78 million units since its debut in 1996 (Clement 2022). Mobile gaming applications have also been influenced by zombie forms. As of March 2021, the IOS gaming application *State of Survival: Zombie War* was grossing over $900 thousand a day (Clement 2021). In June of 2022, this app was still among the top five gaming apps on IOS (Clement 2022). The zombie form has also entered and solidified within the English lexicon.

Phrases such as "you look like a zombie" after a restless night are not uncommon. In the world of business, the term "zombie" has come to signify, "companies that earn just enough money to continue operating and service debt but are unable to pay off their debt" (Kenton 2021). "Zombie Apps," are "invisible" applications that mobile devices can only find by directly searching for them; a state in which 80-90% of applications exist (Zorraquino 2022). Needless to say, zombies dwell ambiently among us just outside of the screen as ideas and things alike.

The Zombie Forest Expanding Onward

As our trek through the zombie form forest comes to an end, be careful not to stumble over the newer saplings taking root. Their purpose is important, and their ability to alter the world for future generations is of "global significance" as globalized problems create globalized anxieties (Oloff 2012). Our journey has led us through just a few key moments in the rhetorical transformation of cinematic zombies.[2] At each iterative moment of transformation, new forms were brought into being, sparking new understandings inside the film genre and morphing unpredictably outside the silver screen. And they will continue to do so. The zombie has acted as a monstrous projection of societal anxiety, inviting us into the zombie-form forest for dinner, offering to consume our [brains and] fears. As long as the anthropocentric world harnesses anxieties, new zombies will emerge from the forest to gobble them up. From African mythos to a screen near you, the zombie has come a long way and continues to evolve and change with the folx who continue to reinvent them. They will remain a monster with global significance.

Bibliography

"60 Best Zombie Movies of All Time." Stacker. Last modified October 27, 2020. https://stacker.com/stories/4751/60-best-zombie-movies-all-time.

Bishop, Kyle. 2006. "Raising the Dead." *Journal of Popular Film & Television* 33 (4): 196–205. doi:10.3200/JPFT.33.4.196-205.

Bishop, Kyle. 2009. "Dead Man Still Walking: Explaining the Zombie Renaissance." *Journal of Popular Film & Television* 37 (1): 16–25. doi:10.3200/JPFT.37.1.16-25.

---

[2] A few key moments in popular zombie cinema hailing primarily from the USA and the UK. Unfortunately, this text does not even delve into cinematic zombies hailing outside of the "west." The recent increase of zombies forms in Korean and Japanese film as well as the vast depictions found in television have greatly expanded the zombie form forest. Such a limitation offers a whole host of opportunities for scholars considering rhetorical transformation of zombies in other areas and genres.

Boyle, Danny, director. 2007. *28 Days Later*. UK: Fox Searchlight Pictures.

Cahn, Edward L., director. 1957. *Zombies of Mora Tau*. USA: Columbia Pictures.

Centers for Disease Control and Prevention. 2021. "Zombie Preparedness." *Centers for Disease Control and Prevention*, www.cdc.gov/cpr/zombie/index. htm?CDC_AA_refVal=https%3A%2F%2Fwww.cdc.gov%2Fcpr%2Fzombies.htm.

Clement, J. "U.S. Top-grossing IPhone Games 2021." Statista. Last modified March 22, 2021. https://www.statista.com/statistics/263988/top-grossing-m obile-ios-gaming-apps-ranked-by-daily-revenue/.

Clement, J. "Global Top Grossing IPad Games 2022." Statista. Last modified July 21, 2022. https://www.statista.com/statistics/697660/leading-ipad-mobile-games-global-revenue/.

Clement, J. "Resident Evil Game Unit Sales 2022." Statista. Last modified August 16, 2022. https://www.statista.com/statistics/1241675/resident-evil-top-sel ling-games-units-sold/.

Coole, Diana, and Samantha Frost. 2010. *New Materialisms: Ontology, Agency, and Politics*. Durham: Duke University Press.

Crawl Reno. "Reno Zombie Crawl 2022." Crawl Reno. Accessed October 11, 2022. https://crawlreno.com/event/zombiecrawl/.

Davis, Wade, and Carrie Laben. 2017. *The Serpent and the Rainbow*. Ebook.

Dendle, Peter. "The Zombie as Barometer of Cultural Anxiety." 2007. *Monstrous: Myths and Metaphors of Enduring Evil*, Vol. 38, 45–57.

Dendle, Peter. 2001. *The Zombie Movie Encyclopedia*. Jefferson: McFarland. 211–212.

Finlay, Craig. 2014. "Sustainable Brains: Deep Ecology and Dawn of the Dead." *Journal of Humanistic & Social Studies* 5 (1): 131–43.

Fleischer, Ruben, director. 2009. *Zombieland*, USA: Sony Pictures Releasing.

Fleischer, Ruben, director. 2019. *Zombie Land: Double Tap*, USA: Sony Pictures Releasing.

Forster, Marc, director. 2013. *World War Z*, USA: Paramount Pictures.

Fresnadillo, Juan Carlos, director. 2007. *28 Week Later*. UK: 20th Century Fox.

Gries, Laurie. 2015. *Still Life with Rhetoric: A New Materialist Approach for Visual Rhetorics*. Boulder: University Press of Colorado. Kindle.

Halperin, Victor, director. 1932. *White Zombie*. *Youtube*. www.youtube.com/w atch?v=vd88ogGoBmk.

Jarmusch, Jim, director. 2019. *The Dead Don't Die*, USA: Focus Features.

Kenton, Will. "Zombies." Investopedia. Last modified August 31, 2021. https://www.investopedia.com/terms/z/zombies.asp.

Lauro, Sarah J. 2015. *The Transatlantic Zombie: Slavery, Rebellion, and Living Death*. Rutgers University Press. EBook.

Levine, Caroline. 2016. *Forms, Literary and Social*. Standford Press, arcade.sta nford.edu/sites/default/files/article_pdfs/Dibur-v02i01-article07-Levine. PDF.

Levine, Caroline. 2017. *Forms: Whole, Rhythm, Hierarchy, Network*. Princeton: Princeton University Press. Kindle.

McCarthy, Niall. "Infographic: 90% Of All IOS Apps Are Zombies." Statista Infographics. Last modified September 5, 2016. https://www.statista.com/ chart/ 5715/90-of-all-ios-apps-are-zombies/.

Morton, Timothy. *The Ecological Thought.* Cambridge: Harvard University Press, 2010.

Murnau, Friedrich W., director. 1922. *Nosferatu.* Germany: Prana Film.

Oloff, Kerstin. "'Greening'the Zombie: Caribbean Gothic, World-Ecology, and Socio-Ecological Degradation." *Green Letters* 16, no. 1 (2012): 31-45.

Pop, Doru. 2014. "The Desecration of Bodies. Re-Animating Undead Mythologies in Cinema." *Ekphrasis (2067-631X)* 12 (2): 110–30.

Romero, George A., director. 1968. *Night of the Living Dead,* USA: Continental Distributing.

Romero, George A., director. 1979. *Dawn of the Dead,* USA: United Film Distribution Company.

Romero, George A., director. 2005. *Land of the Dead,* USA: Universal Pictures.

Rossi, Benedetta. 2015. "African Post-Slavery: A History of the Future." *The International Journal of African Historical Studies* 48 (2): 303–24.

Sekely, Steve, director. 1943. *Revenge of the Zombies,* USA: Monogram Pictures.

Sekely, Steve and Yarbrough, Jean, directors. 1941. *King of the Zombies,* USA: Monogram Pictures.

Snyder, Zack, director. 2021. *Army of the Dead.* USA: The Stone Quarry.

Spiro, Mia. 2013. "Containing the Monster: The Golem in Expressionist Film and Theater." *Space Between: Literature & Culture, 1914-1945* 9 (1): 11–36.

Wegener, Paul and Galeen, Henrik, directors. 1915. *The Golem: How He Came into the World. YouTube.* https://www.youtube.com/watch?v=2A0lMPde6q8.

Wonser, Robert, and David Boyns. 2016. "Between the Living and Undead: How Zombie Cinema Reflects the Social Construction of Risk, the Anxious Self, and Disease Pandemic." *Sociological Quarterly* 57 (4): 628–53. doi:10.1111/tsq.12150.

Wright, Edgar, director. 2004. *Shaun of the Dead, UK:* Rogue Pictures.

YouGov. "Zombies." YouGov. 2017. https://d25d2506sfb94s.cloudfront.net/cu mulus_uploads/document/phqmwnnd80/Results%20for%20YouGovNY%2 0(Zombies)%20223%2010.25.2017.pdf.

Zorraquino. "Zombie Apps." Zorraquino. Last modified 2022. https://www. zorraquino.com/en/dictionary/technology/what-are-zombie-apps.html.

Chapter 5

Monstrous Gatekeepers – Eco-gothic Bodies in Video Games

Morgan Kate Pinder

Deakin University

Abstract: As we edge closer to the looming ecological crisis of the Late Anthropocene, the fragility of the structures that insulate the human from the unpredictable violence of nature have become increasingly apparent. Ecophobia, that is, the irrational fear of nature and the non-human ecology, manifests across media. However, very few mediums let you walk through those narratives, choose your own path, and be held responsible for a chain of cause and effect. This chapter deals with the transgressive and abject ecoGothic monsters that stalk video games. Rather than being one of many, they are anomalous and 'unnatural.' These video games have the primary ecoGothic feature of the abject or monstrous Gothic body, which is hybridized, mutated, or in some way transgressive of species. This is often expressed through the instability of form and fluidity of species. Some harken back to the degeneration theory of the Victorian era; others engage with 20th-century distrust of difference and the unknowable and still further are symptomatic of human hubris and interference. Despite the apparent malevolent nature of these videoludic monsters, their status as evil is often problematized through their vulnerability to the same vast and unfathomable forces as the player character. From games like *Sekiro* (FromSoftware 2019) that are structured around punishing boss fights connected through supernatural and ecological crises to puzzle games such as *The Return of the Obra Dinn* (Lucas Pope, 2018) in which the true monstrosity is gradually revealed, the monsters themselves are also victims. They are rendered monstrous through their trauma and otherness. This may be achieved through monstrous 'technologies' such as hybridity, contamination, and unfathomability. Through video game narratology and eco-gothic theory, I will explore the complex connections between ecophobia and the video game monsters that stand between the player and their objective.

Keywords: Monsters, Levinas, Vulnerability, Ethics, Houshang Golshiri, Tale of the Fisherman and the monster

***

The deceptively peaceful, snow-covered Sunken Valley of *Sekiro: Shadows Die Twice* (FromSoftware Inc. 2019) is home to a vast array of hostile creatures that pose a very real threat to the eponymous hero and player-character. But this dangerous valley stands between the warrior and their purpose, so there is no option but to continue through this strange subversion of the hero's journey, through the ruins of giant statues, and into the realm of the monkeys. As Sekiro enters a deep crevasse, the player sees the elongated limbs and hunched posture of a great ape sitting in a shallow lotus pool, his features are a grotesque parody of a primate. A sword sticks out of his neck, and he greedily drinks from the water around him. The vulnerability of the human form is laid bare when compared to the enormous simian. The creature leaps at the comparatively tiny warrior, and the deadly dance of a FromSoftware boss fight begins. This is how players meet the Guardian Ape of *Sekiro: Shadows Die Twice*. This magnificent creature is more than a monster, the eco-gothic body of the Guardian Ape brings with it the eerie and unsettling qualities of abjection and transgression. By transgressing the anthropocentric view of human dominance and human systems of categorization, the Guardian Ape is tapping into our fear of the other, the big bad ecosystem that human civilization has spent generations building walls to keep out.

As we edge closer to the looming ecological crisis of the Late Anthropocene, the fragility of the structures that insulate human society from the unpredictable violence of nature has become increasingly apparent. Ecophobia, which is cited by Simon Estok as the irrational fear of nature and non-human ecology (Estok 2018), has many manifestations across media narratives. Literary and cinematic monsters such as Melville's *Moby Dick* (Melville 2013) and abstracted invasion narratives like *Annihilation* (VanderMeer 2015) have encapsulated the vulnerability of the human form and the fear of the ecological other. However, very few mediums let you walk through those narratives, choose your own path, and be held responsible for a chain of cause and effect. Ecophobia is distinct from grounded fears about the environmental crises of the Anthropocene. It, instead, is the distorted representation of environmental fears through the gothic and the supernatural. Rather than fears about the catastrophic, slow violence of climate change, it transforms that violence into one of terrible vengeance and immediate, focused terror. Estok's ecophobia hypothesis interrogates the Romanticized notion of the human reverence of nature by highlighting fear-based and anthropocentric reactions to that which we cannot control or understand (Estok 2018). It is the fear of the perceived other that helps us determine what is friend or foe as we stumble through digital forests, keeps us on a hair trigger running through the corridors of a zombie-infested wasteland, and disarms us when we encounter the hybridity and power of the eco-gothic boss. Sebastiano Cossu posits that bosses are not only often climactic villains distinct from "regular enemies" in their narrative function but also "teachers" (Cossu 2019). Battles with these non-player characters, often referred to as 'boss fights,' may introduce a new mechanic or act as the threshold to a new mode of gameplay. As the monster is on the threshold of a pivotal moment of achievement, they may require the player to make narrative choices or gain mastery of a new skill to overcome them.

This chapter deals with the transgressive and abject eco-gothic monsters that stalk video games. Rather than being one of many, they are anomalous and 'unnatural.' These video games feature the abject or monstrous eco-gothic body, which is hybridized, mutated, or in some way transgressive of species. This is often expressed through the instability of form and fluidity of species. Some harken back to the degeneration theory of the Victorian era (Hurley 2004); others engage with twentieth-century distrust of difference and the unknowable and still further are symptomatic of human hubris and interference (Tidwell and Soles 2021).

Despite the apparent malevolent nature of these videoludic monsters, their status as evil is often problematized through their vulnerability to the same vast and unfathomable forces as the player character. From games like *Sekiro* that are structured around punishing boss fights connected through supernatural and ecological crises to puzzle games such as *Return of the Obra Dinn* (Pope 2018), in which man is revealed as the true monstrosity, the eco-gothic bodies themselves are also victims. They are rendered monstrous through their trauma and otherness. This may be achieved through monstrous 'technologies' such as hybridity, contamination, and unfathomability. Through video game narratology and eco-gothic theory, I will explore the complex connections between ecophobia and the video game monsters in *Sekiro: Shadows Die Twice*, *Inscryption* (Daniel Mullins Games 2021), *Return of the Obra Dinn* and *Until Dawn* (Supermassive Games 2015).

Rather than attempting to convey the full picture of monsters within these games, which often have winding levels and narrative structures, I have chosen to highlight a few of unique ecocritical significance. The post-colonial body of Hannah Washington (*Until Dawn*), the transgressive flora of Leshy (*Inscryption*), and the Guardian Ape detailed above are examples of 'bosses,' anomalous creatures that pose an enhanced threat to the player, whether through difficulty or narrative significance. *Return of the Obra Dinn* approaches depictions of conflict in a non-linear fashion, as a result, focusing on one monster, say the Kraken or the Soldiers of the Sea, would paint an incomplete picture of their ecocritical relevance. As such, I will be approaching the curse of the Obra Dinn as a collective response from the ocean.

In defining the eco-gothic body, it is important to consider ecophobia theories that show our fear of the natural world and the transgressions of these boundaries that result in the tragic and dangerously captivating spectacle of the body in a state of otherness or crisis. The Gothic must identify a line to be transgressed, and in the case of the eco-gothic, that line is usually one of species or human-defined species-based hierarchy. Andrew Smith and William Hughes' edited collection on the eco-gothic contains analyses of these transgressions as well as those of human hubris and violence that result in encounters with monstrous Gothic bodies borne of trauma and corruption (Smith and Hughes, 2016). Of particular interest to this examination of the eco-gothic body in video games is Catherine Lanone's examination of the eco-gothic implications of doomed arctic expeditions in the 1800s (Lanone 2015) and Tom J. Hillard's discussion of the link between Modern American eco-gothic and its historically ecophobic roots (Hillard 2015).

Referring to Tanya Krzywinska's work on Gothic coordinates (Krzywinska 2015) and the Gothic in gaming more generally, it is possible to establish the effect and atmosphere constructed by the interplay of various aesthetic and performative elements of the game (Krzywinska 2017). Similarly, Bernard Perron's work on the structure of horror in video games allows for the definition of the locus of fear and the conditions that create a feeling of dread and unease within the player (Perron 2018). In referring to the importance of affect more generally when confronting an enemy in-game, Aubrey Anable outlines how various in-game elements enact pressures and emotive responses in the player, which will allow for discussions of player engagement that foster empathy for unlikely characters (Anable 2018).

This empathy for unlikely characters leads us to the concept of abjection, which Kelly Hurley deftly explores in their examination of the "Gothic body" in the fin de siècle (Hurley 2004). While on the surface, the Guardian Ape or Hannah Washington may have very little in common with the literary monsters emerging from the late Victorian period, we only have to look at the tragedy of Dr. Jekyll and Mr. Hyde (Stevenson 1992) and the fates of other abject abhuman forms to find that we are dealing with very similar concepts of transformation, hybridity, and loss of self.

It is precisely this transgressive 'thingness' and abjection that links the conventions of the Gothic to Jack Halberstam's technologies of fear, which articulate what it is that makes a monster terrifying (Halberstam 1995). Halberstam uses figures such as Dracula, Leatherface, and Buffalo Bill to illustrate the very specific means each monster uses to terrify audiences. All three challenge the bounds of the fixed corporeal body, appropriating or consuming parts of their prey. This makes them ongoing spectacles of death, reminding audiences of the violence enacted before and the violence that is to come. The act of repeating an act of trauma and violence over and over again puts one in mind for punishingly hard games like *Sekiro,* in which the player-character will die violently, over and over again, at the hands of the same monster. In contrast, puzzle games like *Return of the Obra Dinn* compel the player to closely examine the tragedy of death from many different angles, challenging them to look at the moment of death as an artifact rather than a moment of sickening loss.

Whether in direct confrontation with the player character or as part of a broader puzzle, video games tend to be littered with enemies of various kinds. These enemies create a rising and falling difficulty narrative or threat level that winds its way towards a creature that is often representative of the aesthetic or themes of a stage or the broader game. In the case of the selected games, these bosses can range from the player-character's undead best friend to the actual Kraken. While in puzzle-based games, the boss may be more symbolic in their climactic significance, in combat-based games, they raise the challenge level in several ways. This might include multistage combat with regenerating health or a formidable move set that requires the player to adapt their playstyle. Even more cruelly, the rules of play may change entirely. *Sekiro*, for example, forces the player to study the move set of their opponents, developing an acute temporal and spatial awareness tuned to that creature. In the case of the Guardian Ape, the eco-gothic nature of its corporeal form means that the ape was not acting of its own volition and was itself a host or victim of a parasite. It is only once the parasite has been removed that the Gothic body may finally be defeated.

The vulnerability and tragedy at the center of the narratively complex video game monster may take some additional investigating to find. It may be necessary to look to environmental and optional modular narratives to find their harrowing backstory. For example, while the Guardian Ape isn't beating your character into a pulp, he is busily tending to a flower called The Lotus of the Palace. He is cultivating this flower for its aroma, which attracts female apes in the hopes of finding a new ape. He is lonely, immortal, and a victim of the same parasitic plight as the other creatures in contact with the Fountainhead Waters.

Avenging the Crimes of the Obra Dinn

The eco-gothic presents interesting and subversive ways to critique the violence of humanity and fantasize about the revenge of nature. In *Return of the Obra Dinn*, the ocean does not simply sit idly by while it is pillaged, instead, it rises up, sending wave after wave of creatures to reclaim what the people on board have stolen, dooming the voyage to death and despair.

The player, embodying the auditor, is tasked with reconstructing the voyage after the Obra Dinn is found to be a ghost ship. Lucas Pope's puzzle game was purportedly inspired by real tales of doomed voyages and certainly carries with it the legacy of nineteenth-century ecophobia. This ecophobia was wrapped up in ideas of the hubris of man in traversing where they should not, obsessions that risked lives, and the exploitation and violence of nature as God's creation (Hillier 2009). Rather than the threat exclusively coming from the exterior, humans were stumbling into parts unknown and wreaking havoc. The tragic culpability of the human is gradually revealed in *Return of the Obra Dinn* through non-linear, puzzle-based storytelling that relies on the interpretation and reasoning of the player. Pope draws on elements of the nautical eco-gothic to point to the correlation between the environmental violence of the expedition and its eventual fate. The narrative of this ill-fated voyage draws on a host of eco-gothic conventions such as monstrous nature, the corruption of the human, contagion, and revenge of nature. Linked through memories of their deaths, the interweaving stories of the passengers and crew in the *Return of the Obra Dinn* demonstrate the potential for narrative-driven video games to invoke the eco-gothic meaningfully.

Designed to emulate the record-keeping of the East India Company, the 1807 narrative of *Return of the Obra Dinn* and the lost souls aboard the ship are chronicled in the ship's ledger. It is this massive tome that the player, acting as an insurance inspector, must complete. Through the process of curating and completing this chronicle, the player is implicated in creating the text rather than simply conducting passive observation. Through the supernatural artifact of the *Memento Morte* timepiece, the player can use corporeal remains to be transported back to the exact moment of a character's death. What follows is an explorable fragment of memory that represents the last few moments of a character, which must be investigated to determine their identity and cause of death. The gradual unraveling of this mystery through an acknowledgment of each death onboard evokes a sense of creeping dread, ultimately resulting in horrific revelations about the ecological and social transgressions that took place aboard the Obra Dinn.

As a 'revenge of nature' narrative, the Obra Dinn is characterized by the disconnection of the human from the non-human, that is, the human commits violence to nature, and nature retaliates (Tidwell 2014). Sometimes, the violence in these narratives is overt and singular, such as the shooting of the albatross in "The Rime of the Ancient Mariner," sometimes, it is difficult to define slow violence as in *The Birds* (Hitchcock 1963). Games that follow this narrative tradition share that same divergence of cause, the *Resident Evil* (Capcom 1996) games blame the concentrated works of evil scientists for the zombie-like creatures attacking Racoon City, whereas the cordyceps fungus of *Last of Us* (Naughty Dog 2013) is turning people into monsters with no cause other than that globalization of food sources. In *The Last of Us*, it is up to us to draw connections between human actions and their fate. In these games, the key locus of the eco-gothic effect is the conflict between the human and the non-human, in which human supremacy and exceptionalism are problematized.

The question is, "How do the depictions of plagues and viruses reinforce or subvert the ecophobia centered around uncleanliness, disease, and contamination from the non-human world?"

Narratives that illustrate the intersection of colonialism and environmental exploitation often convey themes of vengeance, justice, and righteousness. Despite the retaliatory nature of the violence aimed at humanity, video games will often charge the player with killing or defeating non-human forces. *Return of the Obra Dinn,* by contrast, requires the player to investigate and bear witness to the bitter conflict between humanity and the ecology of the sea. The auditor doesn't kill or defeat anything, instead, they piece together a tale reminiscent of the "Rime of the Ancient Mariner" (Coleridge 1834) and narratives of doomed voyages from the Romantic Gothic period. *Return of the Obra Dinn* is effectively a non-linear puzzle and mass murder mystery in which the player is charged with reconstructing the terrible events that occurred on board. This revenge of nature tale sees the crew being plagued by disease and misfortune before being hunted by ferocious mermaids, modeled after the terrifying mythical creatures rather than the Disney ideal, giant spider crabs that appear to have humanoid masses protruding from their backs, and the Kraken. Pope deploys the mysterious qualities of the sea and the creatures that live within it to provide an eco-gothic environment that reflects human fears about the unpredictability and power of nature.

Doomed from the outset, the "good ship" Obra Dinn is, in part, on an expedition to steal something valuable from the sea, but the sea fights back. This act of theft and hubris is at the heart of not only the Gothic fiction of the nineteenth century in which the game is set but also the accounts of failed expeditions that have fallen into infamy. Lanone (2015) cites the ill-fated Arctic exploration of Sir John Franklin as a particularly influential cultural narrative of the doomed expedition, in addition to literary narratives of misadventure, such as Walton's framing narrative in *Frankenstein* (Shelley 1832). Like the act of violence that starts in motion the devastating series of events in "The Rime of the Ancient Mariner," the "souls" aboard the ship commit a similar ecological atrocity. This act of theft, whilst arguably more audacious than the killing of the albatross, brings about similar torment, invoking the wrath of the ocean as a collective army.

This army of creatures that rise from the sea are derived from diverse sources, and despite being rendered in a vintage 1-bit monochromatic style, they are detailed visions of monstrosity and uncanny nature. From the mermaids that err on the side of Eldritch or folkloric hybrids rather than modern benign and sexualized humanoids to the hybrid spider crab-like spectacle of the "Soldiers of the Sea," the monstrous individual guardians of the ocean demonstrate ecohorror technologies of the unknown and uncanny. The dramatic eco-gothic spectacle of the Kraken, true to conventions of giant nautical monstrosities, is obscured by its scale and appears as disembodied tentacles that wreak destruction on the boat. But perhaps the most pervasive and difficult-to-anticipate threat from the deep is the disease that plagues the crew, inviting discourse about the disease as a pervasive eco-gothic motif used to rationalize or illustrate persistent and insidious supernatural vengeance.

Whilst the monstrosity of the creatures that emerge from the deep are reflective of entrenched anxieties about the unknown, the cruelty and vindictiveness of humans is an expression of self-reflexive guilt. This guilt is borne out of an understanding of our own culpability in violence and exploitation. Despite the monstrosity and violence of the ocean's army, the violent deaths could be averted through simple acts of ecological atonement and compassion.

The grief-stricken captain demonstrates a fundamental inability to empathize with the non-human, which proves to be his undoing. He is unable to envisage a mode of being with the non-human that does not incorporate domination and human supremacy. This is juxtaposed with the apology offered to the mermaids by the doctor, who demonstrates an understanding of his obligations as part of a broader ecosystem. The entire narrative culminates in a final act of violence, the doctor's murder of his monkey companion, which facilitates the creation of this intricate web of tragedy. The crew of the Obra Dinn fought off disease, hordes of supernatural creatures, and the Kraken, but ultimately, it was the ecological crimes of humanity that killed the "souls" aboard the Obra Dinn.

Until Dawn and the trauma of the Earth

Not all of those aboard the Obra Dinn were directly complicit in the ecological crimes that took place. Some of the earliest victims were claimed by disease before the crime even occurred. Therefore, if we were to view the fate of the Obra Dinn as an act of vengeance, then what implications does that have for the precision of nature in exercising retribution? Are direct and precise consequences beyond the ability or concern of a vengeful ecology? Or is collateral damage an element of the punishment for culturally ingrained acts of ecological violence that have ripple effects throughout nature?

This is an often-silent line of questioning at the heart of narratives that require characters to pay for historical crimes against nature. Such is the case in *Until Dawn*. It is not that teen protagonists are innocent, far from it. Indeed, depending on your choices during the game, you can shape them to be reckless and pitiless monsters whose unrepenting cruelty results in multiple deaths. But ultimately, the origins of the supernatural monsters stalking the teens are far older than the oblivious bullying that qualifies them for death in a teen slasher. These supernatural monsters are the result of ecological violence and exploitation that occurred decades before they were born, exploitation that was part of a pattern of consumption and colonialism stretching back generations. Whether the game makes responsible use of this legacy of trauma or simply appropriates it as a convenient technology of monstrosity is another matter entirely.

Until Dawn uses the conventions of teen horror and contemporary legend to establish themes of cruelty, betrayal, justice, and revenge. In addition to the human tragedy, there is a revenge of nature narrative quietly playing out in the background. The isolated mountain offers a tantalizing unaccountability for young adults but quickly morphs into an eco-gothic labyrinth streaked with the scars of abandoned mining shafts. Drawing from North American First Nation's mythology and the traumatic history of the mountain, *Until Dawn* uses the act of cannibalism and uncanny, animalistic mutations to craft a revenge saga that is tethered to the ecology of the mountain. Centuries of colonialist practices that justify violence and trauma inflicted on land culminate in the deep mountain mining of radium. But this time, they went too far, dug too deep, and released these cannibalistic monstrosities that are expressions of the effect of human exploitation and desperation. *Until Dawn* is following a legacy that Eflin describes as being "the guilty colonial conscience trying to redefine its past until the monster in colonized territory is no longer in the mirror as well" (Eflin 2014). The threat is perhaps best articulated by the "The Stranger" who explains "Should any man or woman resort to cannibalism in these woods, the spirit Wendigo shall be unleashed" (Supermassive Games 2015), making the Wendigo representative of the desperation, violence and consumption of humanity, excising and othering those elements of human nature that are monstrous and uncomfortable.

The introduction of multi-linear choice-based mechanics and a morality system tracks player choices and impacts character relationships, engaging the player in a degree of thoughtfulness about the moral implications of their actions. This, in turn, opens the possibility for a more nuanced mode of storytelling, capable of facilitating discourse about the nature of victimhood and predators. But in a game where your choices purportedly matter, it is the choices that were made before you stepped foot on the mountain that shape the ecocritical meaning of the text. Set in Cree country, *Until Dawn* appropriates an amalgam of Native American stories of the Wendigo to create an audio-visual experience that is often more an interactive creature feature film than a game. But as Tidwell and Barclay note, even the somewhat silly and exploitative creature feature is able to convey "environmental messages and/or interpretations in creature features are directly related to environmental anxieties" (Barclay and Tidwell 2021). The greatest threat to their safety is the aforementioned Wendigo, a spirit that possesses those who engage in cannibalism, borne out of exploitation, desperation and isolation.

As the game starts, there are subtle hints of the underlying threat at the heart of this game, which seems at the beginning to be a pretty standard teen revenge slasher. Dream catchers flit about in the title sequence, and we find out that it is Cree country. Not that this makes a huge impression on our protagonists. Adding to the slasher film feel of the story is the sparse interactivity of the game. Rather than fighting regular enemies or solving regular puzzles, *Until Dawn* relies on the building eco-gothic atmosphere of the isolated mountain and surprise quick time events to build suspense. Failing one of these events could result in long-term consequences for your characters or even death. In a game that purportedly hinges on the "butterfly effects" of choice and layers of accountability and revenge, it conceals much of the information about the cause of the eco-gothic threat in optional modular information. Once discovered, this modular narrative can assist the cast of characters in escaping the Wendigo, but it is entirely possible to get through the game and miss the ecological violence that lies at the heart of the story.

During the game time of *Until Dawn*, the Wendigo finds a host when two sisters, Hannah and Beth, fall to their apparent deaths down a mine shaft. However, one sister survives, and in the cold and isolation of the wilderness, Hannah eventually gives in to her hunger and eats her sister's corpse. Through this act of cannibalism, she becomes monstrous and joins the other Wendigos unleashed onto the world by the exploitative processes of radium mining on the mountain in the 1950s. Hannah not only embodies the video game convention of the ally turned antagonist through possession, but she becomes a vessel for the revenge of nature. She is not aware of her symbolic significance; her only motivation is a gnawing hunger that causes her to hunt her friends. By transforming into an unfamiliar visage with elongated limbs and sharp teeth and feasting on human flesh, Hannah transgresses the boundaries of the human and the nonhuman, of predator and prey. She problematizes societal constructions of the specificity, categorization, and stability of the human form.

Hurley's discussion of the abhuman as the "not-quite-human subject," characterized by the threat of instability and further changes of form, is reflected in the process of transformation (Hurley 2004) and the ability of the Wendigo to mimic the calls of distressed humans. Through cannibalism and the supernatural, Hannah becomes 'abhuman'; a compromised, and consequently less than, human form. Her isolation in the mineshaft is compounded by excesses of trauma; the trauma of her sister's death, the trauma of the lives of miners lost, the trauma of the Cree people, and ultimately, the trauma of the Earth itself.

The ecological hierarchy of *Inscryption*

From a game that arguably appropriates Algonquin mythology to a game that appears to be borne out of urban myth and digital lore, *Inscryption* (Daniel Mullins Games 2021) is situated out of space and time, creating its own expression of nature and ecological violence through the mechanics of the game itself. *Inscryption* lets you know immediately that it will be changing the rules by not giving the player the option to start a new game, only the continue option is available, implying that the player-character, Luke Carder, is not the first person to play this game. It is a self-reflective and metatextual game and, therefore, needs antagonists that are as looming and disorientating as the shifting parameters of the game itself.

In the first stage of *Inscryption*, there is a base card game through which non-player characters and the conventions of the broader game are introduced. It is useful to establish this stage as the key area of focus due to the wildly shifting aesthetics, mechanics, and gameplay across stages. Despite the shifts in genre and dimensions, one constant is that the game uses cards that contain trapped animals and entities. Each animal or entity is attributed health and attack values, as well as "sigils" that govern their behavior. To play a card, the player must sacrifice an animal of "lesser value," which in turn will be sacrificed for a "higher value" card. This ranking of ecological value is not the only part of the stage laden with ecocritical meaning. Your opponent, the tree-like Leshy, is a uniquely eco-gothic creature who is, in many ways, inseparable from the game he plays.

The card game's hierarchical categorization of the environment harkens back to an anthropocentric way of understanding nature. Discourse about systems that value the ecology based on human interests and morality from an Anglocentric viewpoint inevitably intersect with the Great Chain of Being:

> The legacy and prevailing attitude of world religions reside in their transcendental attitudes and Great Chain of Being anthropocentrism (i.e. humans exist in a hierarchy that places them above and separate from lower forms of life in nature). (Gras 2010, 1)

Where *Inscryption* departs from the Great Chain of Being is in the unexpected integration of the human into the deck of playable cards. Rather than being inherently more valuable or powerful than other cards, they are afforded an additional, inherent individuality, but the strategic value of the human cards remains in line with the non-human. The exception being the cards created by the player-character as they lose the game and are trapped in the card by Leshy, which can be overpowered based on the combination of cards offered.

Leshy, the scribe of beasts, is the first and certainly the most prominent of the eco-gothic bodies we encounter. He appears to be made of wood, yet he whittles wooden pieces for the game board, if not from his own flesh, then from the same material as him. Halberstam notes that "skin houses the body and it is figured in Gothic as the ultimate boundary, the material that divides the inside from the outside" (Halberstam 1995). But Leshy has no such vulnerable interior, and this is one source of his monstrosity, his otherness, and ambiguity that defies the anthropocentric rules that define his game. He is corporeally both human and fauna, transgressing boundaries of species and visibly sharing his physical space with fungus and moss. He is a tree-man in the woods, playing with little wooden figurines and cards, just waiting for a worthy adversary. While he is ultimately part of a broader, metatextual video game, he has no motivation beyond keeping you in this cabin, keeping everyone in this cabin, and playing games. He rolls out a series of crudely designed maps for the player-character to traverse, each representing a biome; the woods, the wetlands, the mountains, and finally, the purple-hued surrounds of Leshy's cabin. Each map has a relevant boss and introduces new cards featuring animals from that biome that Leshy has no doubt captured and imprisoned with his magic camera.

Leshy masquerades as multiple characters that complicate the game and are often all we see of our mysterious opponent. These identities are tied up in the mode of using the environment as a resource. According to the four modes of environmental representation outlined by Abraham and Jayemanne, when the environment is depicted as a resource in video games, "this is the environment as something to be exploited. Games deploy this relationship whenever they utilize extractive or collecting mechanics for the sake of development, deployment or creation" (Abraham and Jayemanne 2017). While the player is not directly implicated in this process in the same way as they might be in games like *Minecraft* (Mojang 2011), some processes symbolically mimic the commerce and environmental destruction associated with using the environment as a resource. The most obvious and destructive of these processes is the use of animals for combat. The player deliberately puts animal cards in harm's way to protect themselves and effectively manipulates the environment to turn against itself. We know these are not merely representative of real animals but are trapped creatures due to the information we have about Leshy's construction of the cards and the communication that the player-character has with select cards.

Antagonist characters facilitate this multifaceted procurement, processing and trade of the ecology; The Angler, The Prospector, and The Trapper, who is the flipside of the Trader mask. Alter egos that play a more neutral role include the Wood Carver and The Mycologist, who not only possesses the abilities of fungus to replicate through fission and mutation but embodies this ability through their second head. The Mycologist is able to combine cards of the same type to make one stronger card. Indeed, each of the alter egos possesses mechanics that shape the game and are tethered to some real-world ecological truth.

Fungal bodies present unique challenges to the human body as a single, unified system. The ambiguity of fungal forms and their complex relationships with other elements of the ecosystem are at odds with the human misconception of the body as separate and contained. These challenges to the liminality of species are further compounded by associations with decay and disorder; "the dysmorphic fungal body instead poses the threat of human devolution and a degrading return to a less organized primordial state of being" (Camara 2014).

The game mechanics are governed by a symbolic interpretation of ecological phenomena. Leshy's games could be seen as an attempt to grapple with the value of life and the relationship of the human with the non-human through iconography and symbology. Unlike survival horror games that simply utilize puzzles as distinct and separate "set pieces" away from the action (Kirkland 2009), the puzzles in these games represent the bulk of the gameplay. These are puzzle video games that derive eco-gothic effects from the use of living things as puzzle pieces, often ascribing them a value based on their hierarchy in the biosphere. There is an element of the logic of Bram Stoker's Renfield (*Dracula*, Stoker 1995) in these puzzle mechanics in which the animals at the bottom of the food chain are sacrificed to obtain those further up, who are then in turn sacrificed to meet a greater goal. The player is staging a monstrous re-enactment of ecologies to meet their own goals.

In the same way that Renfield feeds flies to spiders and uses those spiders to catch a bird, the player sacrifices squirrels to pay for animals considered to be of greater value, such as the elk, who will, in turn, be sacrificed for a more useful creature. This condition is typified by the sacrifice and consumption, which Doctor Seward terms zoophagia, calling Renfield a "zoophagous (life-eating) maniac; what he desires is to absorb as many lives as he can, and he has laid himself out to achieve it in a cumulative way." The player has been locked into this cycle of escalation and cumulative consumption and must now find a way to break this pattern of suffering.

Leshy has deliberately and meticulously crafted this "carefully curated cycle of life and death" in a bizarre escalation of his role within the program as the scribe of beasts. Any doubt we have about his intentions is cleared up in stage two when he clearly articulates this. He is not merely playing a game, he is playing an ecology and ecology that cannot function without the player. So, he sits alone and abject, himself a prisoner, a victim captive in an artificial structure who has seized what little power he can, playing out a macabre game of life and death. Despite the illusion of organic matter, his body is constructed from pixels and code, a creature of science fiction that is only representative of something real, natural, and material.

Conclusion

Through the bittersweet tragedy of the Guardian Ape beset by a cruel parasitic force, *Sekiro* effectively blurs the boundaries of accountability and heroism. Is it truly heroic to attempt to kill this creature that has its own emotional pain, aspirations, and internal motivations? The defeat of the ape accomplishes nothing, the immortal creature continues to suffer and amble headless through the valley. Similarly, the voyage of the Obra Dinn accomplishes nothing, its stolen cargo is thrown overboard. The retribution and righteous fury of the ocean enacted by the bizarre eco-gothic bodies that rise from the ocean ultimately achieve its end. The thieves are held to account and the treasure is returned to the deep. The deep mountain mining of *Until Dawn* cannot be so easily remedied. Instead, we are confronted with the ongoing corruption of the human body by creatures tethered to cycles of trauma and violence. Just as inescapable cycles of trauma play out in the mines beneath the mountain, the card game at the center of *Inscryption* imprisons the player-character in an ecological game of sacrifice with one of the most explicitly eco-gothic in recent video game design.

The cycles of victimhood, revenge, and control enacted through the eco-gothic bodies in *Sekiro, Return of the Obra Dinn, Until Dawn,* and *Inscryption* draw upon deep-seated fears and anxieties about the environmental other. Rather than considering the human as an intrinsic part of the environment, the eco-gothic highlights the artificial barriers between the human and the non-human, preying on the anxieties of anthropocentric thinking. 'Scary' video games and those that deploy the technologies of fear rely on the ambiguous and the monstrous to make the player complicit in the ecological tragedies of these abject creatures, which are inextricably interconnected with their ecologies.

Bibliography

Abraham, B.J., and Darshana Jayemanne. 2017. "Where Are All the Climate Change Games? Locating Digital Games' Response to Climate Change." *Transformations*, 30.

Anable, Aubrey. 2018. *Playing with Feelings*. University of Minnesota Press. https://doi.org/10.5749/j.ctt20mvgwg.

Barclay, Bridgitte, and Christy Tidwell. 2021. "Introduction Mutant Bears, Defrosted Parasites and Cellphone Swarms: Creature Features and the Environment." *Science Fiction Film and Television* 14, no. 3: 269-277.

Camara, Anthony. 2014. "Abominable Transformations: Becoming-Fungus in Arthur Machen's The Hill of Dreams." *Gothic Studies* 161: 9-23.

Capcom. 1996. *Resident Evil Series*. Capcom.

Coleridge, Samuel Taylor. 2009. *Rime of the Ancient Mariner: And Select Poems / Samuel Taylor Coleridge; Edited by Frederick H. Sykes*. Waiheke Island: Floating Press.

Cossu, Sebastiano M. 2019. "Designing Bosses." *Game Development with GameMaker Studio 2: Make Your Own Games with GameMaker Language*, 231–40.

Daniel Mullins Games. 2021. *Inscryption*. Devolver Digital.

Eflin, Jackson. 2014. "Incursion Into Wendigo Territory." *Digital Literature Review* 1: 9–19.

Estok, Simon C. 2018. *The Ecophobia Hypothesis*. United States: Routledge. https://www.taylorfrancis.com/books/9781315144689.

FromSoftware Inc. 2019. *Sekiro: Shadows Die Twice*. Activision JP.

Gras, Vernon. 2010. "Dialogism as a Solution for the Present Obstacles to an Ecological Culture." *Local Natures: Global Responsiblities*: 1–9.

Halberstam, Jack. 1995. *Skin Shows*. Duke University Press.

Hillard, Tom J. 2015. "From Salem Witch to Blair Witch: The Puritan Influence on American Gothic Nature." *EcoGothic*: 103–19. Manchester University Press.

Hillier, Russell M. 2009. "Coleridge's Dilemma and the Method of "Sacred Sympathy": Atonement as Problem and Solution in The Rime of the Ancient Mariner." *Papers on Language and Literature* 45, no. 1: 8-36.

Hitchcock, Alfred. dir. 1963. *The Birds*. Universal-International Pictures.

Hurley, Kelly. 2004. *The Gothic Body: Sexuality, Materialism, and Degeneration at the Fin de Siècle*. Cambridge University Press.

Kirkland, Ewan. 2009. "Storytelling in Survival Horror Video Games." Horror Video Games: Essay on the Fusion of Fear and Play. McFarland & Company, Inc 62-78.

Krzywinska, Tanya. 2015. "The Gamification of Gothic Coordinates." *Revenant: Critical and Creative Studies of the Supernatural* 1, no. 1: 58–78.

Kryzwinska, Tanya. 2017. "Gothic American Gaming." *The Cambridge Companion to American Gothic*: 229-242.

Lanone, Catherine. 2015. "Monsters on the Ice and Global Warming: From Mary Shelley and Sir John Franklin to Margaret Atwood and Dan Simmons." *Ecogothic*: 28–43. Manchester University Press.

Melville, Herman. 2013. *Moby-Dick* (Penguin Classics*)*. Penguin.

Mojang. 2011. *Minecraft*. Mojang Studios.

Naughty Dog. 2013. *Last of Us*. Sony Computer Entertainment.

Perron, Bernard. 2018. *The World of Scary Video Games: A Study in Videoludic Horror*. Bloomsbury Publishing USA.

Pope, Lucas. 2018. *Return of the Obra Dinn*. 3909 LLC.

Shelley, Mary Wollstonecraft. 1985. *Frankenstein*. Penguin Classics. Harmondsworth, Middlesex, England; New York, N.Y., USA: Penguin Books.

Smith, Andrew, and William Hughes. 2016. *EcoGothic*. Machester University Press.

Stevenson, Robert Louis. 1992. "The Project Gutenberg EBook of The Strange Case Of Dr. Jekyll And Mr. Hyde, by Robert Louis Stevenson." https://www.gutenberg.org/files/43/43-h/43-h.htm.

Stoker, Bram. 1995. *Dracula*. https://www.gutenberg.org/ebooks/345.

Supermassive Games. 2015. *Until Dawn*. Sony Computer Entertainment.

Tidwell, Christy. 2014. "Monstrous Natures Within: Posthuman and New Materialist Ecohorror in Mira Grant's 'Parasite.'" *Interdisciplinary Studies in Literature and Environment* 21, no. 3: 538–49.

Tidwell, Christy, and Carter Soles. 2021. *Fear and Nature: Ecohorror Studies in the Anthropocene.* Vol. 8. Penn State Press.

VanderMeer, Jeff. 2015. *Annihilation.* The Southern Reach Trilogy, Book one. London: Fourth Estate.

Chapter 6

The Monstrous Gaze: Examining the Camera in Horror Film

Mychal Reiff-Shanks

Georgia State University

Abstract: The Monster has been the foundation of horror since its creation, from the literary Universal Studios monster to the 1970s slasher killer to now the socially conscious killer/monster. Interestingly, with the transition to human monsters, the camera became more monstrous, as demonstrated in the 70s, utilizing the killer's POV (point of view). The camera becomes linked to the monstrous as a literal killer—as described previously—and what I argue in this chapter, through its phenomenological viewpoint as viewing and viewed, which I correlate to the similar dynamic of monster and victim. I argue that a new form of monstrous has risen out of the horror genre exhibited in the camera. For this chapter, I define monstrosity using Patricia MacCormack's definition, emphasizing hybridity. Through this framework, I argue that the camera is monstrous due to its hybrid nature as both viewer (in the cinematic world) and viewed (by the audience). However, to explore further, I posit that the hybrid and nonconformity of the camera stems from it being an indestructible victim, a contradiction in itself, creating a monster/victim dynamic, an inherently vulnerable and precarious viewing position for the audience. Two filmic examples that highlight this monstrous relationship of the camera are *What We Do In The Shadows* (2014), a New Zealand horror-comedy, and the modern remake, more retelling, of *The Invisible Man* (2020). The camera in these films takes on the perspective of a victim who exists in and out of the filmic space, highlighting the dangers of their filmic worlds yet posing no mortal risk to the camera. For the most part, the camera and audience are never in real danger. Nevertheless, for horror to succeed, the camera must make the audience believe that danger could happen to the camera and, by extension, the audience. The gaze in these films is not only monstrous because of their link to the monster—as seen from the killer's POV—but also their potential agency against them, creating a subversive gaze of hybridity. The camera's gaze is one of a victim—in danger and highly observant—yet it does not conform to this ideology. Instead of running away, it continues to put itself in harm's way, creating vulnerable invulnerability. Similar to the camera being viewer/viewed, the camera in these films is victim/monster, visualizing the audience's dichotomy within horror.

Keywords: Monster, victim, killer POV, camera gaze, hybridity

***

The monster has been the foundation of horror since its creation. Often depicted as violent, bloodthirsty, and dangerous, the monster has become synonymous with evil, an antagonist with a propensity for violence. However, the form of the monster has changed over the decades, with the early 1900s-1950s being the literal monsters of Frankenstein, Dracula, and Wolfman, all based on their literary predecessors popularized by Universal Studios. By the 1970s, the monster had moved away from the supernatural non-human to the human killer. A suburban terror ready to mutilate the nuclear family by killing teen victims. These monstrous human elements continue in horror movies today with the addition of focusing on marginalized groups and social issues, as seen in Jordan Peele's debut film *Get Out* (2017).

Interestingly, with the transition to human monsters, the camera became more monstrous, as demonstrated in the 70s, utilizing the killer's POV (point of view). *Halloween* (1978) begins with the POV sequence of a young Michael Myers killing one of his sisters on Halloween night. In *Black Christmas* (1974), the killer is represented only through POV for most of the film. Even *Jaws* (1975) uses it for its non-human killer with its iconic underwater shots and third-act reveal of the shark. The camera becomes linked to the monstrous as a literal killer—as described previously—and what I argue in this chapter, through its phenomenological viewpoint as viewing and viewed, which I correlate to the similar dynamic of monster and victim. I argue that a new form of monstrous has risen out of the horror genre exhibited in the camera.

For this chapter, I define monstrosity using Patricia MacCormack's definition, emphasizing hybridity. Through this framework, I argue that the camera is monstrous due to its hybrid nature as both viewer (in the cinematic world) and viewed (by the audience). However, to explore further, I posit that the hybrid and nonconformity of the camera stems from it being an indestructible victim, a contradiction in itself, creating a monster/victim dynamic, an inherently vulnerable and precarious viewing position for the audience. Two filmic examples that highlight this monstrous relationship of the camera are *What We Do In The Shadows* (2014), a New Zealand horror-comedy, and the modern remake, more retelling, of *The Invisible Man* (2020). The camera in these films takes on the perspective of a victim who exists in and out of the filmic space, highlighting the dangers of their filmic worlds yet posing no mortal risk to the camera. For the most part, the camera and audience are never in real danger. Nevertheless, for horror to succeed, the camera must make the audience believe that danger could happen to the camera and, by extension, the audience. The gaze in these films is not only monstrous because of their link to the monster—as seen from the killer's POV—but also their potential agency against them, creating a subversive gaze of hybridity. The camera's gaze is one of a victim—in danger and highly observant—yet it does not conform to this ideology. Instead of running away, it continues to put itself in harm's way, creating vulnerable invulnerability. Similar to the camera being viewer/viewed, the camera in these films is the victim/monster, visualizing the audience's dichotomy within horror.

Defining Monstrous

In Patricia MacCormack's chapter "The Queer Ethics of Monstrosity," she describes the monster as the following:

> The monster is alterity as both wonder and horror, as the limit of humanity and proof that the human always exceeds the parameters of what we think it is capable of. The monster crosses species and boundaries; it is hybrid, metamorphic, but it is not properly something that is so much as something that fails to be something else—the traditional dominant human subject. (MacCormack 2012, 257)

The defining quality of the monster for MacCormack is its hybridity or failure for conformity. With slasher killers, they fail to perform heteronormativity, thus failing to perform their masculine patriarchal function. Dracula fails to be human, thus needing to drink human blood. The Other is the foundational tension of Gothic horror. MacCormack continues with:

> The other thus fails to pass as subject defined by mind over body or embodied mind. Rather the subject is territorialized by color, sex, age, and other trajectories of signifying difference. Monstrosity is at its most spectacular when it is visible deformity in form or action. Monstrous bodies are also those that have certain qualities—sticky, not demarcated, compelling in spite of their repugnance, interspecies, multiple, or generally resistant to both signification and subjectification. (ibid.)

MacCormack's definition of the monster, I argue, applies to the camera. The camera throughout scholarship is defined by its lack of distinction. The camera exists in the filmic world yet is acknowledged as outside of it. It is both viewing and viewed, making the concept of the camera monstrous in its inherent hybridity within film. Nevertheless, it is a tool for the audience and the film world, yet unable to exist in both. In horror, the camera's gaze embodies the monster and victim.

Many scholars argue that POV creates identification, such as Carol J. Clover, who states:

> But let us for the moment accept the equation point of view = identification. We are linked, in this way, with the killer in the early part of the film, usually before we have seen him directly and before we have come to know the Final Girl in any detail. Our closeness to him wanes as our closeness to the Final Girl waxes—a shift underwritten by story line as well as camera position. (Clover 2015, 93)

I agree with Clover's theory on identifying with the killer and the final girl. However, I argue that this identification is happening simultaneously for the audience, which is where the tension of horror resides. Though the terms I am using, monster and victim, can be applied to individuals within the character world (killer/final girl), I use these in their broader metaphorical forms. My definition of monster I stated above, however, victim I define as one who lives in precarity. This role can be linked more to a narrative character like the final girl, but it could be for the camera's body as displayed in the filmic examples later demonstrated in this chapter. The camera lives within the realm of precarity as it balances its presence within two worlds. When thinking of the monster/victim dynamic as a theoretical tool, I turn to Daniel Morgan's piece "Where are we?: camera movements and the problem of point of view," he dissects the use of POV in both film and scholarship, he argues that scholars have ignored POV when discussing camera movement. Morgan uses Richard Wollheim's internal/external spectator, saying,

> …the external spectator marks the position that we take up outside the world of the work of art, the position of the viewer; the internal spectator, by contrast, picks out a viewing position within the work and the 'virtual space' it creates. Wollheim emphasizes that our relation to the internal spectator—the 'spectator in the picture'—is not based on identification: we do not inhabit this position, and it remains explicitly distinct from our visual point of view. Yet its presence colors how we parse the fictional world being shown. (Morgan 2016, 236)

I apply Wollheim's internal/external spectator theory to my monster/victim dynamic. Within horror, the violence experienced on screen the audience does not identify, but because of the camera, the audience feels the effects of danger and protection. Morgan continues with Wollheim, stating, "The internal spectator creates a refraction of sorts, splitting the beam that connects the viewer to film world into different spectatorial positions dispersed within the image. We are not 'at' the viewpoint established by the camera, nor that of a character. Instead, we are able to simultaneously inhabit multiple positions within the world of the film" (Ibid. 238). I believe these multiple positions Morgan mentions within horror are victim and monster. Morgan is curious about the distinction when the camera rejects the character's POV, such as when the eyes we thought we were looking through come into view and our perception of these moments, which he coins 'perceptual games.' However, perceptual games can only exist in epistemological fantasies, which he defines as "one of being at a place we cannot be, a place we are barred from inhabiting" (Ibid. 242). He continues asserting, "We are not with the camera in the world of the film but we *want* to be there, and the way films incite the desire to be at the position of the camera, to be moving with it, allows us to believe in something that is not, strictly speaking possible for us to do" (Ibid.). What Morgan is theorizing is the effect of horror on the camera.

Using feminist scholarship, Linda Williams, in her piece "When the Woman Looks," argues that women identify with the monster in classic horror films because she recognizes a shared identification.

> The female look—a look given preeminent position in the horror film— shares the male fear of the monster's freakishness, but also recognizes the sense in which this freakishness is similar to her own difference. For she too has been constituted as an exhibitionist-object by the desiring look of the male. There is not that much difference between an object of desire and an object of horror as far as the male look is concerned. (Williams 2015, 23)

Unfortunately, with modern horror, the monster's identity becomes hidden with POV shots from the killer's perspective. William continues, "This 'non-specific male killing force' thus displaces what was once the subjective point of view of the female victim onto an audience that is now asked to view the body of the woman victim as the only visible monster in the film" (ibid. 33). The woman's gaze is no longer turned to a monster but becomes monstrous and turns onto her. She becomes a victim and killer, and her looks result in her death. Using Williams, the monster/victim concept I am theorizing has the potential in horror films for re-centering the gaze through marginalized identities, especially with films using oppressive structures as the monsters in the narrative.

With these theorizations of the gaze, Adam Charles Hart argues that this previous identification with the killer POV, the POV shots from the killer's perspective where the killer is unseen and is seen commonly in 70s slasher films, is a false identification with the killer.

Rather than being imbricated within the logic of suture, killer POV abstracts the look, removing it from reference to a familiar or concrete character who is doing the looking. Instead, it presents the act of looking to the audience and thus should be understood as a depiction *of* a look. That is, the look itself is just as much the object of the camera's gaze as are the victims-to-be who appear on camera. (Hart 2018, 77)

The audience's identification is not with the unseen killer but with the threat of the monstrous camera. The camera's presence as it stalks, lurks, and—with the addition of sound—breathes as it watches possible victims, causing the audience to have a moment of sympathy for the victim due to the power of the camera gaze and knowledge of that gaze. Patricia MacCormack theorizes a possible reason for this breakdown between camera, audience, and character: "The monster represents two vulnerabilities in the system of the singular—the abject as the collapse between subject and object, I and other, demarcated and integrated. It also shows to the I that it is always and already part of this collapse" (MacCormack 2012, 263). This collapse is seen in the killer's POV. The camera becomes monstrous because, as the monster, it controls our gaze. This is further proven by the fact that the killer is unkillable during these shots only when the killer is revealed in a reverse shot to the Final Girl that he or she is vulnerable enough to be killed (Hart 2018, 80-81). The killer becomes vulnerable when their identification with the audience is broken, for the camera and, by extension, the audience cannot be killed in the filmic world. This is the moment Clover mentions when the audience identifies with the Final Girl because she gazes upon the monster in a long-denied reserve shot. However, I would characterize this shift in gaze as one of a monster/victim.

Filmic Examples

What We Do In The Shadows is a 2014 New Zealand horror comedy mockumentary about a group of vampires living together in an apartment in Wellington, New Zealand. Due to the mockumentary format, the camera is a voyeuristic observer copying the direct cinema style, using moments of cinéma-vérité for comedic effect. In direct cinema, the camera is only there to capture reality and not to be acknowledged. The crew's involvement on screen is never seen, only briefly referenced by those on-screen with glances at the camera and talking-head interviews. Throughout the movie, the safety of the human film crew is mostly forgotten. Though the audience is aware of their existence and, in some instances, fears for them, they—the fictional film crew—are unfazed by their dangerous situation of filming vampires. In a scene later in the film, the vampires and Stu (Stu Rutherford), their human companion, attend an annual vampire ball. At the event, it is revealed to the rest of the partygoers that Stu is human and becomes a potential victim. Events quickly escalate as the vampires try to eat Stu before being stopped by Vlad (Jemaine Clement). The scene's tension comes from Stu being vulnerable as a human, putting him in precarity. However, the camera crew seems to go relatively undetected even though it is verbally confirmed that they are also human, even though up to this point in the film, the audience has yet to receive visual confirmation. During the scene, the crew is called into question about their presence, and Vlad does claim that they cannot eat the camera guys except maybe one (Waititi and Clement 2014). Though there is a brief moment of the threat, it is felt more for Stu than the camera crew.

The camera crew in *What We Do In The Shadows* takes on a similar role as the killer POV that Adam Hart defines. Their presence in the film is more monstrous than the monsters they document. They are invincible to any harm for the majority of the film, and this is because they are never seen. This lack of confirmation makes the camera the disembodied audience in the narrative world, as we view events yet are not in any real danger like the monsters. Morgan points out, "The camera, then, resides within a spatial world that extends all around it, and this allows us, as viewers, to experience the world of the film as if we were at a position within it" (Morgan 2016, 225). The audience embodies the camera crew; however, the crew also embodies the audience. In the narrative world of *What We Do In The Shadows*, the camera inhabits a heterotopic space that encapsulates the hybridity of the monster within it. Foucault's concept of the heterotopia is an in-between place of a utopia, which is not real, and reality. He uses the mirror as an example, saying:

> The mirror functions as a heterotopia in this respect: it makes this place that I occupy at the moment when I look at myself in the glass at once absolutely real, connected with all the space that surrounds it, and absolutely unreal, since in order to be perceived it has to pass through this virtual point which is over there. (Foucault 1984, 4)

Like the mirror, the camera and the cinema are both technologies that can create heterotopic spaces. The crew in *What We Do In The Shadows* seems to occupy a heterotopia due to their access to the camera being both in the dangerous spaces as their subjects yet removed from the space through the camera. Their presence in the film is both necessary and real yet ignored and forgotten. Similar to the heterotopia of the movie theater, Foucault comments, "...the theater brings onto the rectangle of the stage, one after the other, a whole series of places that are foreign to one another; thus it is that the cinema is a very odd rectangular room, at the end of which, on a two-dimensional screen, one sees the projection of a three-dimensional space" (ibid. 6). Heterotopias are liminal spaces and thus are temporary. What is also temporary is the invincibility of the camera in horror, which creates tension in the monster/victim dynamic. This is exhibited in the scene following the vampire masquerade.

The main characters and crew leave the party unscathed following the previous scene. They then run into a group of werewolves, whom they have tussled with previously in the film. As the werewolves begin to transition under the full moon, they warn everyone, including the camera crew, to run. As the vampires, Stu, and crew take off to escape the bloodlust of the werewolves, one cameraperson is not as lucky. Caught on camera is one of the crew members being attacked and killed by a werewolf. This is the first and only instance of the crew on screen. This scene takes on two horror perspectives, the first being the killer's POV, which denies the reverse shot, creating tension in the audience and the perceived invulnerability of the cameraman. Second, in this scene, the audience is finally granted the reverse shot, showing the vulnerability of the crew as the cameraman is killed on camera. This scene begins to take on filmic aspects of found footage. Hart discusses the shift from killer POV to found footage camera style in horror.

> Whereas killer POV indicates something approaching invulnerability and omniscience, the diegetic camera signifies utter vulnerability because neither the viewer nor the cameraperson—whose views are here aligned—knows what exists beyond the edges of the frame: we do not know who else might be looking or where they might be looking from. (Hart 2018, 82)

This is one of the few moments where the audience feels threatened, not for another character but for ourselves. The chase begins with the camera running and the sound of heavy breathing. Suddenly, a werewolf lunges from the darkness at the camera. The camera falls, and only then can the camera disengage from the camera's subject (the cameraman) as the audience gazes upon the bloody camera operator. The camera still runs as the dead body of the cameraperson lies in front of the camera, but even then, the footage is obscure, and the body is hard to recognize.

The camera becomes disembodied and turns into an object for this brief moment. The audience is no longer attached to an unseen body but has become an object looking. Vivian Sobchack theorizes that objects do have the ability to look back.

> Thus, when we visually engage an object that seems to 'look back' at us and that momentarily startles, intimidates, and fixes us with its 'irrational' autonomy, it seems obdurate and opaque, decentering us and undoing the mastery and privilege of our vision—and this because its full significance and presence not only eludes but also refuses human comprehension and reduction. (Sobchack 2004, 93)

The camera is a monstrous object and subject because the camera exists outside of the human. The camera's body, as discussed in phenomenology, though linked to the human body, can and does exist as a non-human entity because the movement of the camera is beyond human. The humorous tension of *What We Do In The Shadows* comes from the reversal of expectations. The vampires, usually associated with seduction and intelligence, are nerdy and imbecilic. The humans behind the camera, though the prey of the filmic subjects, the vampires, carry the power of the monster through the use of the camera. It is when they lose that power that they become victims again. This carries over to the television spin-off show of the same name. Within the pilot episode, the crew's presence is addressed when one of the vampires of the high council, Baron Afanas (Doug Jones), visits the three main vampires, Lazlo (Matt Berry), Nadja (Natasia Demetriou), and Nandor (Kayvan Novak). After receiving the Baron's coffin, the three vampires, plus their familiars, await for the Baron to emerge. Once he does, the Baron drinks the blood of the closest familiar, making Guillermo (Harvey Guillén), Nandor's familiar, hyperventilate, as it easily could have been him. However, the film crew is visibly unfazed. The Baron begins a speech, which he interrupts himself, noticing the cameras. The following exchange occurs:

> Lazlo: It's a documentary crew. They're cameras.
>
> Nandor: It's like they're not even here.
>
> Baron: They're filming me?
>
> Lazlo: Yes.
>
> Nandor: Just pretend like they're not there. It's kind of a natural piece. You were saying, Baron? (Waititi 2019)

The scene continues, but the brief acknowledgment of the crew puts them in a victim role as the acknowledgment of their presence creates precarity; however, it is quickly returned to the monstrous as the Baron accepts their presence.

In the retelling of *The Invisible Man* (2020), the film follows the story of Cecilia (Elizabeth Moss), who escapes one night from her abusive boyfriend. Weeks later, she discovers he has killed himself but believes she is being stalked by him even though she cannot see him, and he is presumed dead. She uncovers a secret suit he has created that is made entirely of cameras that allow him to be 'invisible.' She fights and eventually kills her boyfriend, freeing herself from his abuse. The narrative plot of the story is from Cecilia's perspective, which the audience sympathizes with and identifies with her. I bring this film as an example of the monstrous camera for two reasons. The first is that the monster in this movie is made of cameras, and the camera's gaze tortures and haunts Cecilia. The suit Adrian, Cecilia's abusive partner, creates to gaslight Cecilia is made of tiny cameras that cover his body. The camera takes on the literal form of a monster.

The Invisible Man—a book by H.G. Wells filmed and distributed by Universal Studios in 1933—follows Dr. Jack Griffin, a scientist who turns himself invisible but goes mad in the process, turning into a murderer. The changes from the original to this retelling speak on the current cultural moment as the story focuses away from the Invisible Man and more on Cecilia, a victim of this man. This is reflected in the camera movement. Throughout the film, the camera pans away from Cecilia to empty spaces or lingers in spaces. In one instance, Cecilia puts away clothes on one side of the room; the camera pans to the other side, where nothing is visibly present. Eventually, Cecilia enters the frame after the camera has already moved. The *Invisible Man* utilizes the monster/victim dynamic, but unlike *What We Do In The Shadows*, the camera exists outside of a narrative human, adding more to the monstrous camera.

Going back to Sobchack's object gaze, she continues with, "Looking *back* at us, the significant object also looks *beyond* us to an *expanded*—if deferred— *field* of visuality and meaning that subsumes and absorbs the reductive, if invested and consequential, questions asked of it by our contingent, local, and personal gaze" (Sobchack 2004, 93). The camera is both object and subject in the narrative and to the audience. The abuse that Cecilia endures is due to the camera, both the literal and filmic cameras. However, it also subverts the killer's POV to reveal the narrative killer to the audience before the characters. Locked in a mental hospital after being presumed to have killed her sister, Cecilia screams as she is tied down. She yells that she sees Adrian as the camera reverses shots to an empty corner of the room.

In *Invisible Man*, the camera is already in the monster/victim dynamic as the filmic camera hints at the threat of the literal camera monster (Adrian's tech suit) with panning and reverse shots of empty spaces. However, as Clover suggests in the change of identification from killer to final girl, Cecilia's gaze changes from victim to monster. As the camera is already aware of the monster's presence, making the audience aware of his presence, Cecilia must catch up with the audience's gaze. Not until the movie's end does her gaze become monstrous. The film ends in a more poignant but subdued fashion, with Cecilia killing Adrian in his home with his device by slitting his throat the same way he killed her sister. Cecilia becomes the monster/camera, and instead, Cecilia and the audience reaffirm that both are the holders of the gaze through the camera. She wields the phallic power of the camera and the gaze through Adrian's death and in the film's last frames as Cecilia stares back at the audience.

Conclusion

Horror film has always utilized the camera in exciting and compelling ways to enhance the creation and experience of horror. When watching a horror film, the camera is part of the audience's tension. As discussed in this chapter, part of this tension is because the camera takes on a hybrid rule of monster and victim through the gaze. Monster is usually associated with negative connotations. However, using Patricia MacCormack's definition of monstrosity, I use the monster in the context of something unable to perform as one thing or lack conforming. The hybrid nature of the monster creates a broader usage to be applied to the camera. However, the camera is not only monstrous but also a victim. The victim is an agent of precarity as the camera is a liminal agent within the filmic world. The threat of the camera acknowledgment creates unease within the audience as the camera's gaze is momentarily threatened. The monster/victim dynamic is the crux of horror tension. I argue that the camera is the embodiment of that dynamic. With the two filmic examples—*What We Do In The Shadows* and *The Invisible Man*—the monster/victim gaze of the camera becomes murkier and more complicated. The camera acts similar to the killer POV of the slashers of the 1970s as the camera becomes invincible, unable to be harmed or killed for the time being. However, unlike the killer POV, the camera cultivates an aura of possible harm that could be inflicted on it, similar to the final girl/victim within these shots.

Nevertheless, the camera body is the possible victim, as well as those on screen. In *What We Do In The Shadows*, the monster is the camera through the embodiment of the unseen documentary camera crew. Though in dangerous and life-threatening situations, their precarity is ignored until the end, when it is reality. However, that is quickly glossed over. Their victimhood is an illusion for jokes. In *The Invisible Man*, the monstrous camera takes a literal approach as it tortures Cecilia. Nevertheless, she utilizes the camera for her survival and freedom, takes that power from Adrian, and becomes the monster with the camera. Outside of the narrative, the camera can see danger even though Cecilia cannot make the audience aware of it while also participating in it. With the shift towards nuanced, diverse storytelling, the monster/victim dynamic becomes more nuanced. With the slasher films, siding with the monster and final girl, as Carol J. Clover and Linda Williams point out, feels unbalanced and sadistic. However, with more horror focusing on marginalized narratives and social issues, the monster/victim dichotomy I theorize here could give a chance for agency amongst groups that previously did not have any. The gaze is a tool of power that, for so much of filmic history, was granted to specific groups of people. However, the camera and audience have the power to change that gaze into something revolutionary, which is part of horror's genre legacy.

Bibliography

Clover, Carol J. 2015. "Her Body, Himself: Gender in the Slasher Film." In *The Dread of Difference: Gender and the Horror Film*, edited by Barry Keith Grant, 68-115. Austin: University of Texas Press.

Foucault, Michel. 1984. Translated by Jay Miskowiec. "Of Other Spaces: Utopias and Heterotopias." In *Architecture/Mouvement/Continuité*. 1-9. France: Architecture/Mouvement/Continuite.

Hart, Adam Charles. 2018. "Killer POV: First-Person Camera and Sympathetic Identification in Modern Horror." In *Imaginations* vol. 9, no. 1, 69-86. Alberta: University of Alberta.

MacCormack, Patricia. 2012. "The Queer Ethics of Monstrosity." In *Speaking of Monsters: A Teratological Anthology*, edited by Caroline Joan S. Picart and John Edgar Browning, 255-265. London: Palgrave Macmillan.

Morgan, Daniel. 2016. "Where are we?: camera movements and the problem of point of view." In *New Review of Film and Television Studies*, 14:2, 222-248. England: Routledge.

Sobchack, Vivian. 2004. "The Expanded Gaze in Contracted Space: Happenstance, Hazard, and the Flesh of the World." In *Carnal Thoughts: Embodiment and Moving Image Culture*. Los Angeles: University of California Press.

Williams, Linda. 2015. "When the Woman Looks." In *The Dread of Difference: Gender and the Horror Film*, edited by Barry Keith Grant, 17-36. Austin: University of Texas Press.

Filmography:

Clement, Jemaine, writer. *What We Do In The Shadows*. Season 1, episode 1, "Pilot." Directed by Taika Waititi, featuring Kayvan Novak, Matt Berry, and Natasia Demetriou. Aired March 27, 2019, in broadcast. FX Networks, 2019, https://www.hulu.com/watch/e03add94-3392-45a3-b036-034cb00ae9d0.

Waititi, Taika, and Jemaine Clement, dir. *What We Do In The Shadows*. 2014; Burbank, CA: Paramount Pictures, 2014. Digital.

Whannell, Leigh, dir. *The Invisible Man*. 2020, Burbank, CA: Universal Pictures, 2020. Digital.

Further Reading:

Benshoff, Harry M. 2015. "The Monster and the Homosexual." In *The Dread of Difference: Gender and the Horror Film*, edited by Barry Keith Grant, 116-141. Austin: University of Texas Press.

Choi, Jinhee. 2005. "Leaving It up to the Imagination: POV Shots and Imagining from the Inside." *In The Journal of Aesthetics and Art Criticism* 63, no. 1, 17-25. Oxford: Oxford University Press.

Doane, Mary Ann. 1980. "The Voice in the Cinema: The Articulations of Body and Space." In *Yale French Studies*, no. 60, 33-50. New Have: Yale University Press.

Rubin, Rebecca. 2018. "Diverse Audiences Are Driving the Horror Box Office Boom." In *Variety*, October 25, https://variety.com/2018/film/box-office/horror- movies-study-1202994407/.

Savoy, Eric. 1998. "The Face of the Tenant: A Theory of American Gothic." In *American Gothic: New Interventions in a National Narrative.* Iowa City: University of Iowa Press.

Williams, Linda. 1991. "Film Bodies: Gender, Genre and Excess." In *Film Quarterly,* 2-13. Los Angeles: University of California Press.

Wood, Robin. 2018. "An Introduction to the American Horror Film." In *Robin Wood on the Horror Film: Collected Essays and Reviews.* Detroit: Wayne State University Press.

Chapter 7

"You Are Trespassing in My House": Subverting the Gaze in Jennifer Kent's *Monster* and *The Babadook*

Adam P. Wadenius
Cosumnes River College

Abstract: Amelia, the main protagonist of Jennifer Kent's *Monster* (2005) and *The Babadook* (2014), is not your typical horror film female—sexual object, body in the throws of ecstasy, the monstrous feminine. She's a diverse woman going through an intense period of emotions in the years after her husband Oskar's death, and the spectator is positioned to identify with her complexity as a woman and mother. Vivian Sobchack argues that the horror films of the 1960s "contain, work out, and in some fashion resolve the contemporary weakening of patriarchal authority." Many horror films start out with the absent father as a symbol of patriarchy in crisis, but he will typically return, or the film will introduce a suitable replacement in the form of a priest, boyfriend, or lawman to restore repression. When Mister Babadook intrudes into Amelia and Samuel's life, he does so as a signifier of her grief but also of the traumatic void now left in the symbolic order. Throughout both films, spectator identification oscillates between the gazes of the characters as Amelia and the monster wrest for control of her body, home and son Samuel's life. *Monster* and *The Babadook* foreground the tension between Amelia and Oskar, maternal and paternal forces traversing a narrative that explores a bereft mother confronting a monstrous father. In harmony with a reflexive formal style that disrupts time and space by subverting classical conventions of editing and cinematography, Kent's approach produces a counter cinema that, Laura Mulvey argues, is capable of freeing "the look of the camera into its materiality in time and space and the look of the audience into dialectics, passionate detachment."

Keywords: Counter cinema, gaze, symbolic, semiotic, Kristeva, Sobchack, Dayan, Žižek

***

Oscillation & Identification

The opening shot of Jennifer Kent's short film *Monster* (2005) is seemingly an objective one, looking out from under the bed as Samuel hops down from his creaky mattress. Like most objective shots, it functions to establish the context of the scene—in this case, the space where the young boy engages in play and creates his fantasies. At the same time, it situates the spectator in the action, and because there's nothing unique about the shot to suggest otherwise, it can be assumed that it does not emanate from any specific character's perspective. A series of abrupt close-ups immediately follow, one after the next, depicting Samuel as he engages in a pretend conflict with one of his toys: he slams his foot down onto a stuffed monster doll; a low-angle shot frames his face as he looks to the floor; the doll is pictured looking back; drawing his sword from its sheath, he raises it into the air; thrusting the blade down onto the doll's face, each stab is punctuated by a resounding THUD as it strikes. The scene culminates with another low-angle shot from the doll's perspective, watching as Samuel lifts a ceramic bowl over his head before slamming it down towards the camera, wiping the picture to black. A short while later, the same ominous shot from under the bed that opened the film frames Amelia as she walks into Samuel's room. Doing some cleaning, she finds the bowl on top of the doll and picks it up from the floor to examine its face. With these few short interactions, the spectator has been situated into the direct point-of-view of Amelia, Samuel, the monster doll, and unbeknownst to the characters and spectator at this point, the *actual* monster hiding under the bed. In her analysis of slasher horror, Carol Clover argues that spectators are first invited to occupy the point-of-view of the feminine killer, only to later "switch sympathies in midstream" to the masculine final girl (Clover 1992, 46). Spectator identification becomes unstable and fluid across sex and gender lines in slasher films, as is the case with Kent's short film.

The opening scene of her feature-length adaptation of *Monster*, titled *The Babadook* (2014), begins with a shot of Amelia attempting to steady her breathing during the sudden impact of a car accident. The sounds of twisting metal echo through the space—a cacophony that accentuates the terror of the moment while also encouraging the spectator to identify with her experience of the crash. Shattered glass ricochets around the cabin, pelting her face and body. In the distance, Samuel's faint voice can be heard screaming for his "mom!" The lights flicker, oscillating dark and light with each turn of the now tumbling vehicle. Suddenly, everything is calm as she looks over to the driver's seat at her husband, Oskar, sitting motionless, unable to return her look. The husband and father-to-be has died, leaving a traumatic gap in the symbolic order. Samuel's voice is again heard, a bit louder this time, just as an intense white light emanates through the windshield and envelops Amelia. Cut to a medium shot that reveals her free-falling into a vast darkness. Samuel's voice is almost at full volume now, calling out for his mother as she passes through the void. Landing forcefully onto her mattress, she's jarred awake from her horrible nightmare to find Samuel standing by the bedside. "Mom, I had the dream again," he whines, having dreamt of a monster himself. It's significant that Amelia is pulled from her frightening recollection by Samuel's calls for his mother. Both *Monster* and *The Babadook* foreground the tension between Amelia and Oskar—maternal and paternal forces—via narratives that explore a bereft mother trying to protect herself and her son from a threatening monster/father. Kent's cinematography is delicately composed to express this theme visually through the use of reflexive techniques such as manipulating the frame rate, blurring the distinction between subjective and objective shots, producing unstable points of identification for spectators, and staging the interface effect. Her subversive approaches to storytelling and formwork in harmony produce a counter cinema that endeavors to "free the look of the camera into its materiality in time and space and the look of the audience into dialectics, passionate detachment" (Mulvey 1975, 816).

Patriarchy in Crisis

The monster in *The Babadook* first appears in the pages of a book called *Mister Babadook*, which is mysteriously found on Samuel's bookshelf. It tells the story of a tall, gaunt figure wearing a black top hat and cloak who intrudes into homes and torments families. You know he's around when you hear, "A rumbling sound then 3 (sic) sharp knocks." Samuel is frightened by the book, and Amelia notices that there are empty pages where the ending should be. She tears it into pieces and tosses it into the rubbish bin, however, that which is repressed in horror films is, of course, bound to return. A few days later, it's morning, and Amelia hears three quick raps at the front door. No one's there, so she pushes it shut. Almost immediately after, there are three more loud knocks: "DOOK, DOOK, DOOK." She opens the door again to find the previously ripped-up copy of *Mister Babadook* lying on the porch. It's been carefully pieced back together, and the once-empty pages are now filled with obscene illustrations of her murdering Samuel, herself, and the family dog. As a representation of the guilt and anxiety that Oskar's death still arouses in her, Mister Babadook arrives as a symbol of patriarchy in crisis, intent on threatening the maternal space of their home. He seeks to restore his paternal authority by reclaiming Samuel and exerting control of Amelia. His intentions are made clear when he calls to her from the basement, disguised as a vision of Oskar. She kisses him and says, "I thought you were dead." "We can be together, you just need to bring me the boy," he replies. Mister Babadook's deception is revealed as the high-pitched sound of cicadas emanate from the background—

the monotonous trilling an indication of the monster's depraved and dangerous presence. "You can bring me the boy," he growls. Amelia turns and runs upstairs, only to be confronted by Mister Babadook's monstrous apparition, now hovering directly above her in the air. For a brief moment, as the monster looms, the two exchange looks, seeing from both Amelia's vantage point and that of the monster's. In situations where Amelia and the monster encounter one another, it can be expected that the spectator's identification will vacillate between the two.

Vivian Sobchack argues that by the late 1960s, popular horror, science fiction, and family melodrama films converge to "test and represent the coherence, meaning, and limits" of the nuclear family under patriarchy (Sobchack 1996, 146). The American family home, once depicted as a "refuge from the social upheavals of the last two decades," has now evolved into a site of turmoil—"the nuclear family has found itself in nuclear crisis" (Ibid). Horror films, in general, tend to affirm fathers and father figures as symbols of strength and power, and the family horror films that Sobchack discusses seek to "contain, work out, and in some fashion resolve the contemporary weakening of patriarchal authority" (Ibid, 147). The patriarch in horror films is often tasked with surmounting the monster as a signal of the restoration of repression: films like *Frankenstein* (1931) and *Poltergeist* (1982) are good examples. In horror films where the father is missing, a surrogate figure may emerge to fill his absence in the time of need, which is the case with Officer Loomis in *Halloween* (1978) or Father Karras in *The Exorcist* (1973). In horror films, the father represents symbolic law (the name of the father), and the absence of the father in *Monster* and *The Babadook* gives rise to intense feelings of anxiety in Amelia and Samuel. There are several characters in *The Babadook* that at first seem like capable substitutes to replace Oskar's authority. Robbie is a friend and potential love-interest who flirts with Amelia in the break room at work. One afternoon, he visits her house to ask her out on a date, however, he's put-off by an argument that she's having with Samuel. Despite repeated warnings, Samuel's been testing his magic tricks in the basement, which is where Amelia keeps her memories of Oskar. Upset, she admonishes him for disobeying; "All of your father's things are down there." "He's my father you don't own him," he screams. Just then, three sharp knocks at the door interrupt their dispute.[1] Robbie stands there looking sheepish, holding a bouquet of flowers and a model airplane kit. Amelia explains that Samuel has been misbehaving, and it becomes clear that Robbie is not prepared for the complexity of the situation. Samuel shouts at her, "I hate you!" Then to Robbie, "She won't let me have a birthday party, and she

---

[1] Robbie arrives unannounced on the porch after knocking three times, in much the same way that the *Mister Babadook* book suddenly re-appears after Amelia destroys it.

won't let me have a Dad!" When faced with paternal responsibility, Robbie acquiesces. After finding *Mister Babadook* on the porch, Amelia believes that she and Samuel are in danger, so she goes to the police to report a stalking incident. At the station, there's a brief moment where she sees a top hat and a long black cloak hanging on a rack behind one of the officers. The figure lurks menacingly in the background with its long, pointy fingers protruding from the sleeves, resembling a raven sitting on its perch. Wherever Amelia goes, her unrelenting grief follows. The officers dismiss her concerns and look at her skeptically, just as the child services workers do when they arrive to perform a wellness check on her home. The welfare officials sent from Community Services inquire about Samuel and his multiple absences from school, insinuating that there will be consequences if Amelia doesn't comply with their recommendations. Along with Robbie and the police, these characters have the potential to stand-in as surrogates for the father, and like Oskar/the monster, they are signifiers of paternal fallibility when they are unfit to fill or resolve the gap left in the symbolic order. As an ever-present reminder of her loss, Amelia's multiple confrontations with impotent figures evoke a narrative tension that is also expressed cinematographically via the oscillating maternal and paternal gazes.

There are a number of deceptive shots in *Monster* that have the dual function of first appearing as objective, only to later be understood as the subjective perspective of the monster. Reconsider the shot looking out from under Samuel's bed towards Amelia's legs as she enters his room to tidy up. The monster is real, it's out of the closet and under Samuel's bed. Each of these shots functions as an exposition of the action, and each is also later comprehended as the monster's subjective, intruding gaze. This technique is further exhibited in the subsequent scene when Amelia is depicted in a low-angle shot that peers at her from within the closet as she tosses the doll inside and shuts the door. A few moments later Samuel approaches the same door, only now it's mysteriously open. Moving cautiously toward the darkened gap, the shot is again composed from inside the closet, looking out through the door frame at Samuel. His eyes widen when he sees something frightening in the darkness, causing him to let out a piercing scream. Amelia comes running from the kitchen, assuring him that what he saw was "just a doll." Samuel snaps back, "No it isn't, it's real…it says it's gonna eat you up!" Sometime later, when Samuel is taking a bath, Amelia goes downstairs to retrieve some clothes from the closet. The now familiar shot, a seemingly objective one looking through the frame of the closet door, stares at her in close-up as she gathers a few items from the shelf. Like Samuel before her, Amelia spies something lurking in the darkened corner. She leans in for a closer look and is startled to see the monster leering back at her with its sinister grin. Upon this revelation, the spectator recognizes that they have been occupying the monster's perspective as he moves about the house, looking out from under Samuel's bed and haunting from within the hall closet.

By calling attention to the manipulative capacity of Kent's direction, it's further understood that objective shots are not to be trusted as such and that, moving forward, the spectator may be situated into the subjective perspective of any character at any time. This type of experimentation with editing patterns, shot framing, and the composition of the mise-en-scène is also apparent in *The Babadook*.

After waking from her nightmare in the opening scene, a series of three shots depict Amelia and Samuel searching the house for monsters: a medium close-up looking out at them from under the bed; a medium shot gazing at them from within the closet; an extreme close-up of an illustration of the Big Bad Wolf from one of Samuel's bedtime stories. The first two shots mirror those seen in *Monster*—they deceptively appear objective, only to be later understood as emanating from the vantage point of Mister Babadook. When juxtaposed with the third, they collectively evoke the looming presence of the monster, hinting at the horrifying violations to come. This is a motif in both films that coincides with static shots of the basement door, boiling pots, empty staircases, sinks filled with dirty dishes, isolated images of barren trees, and short scenes of Amelia and Samuel sitting at the dinner table together in silence. These types of shots resonate with dread because they appear to be objective, however the spectator can never be fully sure that they're not also coming from the gaze of Mister Babadook as reminders of his unrelenting and terrifying presence.

Amelia sees visions of Mister Babadook in various shapes and forms before she first encounters his physical presence.[2] One night, while lying in bed next to Samuel, she hears a screeching noise coming from the kitchen. After a brief moment of quiet, the door to her room slowly opens, and the familiar trilling of cicadas, accompanied by the piercing hiss of Mister Babadook, fills the air in the room. She pulls the thin fabric of the blanket over her head as the monster lets out an intimidating snarl, "Ba-baa-dook-dook-dook." Mustering the courage, she peeks from underneath to see him floating directly above her, moving and convulsing on the ceiling. A point of view shot from Amelia's perspective looks on as he suddenly extends his arms and dives toward her head. The reverse shot is from Mister Babadook's direct point-of-view as he infiltrates her body via her mouth. There is a slight manipulation of the frame rate while this possession takes place, and the fast-motion, jittery effect in the cinematography disrupts the representation of time and space. The quick oscillation between perspectives puts the spectator in a position to identify with a mother grappling

---

[2] For example, when Amelia is doing dishes in the kitchen one evening, she looks across the street at Mrs. Roach and smiles to her. After tending to the dishes in the sink for a brief second, she looks over again to see Mister Babadook standing in the darkness behind Mrs. Roach.

with immense emotional trauma and a paternal monster seeking to reinstate his authority by infecting her mind and taking control of her body. It's immediately clear in the aftermath of this trauma that Mister Babadook has affected a great change in Amelia. She and Samuel begin falling behind on their work and school obligations, her toothache begins to worsen, and she chastises him one night, saying that if he's hungry, he can go and "eat shit."[3] Later that evening, she's sitting fully clothed in the bathtub when Samuel approaches. She sweeps him up and sets him down into the safe, womb-like space of the water. "I don't want you to go away," he pleads. "I'm not going anywhere," she promises. Amelia is struggling, yet she remains in control, comforting Samuel in her maternal embrace.

Mister Babadook persists after Amelia, and in the scene following their encounter in the basement, she hurries to her room and barricades the door in an attempt to keep the monster at a distance. Outsmarting her, he instead enters through the chimney, accompanied by the sharp trilling of cicadas as he slithers his way inside. When she attempts to crawl back to the bedroom door, he removes his cloak and tosses it onto the floor beside her. She repeats to herself out loud, "It isn't real, it isn't real." The monster responds with a resounding "ROAR," affirming he is indeed real. Three shots follow in quick succession: from Mister Babadook's point-of-view, he plunges down towards Amelia's back; a close-up of her face, every muscle clenched in agony; an extreme close-up of her eye dilating, until only the slightest blue ring of color surrounds her large black pupil.[4] Again, the spectator is invited to move back and forth between the subjective gazes of Amelia and Mister Babadook. In *Monster* and *The Babadook*, Kent is undermining symbolic structures by telling stories about paternal figures in crisis and heroic mothers who find peace within themselves. This functions in concert with her formal style, which challenges the spectator's expectations by creating unstable points of identification, oscillating the gaze, and exploring the borders that separate objective and subjective shots.

Counter Cinema

Amelia, the main protagonist of *The Babadook*, is not your typical female horror film heroine. Unlike Marion in *Psycho* (1960), she is not a fetishized object or an out-of-control body in the throes of ecstasy like Megan in *Re-Animator*, nor is she the vengeful monstrous feminine like the titular young woman from *Carrie* (1976). All three archetypes depict horrific fantasies about

---

[3] The concept of the abject is evoked, similar to the opening scene in DePalma's *Carrie* where Chris says to Carrie, "You eat shit!"

[4] Evoking a similar sense of psychological dread as the shot of Marion's eye in Hitchcock's *Psycho* just after she's been murdered in the shower.

women as alluring sexual objects, threatened bodies in need of rescue, or monstrous Others driven to mass killing sprees. Each of them is forced into one of two dichotomous positions—either worthy of reward for their subordination or in need of punishment for their sins against patriarchy. In her essay "Women's Cinema as Counter Cinema," Claire Johnston discusses the patriarchal discourse of popular American cinema as one where the camera captures "the 'natural' world of the dominant ideology" (Johnston 2004, 4). Women's cinema has to function as an affront to hegemonic film structures; "it cannot be 'captured' on celluloid with the 'innocence' of the camera: it has to be constructed/manufactured. New meanings have to be created by disrupting the fabric of the male bourgeois cinema within the text of the film" (Ibid). Amelia is a diverse woman going through an intense period of emotion during the six years following her husband's death. She loves her son, Samuel, though she has trouble showing affection to him. She has a close relationship with an adoring neighbor, engages in meaningful interactions with her colleagues at work, fights with her sister, and her sexual frustrations are highlighted in a scene where Samuel accidentally interrupts her while she's trying to masturbate. These are all important characteristics for strengthening the spectator's sense of identification with her as a complex female protagonist undergoing emotional trauma, while at the same time, they highlight the fact that the monstrosity of the film does not emanate from any aspect of her womanhood or femininity. The monster in the film is her repressed memories of Oskar's death, figured as the threatening, shadowy ghoul named Mister Babadook. Not only is Amelia reminded of Oskar's death every time she's in the presence of potential surrogates, but she's visibly shaken when interacting with Samuel, and her feelings of guilt and anxiety about his birth have created a distance between them. When speaking to a stranger at the grocery store, with friends at a birthday party, or during conversations with her sister, Amelia's pained expressions and outbursts of anger at the mention of Oskar's death are reminders of the immense sorrow she carries. At the beginning of *The Babadook* the spectator is installed into Amelia's nightmare and observes her recollection of the car accident that killed her husband, which also took place on the day Samuel was born—the day she became a mother. At the beginning of the film, Samuel's voice wakes Amelia from her nightmare, in the same way that in *Monster,* just after the monster infiltrates Amelia's body, Samuel's voice calling out for "mommy" jolts her from a temporary daze. In both *Monster* and *The Babadook,* Amelia's maternal nature is highlighted from the onset, and its subversive character is articulated through multiple stagings of the interface effect.

Daniel Dayan's essay "The Tudor-Code of Classical Cinema," argues that through the system of the suture, classical cinema functions to "mask the ideological origin and nature of cinematographic statements," thus revealing itself as "the ventriloquist of ideology" (Dayan 1974, 31). Within the system of the suture, the meaning of a shot is always dependent on the shot that follows, therefore making each filmic statement an "incomplete part of a whole yet to come" (Ibid). Slovenian philosopher Slavoj Žižek discusses the logic of suture in three elementary steps. The spectator is first "confronted with a shot, finds pleasure in it in an immediate, imaginary way, and is absorbed by it" (Žižek 2001, 32). Their engagement is soon undermined by the realization that they sit passively within a construct, under the control of the "Absent One (or, rather, Other) who manipulates images behind my back" (Ibid). What follows is a reverse shot from the place of the Absent One, "allocating this place to its fictional owner, one of the protagonists" (Ibid). The spectator, fully engaged with the events on screen, is subjectively sutured into the narrative by the filmmaker. While suture is an important formal mechanism for maintaining an imaginary sense of identification with the characters, Žižek suggests that the fundamental ideological function of suture is to hide the notion that Jacques Lacan's 'big Other' does not exist. In Lacanian psychoanalysis, the big Other is "the regulation of the domain of symbolic mandates" and functions as the agency for which one has to maintain an appearance—"'God' in a theocracy, 'the Party' under Stalinism, or 'the People' in today's China" (Žižek 1997, 1). All of the subject's thoughts and actions stand in relation to the big Other, and because "the big Other does not exist," Žižek argues that one can occasionally glimpse its fictional status (Ibid, 2). In other words, the in-existence of the big Other directly correlates to an acceptance of, and trust in, symbolic law; we know very well the big Other doesn't exist, yet we make believe it does so that we can go on as proper subjects within the symbolic order. The cinematographic style and editing patterns of the classical and other patriarchal forms of cinema function to suture the spectator into the narrative, thus concealing the fictional status of the big Other. Women's and other forms of art cinema, the avant-garde, and experimental filmmaking can function to reveal the fictional status of the big Other in moments when suture fails to keep the spectator properly oriented in the narrative. An awareness of the fictional status of the big Other results in a breakdown of "symbolic efficiency," rendering it vulnerable to violent disintegration, arousing anxiety in the subject (Ibid). It is here that Žižek introduces the concept of interface:

> "Suture follows the logic of signifying representation (the second shot represents the absent subject - S - for the first shot), while the interface effect occurs when this signifying representation fails. At this point, when the gap can no longer be filled by an additional signifier, it is filled by a spectral object, in a shot which, in the guise of the spectral screen, includes its own counter-shot. In other words, when in the exchange of shots and counter- shots, a shot occurs to which there is no counter-shot, the only way to fill this gap is by producing a shot which contains its own counter-shot." (Žižek 2001, 54)

The interface effect occurs when signifying devices such as suture fail, effectively disengaging the spectator from the narrative. This technique, whereby "the gap between the subjective and objective dimensions of experience is presented within the narrative as a spectral object," is exhibited during several key scenes in *The Babadook* (Skaff and Leubbe 2003, 1). When Amelia and Samuel are reading together in bed, there is a moment where the lights begin to flicker, signaling the eerie presence of Mister Babadook. Startled, Amelia is captured in a close-up shot as she scans the room, expecting to see the monster. Instead, there's a cut to a long shot from her perspective, revealing nothing in the room except her workspace, an old blue chair, some clothes strewn about, and a large armoire with a mirror on its door. Curiously, the reflection of her sitting in bed next to Samuel can be seen in the mirror. Within the system of suture, shot A signifies the presence of the Absent One—a distinct gaze that needs to be filled—while the reverse shot "renders the place from which the Absent One is looking" (Žižek 2001, 32). The ensuing jump cut to a medium shot of Amelia's reflection places the spectator in closer proximity to the image of her, still looking at herself in the mirror as she returns her own gaze. In these two shots, Amelia's look across the room (shot A) signifies the presence of the Absent One, however, the reverse shot B of her staring at herself in the mirror fails to produce the suturing effect. Shot A of Amelia's face as she surveys the cold, empty room is Dayan's description of an "incomplete part of a whole yet to come" (Dayan 1974, 31). A typical reverse shot to this action might offer the perspective of the monster looking back at Amelia in her bed, suturing the spectator into the frightening space. The reverse shot B in this scenario, however, shows Amelia returning her own gaze to the reflection of the mirror, thus signaling the moment "when suturing no longer works" (Žižek 2001, 52). Later, in the scene where Amelia brings Oskar's violin up from the basement, her disjointed perspective is captured in a point-of-view shot of Samuel sitting nervously in the blue chair across the room.[5] The shot slowly dissolves into a slightly canted, medium close-up of Amelia now sleeping in bed. Again, continuity dictates that the reverse shot of her look would be one of Samuel looking back at his mother, fearful of her strange behaviors. Instead, the dissolve resolves Amelia's gaze with another shot of her own sleeping face, failing to suture the spectator into the action.[6] When flipping from channel to channel while watching television one night, Amelia stops on a news report about a woman accused of stabbing her son. In the background of the b-roll footage from the news report, Amelia notices someone staring out of one of the windows of the apartment building where the tragedy took place. A wipe

---

[5] The image goes in and out of focus to suggest her eyes are adjusting to the light of the space, as well as signaling that a monstrous presence has invaded her body.

[6] Effects like this and others (manipulating frame rates, e.g.) also function to create ellipses that play with time and space.

situates the action closer, and it is clear that the person looking back at her from the screen is her smiling doppelgänger. Cut to a close-up of the maniacal face, leering from the television, then a cut back to Amelia as the lamp next to her sparks and fizzles out. Again, continuity is subverted by the reflexivity of a moment where Amelia is put into a position to exchange gazes with herself. In each of these examples, the interface screen field steps in "when suturing no longer works" as a "direct stand-in for the 'Absent One'" (Ibid). In *Monster* and *The Babadook*, continuity techniques like shot/reverse shot patterns effectively suture the spectator into the narrative, concealing the fiction of the big Other. In moments when suture fails—when objective and subjective shots are subverted, ellipses manipulate time and space, or the interface effect is foregrounded, these forms of stylistic experimentation sever the spectator's imaginary sense of identification with the characters, highlighting the breakdown of symbolic efficiency by threatening to reveal the big Other as a delicate fiction. This urges the spectator to consider the conclusiveness of the reality presented on the screen and introduces the potential for the authority of the big Other to be radically re-articulated in maternal terms.

Semiotic Cinema

In her essay "Revolution in Poetic Language," Julia Kristeva presents an argument for a "theory of signification based on the subject, his formation, and his corporeal, linguistic and social dialectic" (Kristeva 1983, 15). She designates the symbolic (clear, meaningful communication) and the semiotic (expression of bodily drives and feelings) as two modes of the signifying process that constitute language. The space of the semiotic originates in the *chora*, an unrepresentable, pre-linguistic space that is "connotative of the mother's body…the 'pre-symbolic'—a manifestation—especially in art, of what could be called the 'materiality' of the symbolic: the voice as rhythm and timbre, the body as movement, gesture, and rhythm" (Lechte 1990, 129). Kristeva is careful in her analysis to discuss the import of both the symbolic and the semiotic as a way to consider "the mothers 'place' as *chora* as well as the place of the father as the embodiment of the symbolic Name-of-the-Father" (Ibid, 130). The semiotic and the symbolic exist in a fragile symbiosis. Without the symbolic, "there would be no art as we understand it in western society because there would be no language as communication," and without the semiotic, "the symbolic would lack any form of materiality with the result that there would still be no art or language as communication" (Ibid). As representations of the signifying process, *Monster* and *The Babadook* call specific attention to the dialectic oscillation between semiotic and symbolic forces.

During the climactic moments of *The Babadook*, the spectator occupies Amelia's hazy subjectivity as she wakes up on the basement floor, her limbs tied with rope and her body still under attack by the perverse invasion of the monster. Afraid for his life, Samuel begs for her to continue fighting, "I know you don't love me, the Babadook won't let you. But I love you mom and I always will." She lets out a maniacal laugh that immediately turns to sobs of anguish, signifying the abject tension of her condition as Samuel's mother, possessed by a paternal monster. The spectator recalls the opening moments of the film, where Samuel rouses Amelia from her wicked nightmare by shouting for his "mom." "You have to get it out," he says. In a state of division, Amelia lifts her hands to Samuel's neck and begins to strangle him while at the same time fighting the urge to give in to Mister Babadook's control. Gasping for air, Samuel raises his hand to her cheek and gently caresses her face, again appealing to her maternal instincts.[7] She's able to resist the monster's impulses and quickly pushes Samuel to the side before doubling-over and vomiting a viscous black goo onto the floor.

After abjecting his presence from her body, Amelia must surmount the monster, who retreats upstairs to hide in her bedroom. Before emerging from the darkened void in the corner of the room, he forces her to re-experience the moment when Oskar is decapitated in the auto accident. He then takes his hideous, threatening form in an attempt to intimidate her, but she summons the courage to stand up and scream, "You are nothing. This is my house. You are trespassing in my house. If you touch my son again, I'll fucking kill you!" Clutching Samuel in her arms and emboldened by the restoration of the mother-son bond, she asserts control of her grief, rendering the monster powerless as his slender frame falls limp to the ground.[8] She moves slowly over to his lifeless body when a sudden cut positions the spectator into the monster's point of view, bursting into the air. Now enveloped by the same white light that illuminated the space of her nightmare in the opening scene, Amelia stands motionless in front of the ghoul as he howls directly in her face. Still occupying the monster's point-of-view, the shot tracks to the right, out of the room, and down the stairs to the basement door, where it slams shut. Amelia secures the lock, and she and Samuel embrace. Amelia has accepted Oskar's death, and though she will never be fully rid of the sorrow she harbors, she's in control and can revisit him whenever she wishes. Mister Babadook/Oskar will always be kept safe subordinate, because there is "no narrative resolution for patriarchy" in the film, "except the denial or death of the father," which functions to symbolize "the death of the future" (Sobchack 1996, 159). This is further illustrated in the subsequent scenes, as she is able to openly discuss Oskar's death with both the child service workers and Mrs. Roach without any signs of

---

[7] This is another example of Kent manipulating time and space by distorting and exaggerating Amelia's movements as she struggles to rid herself of Mister Babadook's presence.

[8] The scene is reminiscent of the climactic moments of Wes Craven's *Nightmare on Elm Street*, when Nancy turns her back on Freddy to strip him of his power.

emotional stress. The final images of the film are of her and Samuel in a warm embrace, at peace with each other in the maternal space of the semiotic *chora*. *Monster* concludes with a similar confrontation between maternal and paternal energy. Amelia, watching as Samuel is beset by the monster, threatens, "Leave him alone! If you come back here without my permission, I will kill you, do you understand? I mean it!" The monster relents. Amelia and Samuel fall backward into bed, where she caresses him, awash in a bright white embrace of semiotic light. In the final scene of the film, Amelia pours some milk and sets it down in front of the closet. The image of the monster's spindly hand snatching-up the glass is a signifier of maternal desire, an acknowledgement of the mother's role in signifying processes, and a reminder of the abject tension that remains between symbolic and semiotic structures.[9]

As instances of semiotic cinema, *Monster* and *The Babadook* stage narratives about maternal heroines who confront paternal monsters that ultimately resolve with the death or denial of the father and the restoration of maternal love, agency, and symbiosis with her child. This demonstration of the fragility of symbolic structures functions in concert with Kent's experimental formal style to "violently interrogate" the gaze of the characters and spectator, upsetting the established "language of the cinema" by revealing the fiction of the big Other (Johnston 2004, 4). Her counter cinema subverts traditional representations of symbolic fatherhood, re-articulating its power and authority in maternal, semiotic terms, to produce filmic experiences of "the 'feminine' coming to disrupt the Name-of-the-Father as the embodiment of the paternal function (of father/mother/child triad), and thus, the symbolic as the order of language and signification" (Lechte 1990, 5).

Bibliography

Carpenter, John, dir. 1978. *Halloween*. Hollywood, CA: Paramount Pictures, 2020. DVD.

Clover, Carol. 1992. *Men, Women, and Chain Saws: Gender in the Modern Horror Film*. New Jersey: Princeton University Press.

Craven, Wes, dir. 1984. *A Nightmare on Elm Street*. Burbank, CA: New Line, 2001. DVD.

Dayan, Daniel. 1974. "The Tudor-Code of Classical Cinema." *Film Quarterly* vol. 28, no. 1: 22-31.

DePalma, Brian, dir. 1976. *Carrie*. Los Angeles, CA: 20th Century Fox, 2013. DVD.

Friedkin, William, dir. 1978. *The Exorcist*. Burbank, CA: Warner Brothers, 2010. DVD.

---

[9] See Julia Kristeva's *Powers of Horror* for a discussion of food loathing and the abject qualities of mother's milk.

Gordon, Stuart, dir. 1985. *Re-Animator.* Kew, Victoria, Australia: Umbrella Entertainment, 2018. DVD.

Hitchcock, Alfred, dir. 1960. *Psycho.* Universal City, CA: Universal Pictures, 2012. DVD.

Hooper, Tobe, dir. 1982. *Poltergeist.* Burbank, CA: Warner Brothers, 2008. DVD.

Johnston, Claire. 2004. "Women's Cinema as Counter Cinema." In *Film Theory,* edited by K. J. Shepherdson, Philip Simpson, Andrew Utterson. New York: Routledge.

Kent, Jennifer, dir. 2005. *Monster.* Sydney, Australia: New South Wales Film and Television Office. YouTube. https://www.youtube.com/watch?v=53ZRbiZgB Tk

Kent, Jennifer, dir. 2014. *The Babadook.* Sydney, Australia: Screen Australia, 2020. DVD.

Kristeva, Julia. 1983. *Revolution in Poetic Language.* New York: Columbia University Press.

Lechte, John. 1990. *Julia Kristeva.* New York: Routledge.

Mulvey, Laura. 1975. "Visual Pleasure and Narrative Cinema." *Screen,* vol. 16, issue 3, Autumn.

Skaff, Sheila and Chris Leubbe. 2003. "When an Exception is just an Exception: Slavoj Zizek's *The Fright of Real Tears: Krzysztof Kieslowski between Theory and Post-Theory." Iowa Journal of Cultural Studies,* Fall.

Sobchack, Vivian. 1996. "Bringing It All Back Home: Family Economy and Generic Exchange." *The Dread of Difference: Gender and the Horror Film,* edited by Barry Keith Grant. Austin: University of Texas Press.

Whale, James, dir. 1931. *Frankenstein.* Universal City, CA: Universal Pictures, 2016. DVD.

Žižek, Slavoj. 1997. "The Big Other Doesn't Exist." *Journal of European Psychoanalysis,* Spring/Fall.

————. 2001. *The Fright of Real Tears.* British Film Institute: London.

Chapter 8

Ladies of the Night, What Pop Music They Make: The Monstrous Adolescent in *Jennifer's Body* and *Blue My Mind*

Eleanor Gratz

University of North Carolina at Wilmington

Abstract: "Ladies of the Night, What Pop Music They Make: The Monstrous Adolescent in *Jennifer's Body* (2009, USA) and *Blue My Mind* (2018, Switzerland)" analyzes the revisionist horror practices of women-directed and authored films. This paper was included as a chapter in the Senior Honors Thesis titled "Analysis of Female Adolescent Bodies in Women Directed Horror Films", and received Highest Honors from the University of North Carolina at Chapel Hill. This paper conducts aesthetic analysis in conjunction with canonical film scholarship to redefine gender in horror. I employ scholarship from seminal horror scholars such as Carol J. Clover, Barbara Creed, and Noël Carroll to explore and reposition a new monstrous feminine created when helmed by women filmmakers. Further, the international scope of this paper examines the binding fabric of gendered practices in horror cinema and filmmaking more broadly. Horror scholarship and academia analyzing monstrosity in relation to gender have almost exclusively focused on representations of women on-screen and neglected media produced by women. This paper analyzes revisionist horror history, examining representations of the adolescent body helmed by women filmmakers. I foreground the consciousness of filmmakers operating within the horror genre to subvert and revise traditional narrative and visual language in conjunction with female subjectivity. I analyze the revision of the monstrous adolescent figure as it relates to the intimacy of female friendship, maturation, and sexual identity. Further, I highlight the corporeal nature of these films as a key component of women's cinema. In societies that seek to vilify women, women filmmakers have responded by creating monsters in their own image for audiences to both cower from and embrace.

Keywords: female adolescence, women filmmakers, monstrosity, corporeality, sexuality

***

Horror cinema's operatic sensibilities allow a harrowing and authentic examination of female puberty.[1] In terms of horror rhetoric, the body betrays its host as it begins to take a new form. These changes are uncomfortable and disorienting, yet all the while, one is told how mundane their experience is. The betrayal is emphasized as the body unwillingly begins a metamorphosis, the outcome of which the world already knows. With a new body, the question arises of how to mourn the body that has been lost? Female adolescence is a time of rapid transition and bodily uncertainty. As a girl becomes a woman, she loses the anonymity of childhood, and her body becomes public domain. The world becomes crueler as inhabiting this body invites a sense of everyday lived danger as one finds the world *wants* to hurt women for nothing else but their bodies. Women filmmakers explore feminine experiences in the context of the horror genre by reinvigorating the adolescent horror figure and infusing it with body horror. Horror affords filmmakers the language needed to cinematically communicate the turbulence and emotional violence of female adolescence. Depicting figures engaging in twisted iterations of puberty and burgeoning sexuality, women filmmakers create what I refer to as the "monstrous adolescent."

I begin this chapter by outlining the concept of the female monster as it pertains to the monstrous adolescent. I argue women filmmakers who employ the monstrous adolescent engage with topics of female bonding, maturation, and sexual identity within the horror genre. This chapter continues the work of Patricia Pister's *New Blood in Contemporary Cinema: Women Directors and the Poetics of Horror,* in which she outlines the features of contemporary women-authored horror films as containing an "intimate point of view of the inner experience of the female body," addressing an emotional spectrum of horror aesthetics, and "a poetics of horror is not confined to strict genre boundaries" (Pisters 2022, 3). Further, highlighting Carol J. Clover's scholarship on women and gender in horror films, particularly her discussion of *Carrie* (1976), I compare and outline the history of the monstrous adolescent present in *Carrie*, *Ginger Snaps* (2000), *Jennifer's Body,* and *Blue My Mind.* I argue Women filmmakers revise monstrosity using the monstrous adolescent figure to cinematically explore corporeality, interiority, and burgeoning sexuality as it pertains to the female adolescent experience. I conclude by considering how *Jennifer's Body* and *Blue My Mind* exemplify the presentation of the feminine

---

[1] This chapter examines female monstrosity and puberty yet does not assert womanhood and femininity are predicated on biology. The author recognizes and respects women and femininity in transgender, intersex, non-binary, and queer communities.

monstrous adolescence in horror films, the forethought of women filmmakers crafting nuanced films, and the transnational implications of the monstrous adolescent in the horror genre.

The monstrous adolescent refers to the figure present at the intersection where horror cinema meets the coming-of-age film. Consistent with Pisters' hypothesis of poetics of horror in women's contemporary cinema possessing a genre fluidity, the monstrous adolescent presents itself at the intersection of coming-age-cinema and the horror genre. Moreover, the figure of the monstrous adolescent can be found across genres from Catherine Hardwicke's indie drama *Thirteen* (2003) to the animated feature *Turning Red* (2022). The monstrous adolescent is not exclusive to women characters, but for the purposes of this chapter, I examine only female monsters.[2] The term adolescent refers to an individual's transition from childhood to adulthood, and while the specific age range varies given the individual, within this chapter, I explore adolescence within the teenage years specifically.[3] While this is not reflective of when the onset of puberty occurs, the teen-centric focus removes "terrifying children" and figures like Regan MacNeil of *The Exorcist* (1973). Regan, as a 12-year-old, lacks agency and self-discovery, is infantilized by other characters, and relies heavily on her relationship with her mother. The characters I examine portray distant or complicated relationships with their parents, illustrating a distance from childhood and a confrontation with the boundaries of adulthood.

When defining "monster," I employ Noël Carroll's *Philosophy of Horror, or Paradoxes of the Heart* in which he defines the characteristics of monsters. He writes, "Horrific monsters are threatening. This aspect of the design of horrific monsters is, I think, incontestable. They must be dangerous. This can be satisfied simply by making the monster lethal. That it kills and maims is enough. The monster may also be threatening psychologically, morally, or socially" (43). Carroll argues a monster must threaten one's safety or the social, moral, and psychological natural order. This framework allows for an analysis of the physicality of a monster and the underlying fears a monster illuminates in society, be that biological, sexual, or reflective of a specific time period. Carroll

---

[2] Films focusing on male characters include *Teen Wolf* (1985), *The Lost Boys* (1987), and *My Best Friend is a Vampire* (1987). I argue that these films explore male bodily transformation with levity and revel in the power obtained rather than the humanity lost.

[3] The American Psychological Association within, "Developing Adolescents: A Reference for Professionals" explains the complexity of the term adolescent as, "There is no standard age range for defining adolescence. Individuals can begin adolescence earlier than age 10, just as some aspects of adolescent development often continue past the age of 18. Although the upper age boundary is sometimes defined as older than 18 (e.g., age 21 or 25), there is widespread agreement that those in the age range of 10 to 18 should be considered adolescents."

elaborates further on the importance of impurity in monsters, noting, "[i]mpurity involves a conflict between two or more standing cultural categories" (Carroll 1990, 43). While this chapter invokes Carroll's outline of monstrosity, I also challenge monsters in this chapter, expressing a threat, danger, and impurity that must reckon with the social order when already neglected by that very societal landscape. *Whom* do these monsters threaten? If one is already cast as a monster for their gender or sexuality, would you rather be a monster with fangs or no bite at all?

Employing Carroll's framework, I examine female adolescence within the horror genre and the physical, moral, and social threat female monstrosity poses. Films examined in this chapter illustrate a monster's threatening nature and impurity coalescing with the corporeal horrors of puberty. The physicality of the monstrous adolescent body inspires fear in human characters within the monster's world. Impurity beyond the physical is present in the female figure enacting agency in a patriarchal society. These monsters who retain their femininity are doubly impure. They are both inhuman because of their monstrosity and, as women, are hostile to a patriarchal society. The female adolescent uses the newfound power of monstrosity to act selfishly with a disregard for others. This malicious nature, derived from impurity and heightened physical power, allows these monsters to engage in dangerous, horrific, and, at times, murderous behavior.

I analyze these behaviors and illustrate the physical, moral, and social threat these figures pose both as monsters and as women. In this chapter, I explore the monstrous adolescent in the films *Jennifer's Body* (dir. Karyn Kusama, 2009) and *Blue My Mind* (dir. Lisa Brühlmann, 2017). Employing formal aesthetic analysis, I examine the character's relationship to monstrosity visualized with corporeal transformation, as well as examine the physical, social, and moral threats that each character poses. Further, I situate these monstrous adolescents as they relate to canonical horror films, and the revisions made to the genre by women filmmakers as indicative of a shift in horror's portrayal of the female experience. Drawing on horror scholarship and feminist film theory, I argue women filmmakers revise and reclaim monstrosity to explore female adolescent corporeality, interiority, and sexuality.

The Monstrous Adolescent in Horror Cinema History

Horror films centered on teens that participate in coming-of-age tropes are not a new concept nor are they exclusive to women filmmakers. Carrie White's legacy as a woman and monster in horror cinema casts a large shadow both in narrative structure and visual iconography. Her status and pedigree can be described as the mother of the monstrous adolescent or patron saint of feminine monstrosity. Her impact on horror scholarship and relevancy in contemporary horror filmmaking cannot be overstated. Both Pisters and Clover emphasize the film and character's importance to the genre as Pisters begins *New Blood* with an anecdote on her introduction to *Carrie* and Clover titling introduction to *Men, Women, and Chainsaws: Gender in the Modern Horror Film* "Carrie and the Boys" (Pisters 2022, 1). Clover analyzes *Carrie* in terms of complex and contradictory female representation as well as male audience-identification with female figures. Clover observes, "[w]ith its prom, queens, menstrual periods, tampons, worries about clothes and makeup, *Carrie* would seem on the face of it the most feminine of stories" (Clover 2015, 3). Clover continues her critique of performed femininity, highlighting Carrie's use of violence and how Stephen King refers to Carrie as being more in line with male outcasts. Clover's exploration of Carrie is in the context of how male audiences identify with female figures on screen in the horror genre. Clover argues that Carrie is a female figure disguised as a mistreated high school boy, given the source material of King's novel and De Palma's film. Critical analysis of *Carrie* does not detract from the film's legacy, as many filmmakers and spectators across the gender spectrum enjoy the film's aesthetics and the visualization of female rage that she brings to horror cinema. I argue *Carrie* begins the monstrous adolescent subgenre and in this chapter, I will illustrate how women filmmakers follow her trail of blood to revise her sorrowful tale.

Despite the feminine trappings of prom, tampons, and makeup, Carrie does not engage with elements of female monstrosity present when crafted by women filmmakers. For example, female monsters often inspire horror on a smaller scale, privileging interiority and interpersonal intimacy. Additionally, the promotion of female bonds in horror and the aforementioned intimacy often take place in friendships bordering on romance. The legacy of female horror figures is fraught with characters created almost exclusively by male filmmakers for assumed male audiences. While some figures and films retain nuance without the involvement of women, recent films helmed by women are revising cinematic engagements with corporeality, intimacy, and explorations of queer sexuality.

Jennifer's Body and the Power of Possession

Jennifer's Body has recently seen a cult resurgence counter to the outpouring of negative initial reviews it received. Directed by Karyn Kusama and written by Diablo Cody, the film is a testament to the contradictory rapid progress and harsh backlash in the first decade of the twenty-first century. The recent cult status of the film finds fans among the majority of women viewers for the film's nuance, comedy, and aesthetics visualizing female bonds, bodily autonomy, and queer sensibilities. *Jennifer's Body* features lifelong friends Jennifer Check (Megan Fox) and Needy Lesnicki (Amanda Seyfried). Jennifer, resulting from a failed ritual sacrifice by the occultist boyband Low Shoulder, begins eating humans to remain beautiful and powerful. Needy is forced to reckon with Jennifer's possession within the context of their relationship and stop her reign of devouring their town's young men.

In an interview conducted celebrating the 10th anniversary of *Jennifer's Body,* Cody speaks of the film's recent popularity, "If someone stops me it's always some like 22-year-old who wants to talk to me about *Jennifer's Body* who, to me, that is the coolest thing in the world because it's like I don't even think you could have legally seen this movie when it came out and you found it" (Cody 2019). Since its release, critics and audiences have reexamined the film and considered it a contemporary horror classic. The film expresses a consciousness for the genre and horror film history with homages such as Jennifer wearing Needy's *The Evil Dead* (1981) t-shirt as a *The Evil Dead* poster hangs behind her and a less pronounced visual gag of a bulletin board proclaiming "What Ever Happened to Baby Jane: The Musical" in the Devil's Kettle High School mise-en-scène. *Jennifer's Body's* portrayal of female adolescence cinematically visualizes the violence and lived horror of female adolescence while revising and satirizing with horror tropes and motifs.

Alike in their portrayal of monstrous adolescence coupled with the complexity of the victim/villain/hero classification, *Jennifer's Body* continues the legacies of *Carrie* and *Ginger Snaps*. *Ginger Snaps* features two sisters, Ginger and Brigette Fitzgerald (Katharine Isabelle and Emily Perkins), as Ginger gets her period and is bitten by a werewolf on the same day. Ginger then transforms into a werewolf and murders suburban locals. *Ginger Snaps* has been in conversation with *Jennifer's Body* for the film's similarities in plot and theme. Yet, the latter film revises and expands upon elements of the teen coming-of-age horror subgenre present in its predecessor.[4] Contrary to Carrie and Ginger, who are social pariahs whose bodies become monstrous at the beginning of menstruation, Jennifer is introduced to audiences as a postpubescent teen who possesses power in the realm of high school. She already possesses friendship and popularity, traits often the goal of marginalized characters in coming-of-age films. Her transformation manifests as a possession, an event forced upon her by an occult boy band. Meanwhile, Carrie and Ginger

---

[4] Katarzyna Paszkiewicz's essay "Gender, Genre, and Authorship in *Ginger Snaps*" in *Women Make Horror: Filmmaking, Feminism, and Genre* explains, "There are interesting similarities between *Ginger Snaps* and *Jennifer's Body* critical reception (the latter, nota bene, was accused of imitating *Ginger Snaps* to the point of plagiarizing it)…" (110) she explains the well-noted similarities between the films yet makes no specific reference to the word choice of "plagiarizing." Whether this is to refer to legal action or merely severity of commonality it is unclear.

begin the exploration of their bodies as new women. Conversely, Jennifer is comfortable with her role and identity as a woman. Such as, Jennifer explains to Needy, "We have all the power. Don't you know that? These things? These are like smart bombs. You point them in the right direction, and shit gets real." She explains this while grabbing Needy's breast as if to emphasize detachment regarding the transactional nature of sex and power. For the simplicity and crass nature of Jennifer as a stereotypical cheerleader, she is attuned to the female erotic power she possesses. Audre Lorde defines the female erotic as "a resource within each of us that lies in a deeply female and spiritual plane, firmly rooted in the power of our unexpressed or unrecognized feeling" (Lorde 1984, 53). Jennifer's expression of feminine eroticism marks her as a danger to society and thus speaks to her classification as a monster pre-possession. Her status as an erotic woman who communicates this to the world makes her a target both within a patriarchal society and within the film as a potential human sacrifice. Her self-assured nature and overt sexuality amplify when her body becomes endowed with demonic powers and is cinematically communicated in her method of murdering boys.

Traditionally, in horror cinema, there is a clear distinction between good and evil, hero and protagonists. This is most clear in American slasher films of the 1970s into the 80s. Slashers present the malicious behavior of monsters terrorizing teens simply as evil being present in these villains. However, some horror films do not have as clear a villain for audiences to boo. Carrie is an example of a character that defies categorization, as she inhabits the roles of victim, villain, and hero. Clover explains the relationship between victim, monster, and hero specific to Carrie, "Throughout most of the movie she is the victim of monstrous schoolmates and a monstrous mother, but when, at the end, she turns the tables, she herself becomes a kind of monstrous hero —hero insofar as she has risen against and defeated the forces of monstrosity, monster insofar as she has herself become excessive, demonic" (Clover 2015, 4). *Jennifer's Body* revises this notion, as Jennifer transforms into neither a victim nor a hero, with the reason being that she lacks agency. There is no sense of anger at her abusers or her circumstances. Instead, she delights in her demonic powers. Further, the film does not judge Jennifer as harshly as one could imagine a film about a demon-possessed teen who eats her classmates, but instead, even offers sympathy for Jennifer. The film's sympathetic viewpoint reiterates the horror genre revision of a possession film as Jennifer desperately tries to retain possession of herself.

When Jennifer kills, there is a degree of seduction involved. She picks her victims seemingly at random, the only commonality in her victims being boys who fit within rigid high school archetypes. This random sampling of victims removes the film from categorization as a rape-revenge horror film, as Jennifer is not seeking retribution, only looking for meals where she can find them. In the film, male victims are outside Jennifer's realm of remorse. While the town cries for their lost sons, she does not mourn her victims. Her murders begin with innocence and honesty as she asks her victims to come with her, be that to the woods, a housing development, or an abandoned pool, to which every man agrees. This seduction functions within Barbara Creed's *The Monstrous Feminine* as, "In my view, the definition of sin/abjection as something which comes from *within* opens up the way to position woman as deceptively treacherous. She may appear pure and beautiful on the outside, but evil may, nevertheless, reside within. It is the stereotype of feminine evil— beautiful on the outside corrupt within" (Creed 1993, 42). Jennifer does not use demonic powers to persuade men to follow her, and they take little convincing. They *want* to go with her and think little of the consequences of following a beautiful girl into the dark. This sense of seduction derived from inherent femininity is more consistent with the mythos of sirens, mermaids, and vampires as opposed to films portraying demonic possessions. Sirens, mermaids, and vampires could be described as synonymous with the femme fatale for their sexuality and allure, as the body in question is a site of pleasure and eroticism. Meanwhile, demonic possession uses the female body as a site of conflict rather than presenting the body as alluring. Often, stories featuring demonic or ghostly possession illustrate gendered conflict as a male entity invading a female host, such as in *The Exorcist* and *The Conjuring 2* (2016), and to an extent, *Rosemary's Baby* (1968) and *Demon Seed* (1977). In *Jennifer's Body*, Jennifer appears as the sole inhabitant of her body as it becomes not a site for conflict but an instrument of bloodlust.

Jennifer's murder of Colin Gray (Kyle Gallner), the third in a string of four murders, explores monstrous corporeality and the conflation of monstrosity and sexuality. Colin is a sensitive goth teen whom Jennifer asks to meet at a housing development, motivated by her desire to spite Needy. Jennifer routinely seeks control of Needy's life and sensing her fondness for Colin marks him as her next target. As Colin enters the under-construction house, the interior's unfinished walls, dimly lit with blue light from the window, create a gothic atmosphere. Colin goes further into the house as Akon's "I Wanna Love You" plays eerily, growing louder as he makes his way upstairs and into a room with copious candles lit on the floor, casting a warm glow throughout the room. This is evocative of both a ritual sacrifice and a teenage sexual encounter. There is a gendered role reversal in Jennifer's setting out the candles for the date, a continuation of Jennifer as the pursuer and sexual aggressor. As the encounter progresses, rats scurry across the wooden floors to which Colin, shot in a medium close-up, which is visibly uncomfortable. The blue of the window in the background creates a contrast of warm lighting from the candles, emphasizing a distinction between exterior and interior space. This spatial confusion of the unfinished suburban home housing horror within parallels Jennifer as being beautiful outside while her interior motivation is to devour humans. Jennifer, also in medium close-up, responds to Colin's discomfort as, "I thought guys like you were really into vermin and death and shit." Her dialogue, coupled with the sound of Jennifer unzipping Colin's pants, emphasizes the relationship between sex and death, and the film cuts to the pair filmed at a low angle and framed in a long shot. This framing situates the pair within the copious lit candles, furthering confusion between sex and ritualistic murder. As Jennifer closes in, she is framed in a close-up. A sound like a rattlesnake tail and a deep growl is heard in conjunction with the irises of Jennifer's eyes turning white before shifting back to brown, like an animal's pupils dilating as it gazes at prey. Kusama explains this scene uses subtle digital work to distort Jennifer's face. While not easily identifiable in comparison to her changing eyes on a theatrical screen, the effect is intended to create unease (Kusama 2015, under "Audio Commentary"). Consistent with horror film's portrayals of possession, Jennifer's vocals distort as still framed in a close-up, she commands, "I need you hopeless." This voice, while menacing and reverberating, is not indicative of a male host. Jennifer's vocal presence, despite the distortion, illustrates the film sonically subverting traditional possession motifs. There is no battle between the owner of the body and a foreign demonic entity, but rather, Jennifer is conscious of her actions and derives pleasure from assuming the role of predator. The scene inspires horror while also retaining elements of femininity in Jennifer's voice, face, and, lastly, her body.

The gruesome act of devouring in this scene is not explicit in its use of the body. Instead, shadows of Jennifer positioned atop Colin on the floor are projected onto flesh-colored butcher paper. Jennifer's shadow grows large teeth, rears her head, and releases a guttural howl before diving onto Colin, blood splattering onto the butcher paper indicative of carnage as the camera tracks forward toward their shadow figures slowly. The shadow of Jennifer above Colin is evocative of sexual interaction, yet the layered screams and blood splatter illicit horror. Jennifer's use of her teeth as her primary weapon to kill Colin fosters intimacy and requires his close proximity to her. Jennifer's monstrosity is linked to her physical being. Rather than murder Colin with a knife, traditionally phallic imagery in horror, or negate her body's agency by employing supernatural abilities like Carrie, Jennifer relies solely on her threatening physicality (Stamp 2015, 335). Within this scene, Kusama explains Jennifer's body seen in shadow appears distorted, yet no alteration was made, and that is, in fact, the actress's real body (Kusama 2015, under "Audio Commentary"). This scene highlights the relationship between Jennifer's body and face and how each functions in visualizing and eliciting horror. While there is an overt objectification in the projection of Jennifer's body, there is a separation between the shadow image and the Jennifer audiences have been introduced to earlier. The dark, projected image reads as both feminine and monstrous while maintaining a degree of separation from the flesh of her body. The sequence concludes with Colin's lifeless face filmed in close-up as the camera tracks backward until we see Jennifer in frame crouched next to Colin's torso, cupping his blood in her hands and drinking it. We see no hint of her monstrous form as she appears to us as normal. The horror derives from the incongruent feelings of a beautiful woman slurping blood crouched beside a body so mangled beyond recognition townsfolk would later refer to it as "lasagna with teeth." Jennifer enacts violence that preys on boys and exploits intimacy, yet even more horrifying is how she revels in her newfound evil.

Despite her succubus status, the film sympathizes with Jennifer and allows her a tender moment of humanity in the pre-prom montage. A hallmark of teen films, both horror and not, is the preparing for prom sequence where characters don their dresses and tuxes, coif their hair, readying themselves for a night to remember. *Jennifer's Body* continues this tradition with a rather toned down, mid-western prom get-ready, as Needy's mother curls her hair and she appears in an 80s-style pink dress, a heap of puffy sleeves and ruffles. Meanwhile, Chip's mother gifts him "pink panic" women's pepper spray to ward off the killer with a penchant for young men. The film acknowledges and satirizes gender roles in horror films, as the murder is assumed by the townspeople to be a man. Murders so heinous and gruesome the town only suspects a male murderer and exclude the idea of a cheerleading murderess. The montage concludes with Chip and Needy taking photos with their families and close-up shots of corsages, accompanied by *Panic! At The Disco's* "New Perspective."

Distinct from these instances of parents and their teens is Jennifer readying herself alone in her room. The previous pop music fades and is replaced by ambient sound infused with guitar strumming. The camera, positioned behind Jennifer brushing her hair, tracks forward. In contrast with the dimly lit bedroom, Jennifer appears to be shrouded in shadow despite sitting in front of the lamp on her desk. As we move closer to the figure, we see a clump of hair nestled in Jennifer's hand because of her gentle brushing. There is a mirror on the desk in front of Jennifer, but only once the camera moves to settle behind her shoulder do we see her image reflected in the small mirror. The camera continues forward until Jennifer's mirrored image in close-up takes up much of the screen. Next to the mirrored image of Jennifer on the vanity sits a picture of Jennifer alone, her face bright and smiling. Keeping framed photos of oneself is a comedic visual nod to Jennifer's narcissism. Yet, there is also a sense of sadness. Jennifer, as we see her in the mirror, smears the foundation on her face, and the stark contrast of the foundation shade and her lifeless skin communicates how removed her body has become from who she was previously. Cody explains this scene as "Jennifer is someone who felt secure in her appearance, and to have that taken from her adds a level of sadness to Jennifer's situation" (Kusama 2015, under "Audio Commentary"). Glimpsing the monster covering her face to retain a semblance of normalcy is humanizing as she tries to simulate humanness, inviting the spectator's sympathy.

Sorrow permeates the scene, and yet, it is not remorse for the lives she has taken but rather the loss of control over her body and face. She expresses loneliness and mourning for what she once possessed and exchanged for power. An exchange of familiarity for power reflects how, in puberty, one sacrifices the body they once had for the body society imbues with desire. The ritual of bodily preparation in makeup application is a desperate attempt to maintain control. For Jennifer, her appearance was central to her identity, and a violent act of cruelty forcibly altered it. The juxtaposed images of Jennifer as a monster and as a teenage girl visually communicate the humor of her narcissism and the sadness of her isolation from humanity. Barbara Creed explains horror films where women become possessed as, "Central to these limitations was a strong sense of vulnerability of the body and its susceptibility to possession. They also focus attention on the graphic detailed representation of bodily destruction" (Creed 1993, 31). *Jennifer's Body* challenges this as Jennifer's body was not vulnerable. Instead, her body was unsuited for a virginal sacrifice due to her sexual activity. It is the mistake of assumed vulnerability and virtuousness that creates the demonic possession. The representation of bodily destruction in this film contradicts the extremity of scars and fluids traditionally found in possession films. The bodily destruction is present as a decline of beauty, the prospect of which keeps Jennifer as a slave to her base urges of feeding on humans. There is a relationship between controlling bodily destruction by feeding on humans and even enacting it on oneself, as we see Jennifer holding a lighter to her tongue or slitting her forearm with a pen. The film challenges traditional notions of the possession film and how women are at the mercy of bodily invasion and instead positions a female character who makes conscious decisions to control her body throughout the film.

Depictions of puberty in the film highlight changes to the body and mind, but the alteration of one's face also occurs during this time. Your face is the image that greets you in the mirror daily. Who are you, and who is the person who returns your gaze? Within the horror genre, spectatorship and the gaze are of paramount importance. Linda Williams writes in her essay "When the Woman Looks", "The horror film offers a particularly interesting example of this punishment in the woman's terrified look at the horrible body of the monster...I hope to reveal not only the process of punishment but a surprising (and at times subversive) affinity between monster and woman, the sense in which her look at the monster recognizes their similar status within patriarchal structures of seeing" (Williams 2015, 19-20). *Jennifer's Body*, within the horror tradition, challenges how female characters view monstrosity, as here we see the woman *is* the monster. The use of gaze in this scene highlights the horror of recognizing oneself become a monster and mourning humanity lost. Jennifer illustrates a female monster suffers doubly her status within a patriarchal society as both a woman and monster. For women, there can be a sense of humility that one must possess to be truly beautiful. However, Jennifer neglects feigning bashfulness and takes pride in her appearance. The film could invite audiences to read her misfortune as brought onto herself for her pride and sexual promiscuity, but careful pause is given to moments where Jennifer mourns her losses. Given the female authorship in this film there is an understanding that this bodily loss could easily be portrayed as either solely horrific or comical. Yet, there is nuance to Jennifer's demonic possession. Women filmmakers revise how women engage with monsters by portraying themselves *as* monsters, crafting a monstrous exterior to match the horrors of their lived experience.

Blue My Mind and Transformation as Radical Refusal

Blue My Mind (2017, Switzerland) is the directorial feature film debut of Lisa Brühlmann chronicling the story of a teenage girl, Mia (Luna Wedler), who transforms into a mermaid. Employing Carroll's framework, mermaids warrant classification as monsters for their impurity and categorical confusion of fish and humans residing in one body. The film combines aspects of horror and coming-of-age cinema while breaking from traditional horror narratives in favor of using the distinct element of body horror and realism to exaggerate the harrowing experience of adolescence. Brühlmann has expressed fascination with the mermaid stemming from childhood. Before *Blue,* she explored the figure with her short film, *Hylas und die Nymphen* (2013), inspired by John William Waterhouse's painting *Hylas and the Nymphs.* She explains her intrigue with mermaids and sirens as, for her, they have a sense of anarchy. This representation of power, specifically as they derive it from femininity, makes the mermaid an interesting figure to engage in the horror genre where there had previously been little to no interaction (Brühlmann 2018, under "IFFR Live").

Crucial to the nature of the coming-of-age film is the exploration of sexuality in adolescence. The horror elements of *Blue* derive not only from the body horror of transforming into a mermaid but also from the sexual endeavors of the principal character. The film explores sexuality by framing it as simultaneously deviant and normalized in keeping with the film's European Art Cinema sensibilities. The film portrays Mia seeking hookups via the internet as dangerous and awkward, and yet makes no sweeping statement on virginal purity or punishing characters for having sex. There is an understanding of exploring sexuality and curiosity around sex as a part of adolescence, and the film examines adolescent sexual behavior critically without passing judgment. The film places emphasis on female adolescent sexuality yet transforms the protagonist into a mermaid, a creature devoid of genitalia. Mermaids are traditionally feminine creatures and lack sex organs. This presents a gendered dynamic as employing the mermaid figure removes a central element of fear that is derived from the vagina, with male identification fearing women as the castrated female (Creed 1993, 110). Mia's period serves as a catalyst for her becoming a mermaid, yet through her transformation, the ritual of both menstruation and sexual intercourse will be taken from her.

In *Blue*, Mia's period signals her burgeoning sexuality, which is, in essence, her becoming a woman. The centrality of menstruation in horror is present in horror films and scholarship, as Creed uses the term "menstrual monster" to discuss the figure of the vampire and Carrie White as a witch. She explains how menstruation is central to the power these characters derive and explores the mythos of menstruation being tied to the moon and imbuing women with supernatural powers. In a more contemporary sense, Jennifer Check eloquently states, "PMS isn't real, Needy. It was invented by the boy-run media to make us seem like we're crazy." While Jennifer has not gained the title of menstrual monster, both Carrie White and Ginger Fitzgerald have been described in such terms, and this links their lineages to Mia. Jennifer's cyclical states of waning beauty dependent on consuming humans could be interpreted as representing menstrual cycles, keeping her in conversation with the aforementioned menstrual monsters. Menstruation serves as a visual and symbolic ritual of change where the bleeding wound of shedding the uterine lining acts as a sacrifice of a girl's old flesh to adopt a new womanly form. Creed writes specifically, "[i]n the horror genre however menstrual blood is constructed as a source of abjection: its powers are so great it can transform woman into any one of a number of fearful creatures: possessed child, killer and vengeful witch" (Creed 1993, 83). *Blue* revises the motif of menstruation linked to monstrous transformation by privileging interiority and isolation that reads as reverence. Mia's menstruation, which begins her transformation, links her to the natural world and signals her return to the ocean. Brühlmann articulates the film's conclusion as, "She goes into the ocean and finds her freedom and her peace and also reconnects with her power, with her nature" (Brühlmann 2018, under "IFFR Live"). *Blue* revises previous iterations of women's menstruation as the curse of womanhood that serves only as a source of suffering and a mark of abject shame. While Mia's menstruation and bodily transformation indeed included suffering and a cursed narrative, this is required for her to transcend the limitations of a woman's body and return to nature. Her menstruation serves as a catalyst for her transformation in which she supersedes the body of a woman doomed to face oppression in the patriarchal society and instead finds peace in leaving society.

In her essay "Medusa and the Female Gaze," Susan R. Bowers contrasts how the Medusa myth is retold by male and female artists and authors, respectively. She explores distinct, gendered differences in the treatment of Medusa and the manner in which female artistry has crafted far more sympathetic iterations of

Medusa. She explains the antithesis of the female gaze, "[t]he antidote to the male gaze, and one avenue to women reclaiming their own sexuality, is the female gaze: learning to see clearly for themselves, thus reconstructing traditional male images of women" (Bowers 1990, 218). In *Blue*, this argumentation applies twofold as Brühlmann reclaims and re-contextualizes male-created ideas of nymphs and mermaids by creating a story centered on the intimacy of female bonds and the harrowing experience of possessing a female body experiencing puberty. The inspiration for Waterhouses' *Hylas in the Nymphs* is revised by Brühlmann as she focuses on Mia's transformation and interiority rather than the exploration of a mermaid discovered by a male character. She further reclaims ideas of female sexuality as she provides a protagonist who engages in sexual exploration before ultimately withdrawing from the human world and male-centric ideation of women as accessories to men's sexuality.

In conversation with menstrual monsters in horror, Mia is depicted discovering her first period. The scene begins with Mia in a medium close-up seated on the toilet. Light green bathroom walls create a calm yet sterile atmosphere. The film quickly cuts to a dark red bloodstain on Mia's underwear between her legs. Mia's face shows no signs of shock or alarm, only slight discomfort as she pulls up her underwear, walks to the kitchen counter, and rifles through drawers for a pad or tampon. The camera focuses on a close-up of her hands as they touch the pads and tampons before she settles on a pad. She grabs the pad, and the camera follows as Mia straightens and begins opening the wrapping, only her torso and hands in the frame. After unwrapping the pad, she quickly returns the pad to the drawer and instead reaches for tissues to rectify the bleeding. As she reaches for the tissue box sitting on the bathroom counter, Mia is filmed from behind, and her image in the bathroom mirror shows her facial expressions. The film cuts to Mia in the bathtub with only her face present, her body covered by a sheet of bubbles. Mia slides into the tub as the sounds of water splashing within the tub seem amplified. Her face is seen in close-up as she resurfaces and wipes the bubbles from her face. The film cuts to Mia's hands in close-up, shaving her leg. The camera moves up the length of her body, parroting the movement of her hand moving from her ankle up and settles on her face in the tub. Positioned behind Mia's shoulder, the camera shows her foot with webbed toes within the tub and quickly cuts to Mia's face as she draws in a shaky breath. This scene, while illustrating the catalyst for Mia's transformation, is calm in its unraveling of events. Differing from films such as *Carrie*, the use of blood, while stark red, is not gratuitous. The locker room has been recast as the home bathroom, the interior sphere privileging Mia's privacy and negating the fear of public spectacle. Significant to this scene is Mia's period as an event she explores alone. She does not ask for help from her mother or friends, and there is a cinematic and physical sense of isolation as Mia inhabits the bathroom space.

The use of close-ups to frame hands, legs, and face visually conveys the disjointed nature of the change that Mia will suffer. There is a distinction between body parts, alluding to the disjunctive nature of Mia's experience with her body. Within the world of normal adolescence, she is navigating a rapidly changing body that brings into question ideas of ownership in one's skin. Mia, in the bathtub after finding herself bleeding, symbolizes an attempt to cleanse physically as well as symbolically return to the water as a source of comfort. Within the tub, images of Mia shaving her legs act as both a foreshadowing of self-mutilation as well as a society-approved method of self-destruction. Changing one's outward appearance to the appropriate image with tools used to diminish and destroy. Razors, scissors, and tweezers are mundane grooming tools, as well as devices for Mia's desperate mutilation. Specifically, in this scene, leg hair is a bodily indicator of lost childhood and a burden of grooming. Subscribing to traditional standards of beauty serves as the reason for Mia's shame in her transformation and spurs her to enact bodily mutilation, trying to preserve the body she once knew, the body that society deemed appropriate. Society opposing women's bodies is not exclusive to Mia and is present in the stories of her horror coming-of-age predecessors Carrie, Ginger, and Jennifer.

Mia's classification as a monster comes not from her bloodlust, as she does not pose a threat to others but rather to herself. Aside from devouring fish and punching an older man for making an advance on her, Mia only engages in violence against her own body. While her body is undoubtedly monstrous and horrific with the fusing of appendages and shedding skin, there is no infection of monstrosity to her heart. Applying Carroll's framework of monstrosity, there is an impurity in her being a mermaid as her body is not human, and further, there is a confusion about the categorization of human and fish. Yet, unlike other female horror figures discussed, she does not seek retribution for the wrongs she has suffered or delight in the pain of others. Distinctly different, Mia, in her frustration, only harms herself with the self-mutilation of her legs, and she even acts to aid others, such as saving Gianna at a lake party. These acts both question Carroll's outline of monstrosity and how Mia functions within the horror genre if she defies many of the traditional characteristics held by women characters. Mia's hopeful ending and the nuanced treatment of the Monstrous Adolescent are a product of Brühlmann's crafting a story that not only illustrates the horror of maturation but elevates it with stylistic implementation of dreamlike vignettes and fantastical transformations balanced with realism. *Blue My Mind,* while vastly different in tone and aesthetics from *Jennifer's Body,* shares thematic commonalities and motifs indicative of each film contributing to and revising the monstrous adolescent in horror cinema.

Thematically, *Jennifer's Body* and *Blue* share many commonalities. Both *Jennifer's Body* and *Blue* highlight the loss of bodily control due to forces outside the character's control, this being ritual sacrifice and genetics, respectively. The variance in how each woman adapts to her monstrous change varies from

Jennifer's malicious delight to Mia's somber shame, yet there is a commonality in the loss of identity and bodily autonomy they have incurred. One of the strongest thematic links between the two films that is absent from *Carrie* and *Ginger Snaps* is the portrayal of intimate female friendships that explore queer sexuality. Jennifer and Needy's relationship portrays overt sexual engagement as the two, in a now famous scene, share a kiss. This has inspired readings of the film as Needy's exploration of her sexuality as opposed to a film solely centered on Jennifer's possession. In *Blue*, Mia and Gianna's friendship borders on queer, incredibly intimate, yet never fully realized. The poetics of horror allow for a conflation of female violence and eroticism as the pair engage in bonding activities of choking one another to the point of losing unconsciousness. This eroticism is continued in intimate gazing between the two girls as Gianna tucks a stray hair behind Mia's ear, the motions indicative of a kiss occurring, yet, the pair being joined by their laughing friends spoils the moment. These instances explore the boundaries and spectrum of physicality and pleasure. Women filmmakers revise monstrosity by exploring queer sexuality between monsters and humans traditionally reserved for heterosexual encounters. Returning to Williams' "When the Woman Looks" she examines the phenomenon of the gaze as it relates to the woman and the monster. The woman often possesses desire and sympathy for the monster as she sees her status in patriarchal society reflected in the monster (Williams 2015, 24-25). I position both *Jennifer's Body* and *Blue* as a revision to the horror genre and a contribution to the legacy of the monstrous adolescent through their privileging of queer identity formation and bisexual sensibilities between the monster and the woman. Here, the mirror image of the monster and woman is doubled as the monstrous body is truly the woman's body reflected back to her.

Looking specifically at the characters of Jennifer and Mia, this emphasis on female relationships explores each character's conclusion as reliant on their female counterpart. For Jennifer, she is not killed by the townspeople seeking retribution for their lost boys but rather by Needy. Needy's actions illustrate a tender responsibility to save her lost companion, a rage to rid herself of her manipulative friendship and to avenge her murdered boyfriend. The complexity of their relationship speaks to the nuance with which women filmmakers view the plights of young women. In Mia's case, her relationship with Gianna both saves her from the harsh advances and disgust of men and allows her the strength and ability to return to the sea. The two women present a heartbreaking intimacy to spectators as they must part with one another. Their relationship was unable to flourish on land, indicative of the adversity facing queer youth in contemporary climates. Women filmmakers employ horror genre aesthetics to elevate these relationships with operatic stakes, allowing young women to portray the complex emotional interiority and intimate violence of female adolescent relationships.

This chapter has sought to outline the characteristics of the monstrous adolescent while championing the cinematic prowess of women filmmakers working in the horror genre. The ability of these filmmakers to work with the figure of the monstrous adolescent echoes one another on a transnational scale. The privileging of interiority, corporeality, and sexuality in female adolescence realized within horror aesthetics transcends national boundaries, speaking to a shared experience of feminine maturation. Considering the contemporary global landscape of women horror filmmakers, the monstrous adolescent surely has not shoplifted her last lipstick or devoured her last victim. What makes a teenage girl? The heartbreak, volatility, ephemera of youth, rapid transitions, bodily loss, and intimate friendships must be a part of it. Now, what makes a monster? Someone who suffers lays bare themselves, their body, and their heart, only to be degraded and mocked by society. Perhaps then it is easy to imagine how a teenage girl can be a monster and how she may prefer to be that very creature that stalks the night.

Bibliography

Bowers, Susan R. 1990. "Medusa and the Female Gaze." *NWSA Journal* 2, no. 2 (Spring): 217–35. https://www.jstor.org/stable/4316018.

Brühlmann, Lisa, dir. 2017. *Blue My Mind.* Be For Films. 1 hour 37 min. https://www.imdb.com/title/tt6193454/?ref_=nm_knf_t_1.

Brühlmann, Lisa, dir. 2013. *Hylas und die Nymphen.* 11 min. https://www.imdb.com/title/tt2988516/?ref_=nm_flmg_t_7_dr.

Brühlmann, Lisa. 2018. "IFFR Live: Blue My Mind Interactive Q&A with Lisa Brühlmann." Interview by Winfried Baijens. Uploaded by *International Film Festival Rotterdam*, 7 Feb. 2018. YouTube, 24:13. https://www.youtube.com/watch?v=6s2y3afvcY4.

Carrol, Noël. 1990. *The Philosophy of Horror, or Paradoxes of the Heart.* New York, NY: Routledge.

Clover, Carol. 2015. *Men, Women, and Chain Saws: Gender in the Modern Horror Film.* Princeton, NJ: Princeton University Press.

Cody, Diablo and Megan Fox. 2019. "*Jennifer's Body* Reunion: Megan Fox and Diablo Cody Get Candid About Hollywood (Exclusive)." Uploaded by *ET Live*, 19 Sep. 2019. YouTube, 35:40. https://youtu.be/u2JLRtWlq0o.

Creed, Barbara. 1993. *The Monstrous-feminine: Film, Feminism, Psychoanalysis.* New York, NY: Routledge.

De Palma, Brian, dir. 1976. *Carrie.* Red Bank Films. 1 hour 38 min. https://www.imdb.com/title/tt0074285/companycredits/?ref_=tt_dt_co.

Fawcett, John, dir. 2000. *Ginger Snaps.* Artisan Entertainment. 1 hour 48 minutes. https://www.imdb.com/title/tt0210070/?ref_=nv_sr_srsg_0_tt_8_nm_0_q_ginger%2520snaps.

Kusama, Karyn and Diablo Cody. 2015. "Audio Commentary on the Theatrical Version with Director Karyn Kusama and Writer Diablo Cody" In *Jennifer's Body.* Fox Atomic. 1 hour 42 minutes. Blu-ray Disc.

Kusama, Karyn, dir. 2009. Jennifer's Body. Fox Atomic. 1 hour 42 minutes. https://www.imdb.com/title/tt1131734/?ref_=nv_sr_srsg_0_tt_6_nm_2_q_je nnifer%27s%2520.

Lorde, Audre. 1984. *Sister Outsider*. Trumansburg, NY: Crossing Press.

Paszkiewicz, Katarzyna. 2020. "Gender, Genre, and Authorship in Ginger Snaps." in *Women Make Horror: Filmmaking, Feminism, and Genre*, edited by Alison Peirse, 104-121. New Brunswick, NJ: Rutgers University Press.

Pisters, Patricia. 2022. *New Blood in Contemporary Cinema: Women Directors and the Poetics of Horror*. Edinburgh, UK: University of Edinburgh Press.

Stamp, Shelley. 2015. "Horror, Femininity, and Carrie's Monstrous Puberty." in The Dread of Difference: Gender in the Horror Film, edited by Barry Keith Grant, 329-345. Austin, TX: University of Texas Press.

Williams, Linda. 2015. "When the Woman Looks." in The Dread of Difference: Gender in the Horror Film, edited by Barry Keith Grant, 17-36. Austin, TX: University of Texas Press.

Chapter 9

Watch Out Boys, She'll Chew You Up: Feminine Monstrosity's Linguistic Traps

Ryanne Probst

University of North Carolina at Wilmington

Abstract: In literature, as is true in our culture, the male monster is a creature of multitudes. He can be grotesque but revered; sociopathic but empathized; cold but romanticized. In short: he can be understood. Think of *Wuthering Heights'* Heathcliff or *Red Dragon's* Hannibal Lecter or, for more real-life applications, Ted Bundy as a serial killer or Johnny Depp as an abuser. These men are beloved in part *for* their monstrosity. And yet, stories that feature women as monsters are not as warmly received. Take, for example, the 2020 novel *A Certain Hunger* by Chelsea G Summers, which wrestles with questions of gender and monstrosity. In the novel, Dorothy Daniels is a successful, middle-aged food critic who also happens to be a cannibalistic serial killer. Think *Eat Pray Love*, but the "eat" part involves disemboweling her exes first. Dorothy as a character is nuanced and boundary-breaking, and yet, critical reception of the novel cheapened her character development with descriptors like "naughty pleasure" and "preternaturally hot babe of 51." Why is that? In this chapter, I explore the linguistic trap these critics have fallen into when analyzing Dorothy's character. I argue that part of our fascination with male monsters starts at a language level. That language reinforces empathy and creates space for nuance. And yet, that language does not extend to or has not evolved in the same way for discussions regarding feminine monstrosity. To show this, I analyze the etymology of the words *hero*, *heroine*, and *monster* to show the tension between definitional meaning and cultural meaning. Then, I use elements from Media Theory to pinpoint how that shift in meaning has been further distorted with the popularization of television and the internet. I argue this distortion supplies us with a surface-level lexicon that is weaponized against women to prevent meaningful discourse about feminine monstrosity even in a post-#MeToo era. Monsters may be socially constructed beings, but our critiques of them shouldn't fall into those same traps, not when the recourse for doing so warps our view of real-life women who exhibit monstrous (read: human) qualities as well.

Keywords: feminine monstrosity, sociolinguistics, Monster Theory, Narrative Empathy, media and empathy, Media Theory, women and media, monsters

***

In the fall of 2021, I read a delightfully deranged little book called *A Certain Hunger* by Chelsea G. Summers. The novel follows Dorothy Daniels, a successful, middle-aged food critic who has spent her life *Eat Pray Love*-ing her way towards eternal happiness... *if* that ritual included serial murder. Instead of unlocking her inner peace through carbs and wine in Italy, Dorothy finds that disemboweling her Italian lover makes for a life-altering brisket. Bon appetite. I have a bit of a thing for messy, un-root-for-able women, so I immediately loved this book. Here was a female character who was both a hero and a monster. Deplorable, immoral, unconscionable, and yet extremely likable. Funny, smart, endearing, and yet unquestionably a serial killer. Her victims— the men she beds, kills, and then eats—fell headfirst into their love affairs, with her seemingly unaware of their fatal attraction. As a reader, so did I. I fell for her *because* she was a monster, not in spite of it.

Imagine my surprise, then, to find that the critical reception of the novel had flattened her character with cheap descriptors and one-dimensional reviews. *The Washington Post* summed up the book as nothing but a "naughty pleasure" and reduced Dorothy to a "sexy food critic" and a "preternaturally hot babe of 51" (Corrigan 2020). I can't help but think Dorothy would skewer the reviewer (quite literally) for that last dig. Other reviews have focused more on Dorothy's volatile rage and grotesquely intriguing inner personal monologues. *The New York Times* reviewer Amy Silverberg said of Dorothy that "'anti' might be too weak of a prefix to describe this heroine: she's more of an outright villain" (2020). A *Kirkus* review made similar assertions when labeling Dorothy "a woman who's not just angry, but violent" (2020). This is compared to the character Hannibal Lecter, another cannibalistic serial killer whom Stephen King once called "the greatest fictional monster of our time." "He is no joke," King wrote. "A man like that could steal your heart" (King 2021). Nowhere in the review did King comment on Hannibal's look, age, or sexual wiles. The volatility of Hannibal's character is barely mentioned. Instead, King celebrates Hannibal's nuances, humanizing him with discussion of his comedic prowess and quirky personality.

Both Dorothy and Hannibal's characters are sociopaths, cannibals, and murderers. So, why is it then that Hannibal gets labeled "the greatest fictional monster of our time" while Dorothy is just a "naughty pleasure"? In literature, as is true in our culture, the male monster is a creature of multitudes. He can be grotesque but revered; sociopathic but empathized; cold but romanticized. In short: he can be understood. And this extends beyond a literary scope. Think about the public's treatment of Ted Bundy as a serial killer or Johnny Depp as an abuser. These men are beloved in part *for* their monstrosity. Jeffrey Jerome Cohen's work on Monster Theory tells us that monsters are things socially constructed, born of fear and anxiety and desire. They are "an embodiment of a certain cultural moment—of a time, a feeling, and a place" (Cohen 1996, 4).

Dracula represented a cultural fear of immigrants; Frankenstein a fear of technology and (depending on who you ask) childbirth. Monsters are meant to disrupt societal norms as well as create new norms. Vampires are no longer horrifying but rather represent goth coolness (or, at the very least, conjure images of a shirtless Edward Cullen, chest sparkling, disrupting the libidos of tween girls). Frankenstein is now a campy queer icon. And yet, the legacy of female monsters has not translated in quite the same way.

In reading the reviews for *A Certain Hunger*, I wondered why none of the reviewers had sought to romanticize Dorothy as critics have done with other monstrous characters (hello, Hannibal Lecter). Sexualize and criminalize, sure. But romanticize? How dare we love a woman who kills such nice men. I settled on this: perhaps the language we have to discuss feminine monstrosity has not evolved in the same way as the language we have to discuss male monstrosity. By "we" I mean the powers that be in our larger pop culture landscape—film and book critics, freelancers and staff writers, talk heads on your favorite morning show, journalists-turned-podcasters—whose discussions and critiques set the tone for how every day, non-media people might discuss and critique. There is a difference in how this "we" talks about men and women, and that applies to our monsters as well. In one, we are looking for a redemption arc, a *why*; in the other, we are just looking.

In this chapter, I wrestle with the question of how gender complicates our discussions surrounding monstrosity, especially in this post #MeToo era of American discourse. Who we choose to empathize with is at the center of that complication. In approaching this question, I first analyze the etymology of the words *hero*, *heroine*, and *monster* to show the differences between the definitional meaning of each word and the cultural meaning actually applied to them. Then, I use elements from Media Theory to pinpoint how that shift in meaning has been further distorted with the popularization of television and the internet. I posit that the result of this distortion is a surface-level lexicon that is ultimately weaponized against women to prevent meaningful discourse about feminine monstrosity. Monsters may be socially constructed beings but critiques of them shouldn't fall into those same traps—not when the recourse for doing so warps views of real-life women who exhibit monstrous (read: human) qualities as well.

Tall, Dark, & Sociopathic: Why We Love a (Male) Hero

Before I analyze the linguistic ways in which our lexicon has failed Dorothy and other female monsters, I must first analyze how the lexicon succeeds in shaping heroic male narratives. What does being a hero or a monster even mean? The term *hero* is so rooted in our vernacular that its exact origin story is unknown. There's some debate amongst linguists as to whether the term has Proto-Indo-European roots, originating from the Greek ἥρως *(hērōs)*, or if it has some sort of Pre-Greek origin. What we do know is that its earliest meaning fluctuated between "defender, protector" and "semi-divine and immortal." Early Greek writers like Homer and Hesiod invoked the term to describe great leaders, war veterans, and men whose legacies transcended their mortal bodies (*Online Etymology Dictionary* 2023). Later, the term would be watered down to allow any man to apply it to their character so long as he was "generally admired or acclaimed for great qualities or achievements in any field" (*Oxford English Dictionary* 2023). The divine roots are most important as they suggest an absolution from sin and an allowance for dualities.

I want to emphasize that the term "hero" I've referenced is unquestionably male. It's female iteration, "heroine," pops up in literature around the same time and holds a similar definition. Interestingly, what sets the two terms apart is the contexts in which they are written. The Oxford English Dictionary makes a note that the word "heroine" is usually accompanied by a possessive pronoun or the word "of" (2023). So, for example, Buffy Summers is a heroine *of* mine. Alexandria Ocasio-Cortez is *their* heroine. Olivia Rodrigo is a heroine *to us.* Unlike the hero, the heroine is always attached to others, literally possessed by others, her accomplishments not wholly her own.

The term *monster* has a clearer origin story. The Latin *monstrum* quite literally means "that which reveals," "that which warns" (*Oxford English Dictionary* 2023). Cohen's Monster Theory posits that monsters "like letters on a page" exist "only to be read" (Cohen 1996, 4). Meaning isn't attached to the monster unless we gift it. Power doesn't lie with the monster itself but in what is projected *onto* the monster. In short: heroes create meaning; monsters absorb it. Of course, that meaning is culturally constructed and coded in gender, and because of that, the terms have more than just definitional meaning. In Marianne Govers Hopman's research on the mythical monster Scylla, she suggests that mythical figures generate meaning just as words do. She imagines these figures as symbols and complex signs for "a system of cultural communication" (Hopman 2013, 5-8). These cultural communications are socially bound and reinforce certain norms and ways of knowing. Words are never just words. There are certain narratives infused into those terms. Those narratives then shape societal expectations and the language we use to discuss heroes and monsters. Similarly, Suzanne Keen's theory of Narrative Empathy helps us understand that humans are "story-sharing creatures" by nature, and we rely on certain narratives to shape our understanding of empathy to tell us who to empathize with. The point of this is to train an audience to prioritize certain culturally valued emotional states (Keen 2006, 209). I argue that those "valued emotional states" are gendered.

As a rule, history has supported and championed male narratives, no matter what they are. A classic example of this is Homer's *The Odyssey*. The book is set after the Trojan War during Odysseus' voyage home and spans the course of 10 years. Odysseus is the hero of the story, and yet, his actions don't exactly align with the definitional meaning of hero. During his journey, he blinds the son of a god, spends a year cheating on his wife and living in sin with a sea-witch, damns his crew to starvation and death, steals, lies, and cheats, among other transgressions. He certainly isn't acting semi-divine, nor is he "protecting" anything beyond his own selfish interests to get home. And yet, he is unquestionably a hero. His flaws are considered testaments to his triumphs, if not forgotten altogether, and are unimportant to the plot.

Let's contrast this with another character in the story: Charybdis, a former nymph cursed by Zeus to live out the rest of her miserable existence as a "voracious, man-eating female sea monster, a watery virago" (Zimmerman 2021, 33). She is essentially a whirlpool personified and a barrier to Odysseus getting home. While, technically, she has no physical form, she is canonically gendered feminine (Kapach 2022). Unlike Odysseus, she is given no backstory, no voice. We know nothing of her motivations or interests. Seemingly, her biggest crime is that she refuses to bend to Odysseus' will. It's this act of defiance that brands her a monster. While her motivations aren't made clear in the text, they don't seem to be particularly malicious or ill-intentioned. If anything, she is defending her space against unwanted male intrusion—an act that aligns more with the definitional meaning of hero, not a monster. Here, we see the terms *hero* and *monster* deviate from their definitional meaning to align more closely with their cultural meanings. Odysseus, despite his actual sins and character flaws, is branded as a hero; the words used to describe his journey are overwhelmingly positive. Charybdis, despite her *perceived* character flaws, is branded as a monster; the words used to describe her journey are overwhelmingly negative.

These narratives aren't outdated either. *The Odyssey* made its debut before Christ, and yet the moral of that story (flawed male stories = good; flawed female stories = bad) continues to play out in modern media narratives. Take, for example, the 2022 coverage of the Johnny Depp/Amber Heard defamation trial. Both influential actors in Hollywood, their marriage and divorce served as public fodder for years before culminating in a defamation trial. The trial was explosive in that it was the first time both Depp and Heard had spoken about their relationship in such graphic, candid details. Both parties cited domestic abuse in the relationship, claims that were supported by substantial evidence on both sides and yet only Depp emerged from the trial victorious. Depp won all three defamation charges and a little more than $10 million in damages, though the legal victory feels less important than the one he won with the public (Jacobs 2022). Heard was labeled a liar, crazy, and vindictive. Depp was praised for his valor in surviving the wiles of women. Regardless of the facts of the case, public perception labeled Depp the hero and Heard the monster. Depp's perseverance, like Odysseus's on his journey home, reinforces his heroism and shows how deserving he is of the label "hero." Heard's perseverance shows us the opposite.

The Depp/Heard trial illustrates just how tight a hold these historical narratives continue to have on current conversations. To put things in perspective, the Depp/Heard trial took place in 2022. That's five years after #MeToo started trending on social media, a time period that should have been ripe for discussing women's stories (Corbet 2022). In the year after the movement went viral, Amber Heard wrote an op-ed for *The Washington Post* advocating Congress to give renewed support to the Violence Against Women Act. The piece may or may not have referenced her relationship with Depp (she never mentions him by name). The article would be the centerpiece of the defamation trial. It became the reason Heard couldn't be believed, and she didn't even name her abuser. "Amber Heard and the Death of #MeToo" hailed one *New York Times* opinion (Jacobs 2022). Other headlines called the trial an "orgy of misogyny" (Donegan 2022) that would have a "chilling impact on #MeToo" (Branigan, Heller, and Maloy 2022). Some outlets even mused if the movement was over completely. Dead in the water. The public's perception of Heard showed just how superficial that societal reckoning was. #MeToo may have focused on the disparities in our treatment of women but not in our discussion of them.

I mention these examples because they illustrate that heroism has long been a narrative myth—and a gendered one at that. Male heroes are allowed dualities in ways that female heroines are not. In literature and beyond, women have long since been defined by the Angel/Monster paradigm, a dichotomy that limits them to an either/or scenario. You're either an angel or a monster, a virgin or a slut (Gilbert and Gubar 2020, 17). You can't be both. The dualities myth extends to our understanding of the masculine "hero" as well as its iterations: villains, anti-heroes, Byronic or romantic heroes, and reluctant heroes. What these terms all have in common is that they allow men to be *both*. Let's look at the romantic hero, a hero who defined the Romantic era of literature and is the blueprint for what we know today as the "bad boy." These heroes are rebellious, "deeply jaded, morally superior, and obsessed with lost love" (Palfy 2016, 164). Imagine a heroine being described as deeply jaded and morally superior without the added qualifier of "she was also a bitch." Beyond being morose and broody, romantic heroes are best known for setting their own moral codes (Thorslev 1962, 53). The presence of a moral code is important as it suggests that—despite how twisted and warped their code may be—there is a righteousness to their actions. It's this individualized moral code that adds a level of angst to the text and eroticizes the reader's response. For modern representations of the romantic hero, look no further than *Twilight*'s Edward Cullen (or really any mid-2000s vampire hottie), *90210*'s Dylan McKay, and DC Comics' Batman. Here are men who stand outside the boundaries of society, who were hot *because* they were bad.

Dorothy Daniels is another figure who operates outside the boundaries of society. She is categorically both hot and bad, and yet, we dislike her for it. Beyond her ability to butcher a man and sauté his remains into a Michelin star-worthy cuisine, Dorothy is also an unmarried middle-aged woman with no children (not even a fun dog!) who prioritizes her work and gorges herself on lavish trips and grandiose affairs with unavailable men. Like our other romantic heroes, Dorothy is jaded and morally superior: "I am special, the students intimate. I am valuable… to this, I laughed. I know what I am" (Summers 2020, 25). But she isn't completely morally bankrupt, either. For example, when we first meet Dorothy, she is detailing her murderously glamorous life to us from prison, where she sits convicted of murdering her last lover, Casimir. Instead of expressing remorse or horror for her actions, she reflects on the murder as if it was the tacky execution of a mid-life crisis, her "middle-aged madness, my little red Corvette" (15). It's not that she's sorry she murdered someone, so much as that she's sorry she murdered someone she didn't love. There is a reasoning and a righteousness to her actions, however demented that reasoning may be. Unlike our other romantic heroes, her moral code is one of the things that isolates us from liking her. She's a killer, sure, but it's *who* she kills that's more problematic. Her predilections tend towards attractive, successful men. She kills these men and then consumes them body and soul. That's only cool and sexy when men are doing it to women.

Attractive, emotionally stunted, and morally gray—this is what audiences like about Odysseus, Johnny Depp, and Edward Cullen, but have found problematic in Dorothy's character. Bad boys resonate with us *because* of their dualities. This empathy for male figures is ingrained in our cultural DNA. Jude Doyle's work on the horror genre and femininity suggests that, as a culture, we fetishize female ambivalence, "portraying masculinity as simultaneously attractive and scary and attractive because it is scary" (2018, 95). Did you get all that? We're normalizing scary masculine behavior in order to empathize with it. When men kill and consume women, it's not only expected but captivating. Doyle says that feminine desire—any desire—is the thing that moves her "beyond the reach of our empathy" marking her as a "threat that must be contained or destroyed" (2018, 72). By Dorothy engaging in feminine desire, a desire that results in masculine domination, she is excluded from empathy. Instead, she's labeled naughty, villainous, and angry—all words meant to lessen or destroy the valued emotional state this desire creates.

When looking at cultural narratives of masculine monstrosity, there's an attempt to normalize it by searching for a why. *Did his mother abuse him? Did a girlfriend treat him poorly? Was he depressed?* Our brains search for motivational ways to understand and empathize with the monster. As Keen echoes, it's what we've been trained to do. We value the redemption arc in men. We value villainizing and ostracizing women. This goes back to the very first definitions of *hero*: defender, protector, semi-divine, immortal. Absolution from sin is built into its core meaning, but in order to grant that absolution there needs to be empathy How and for whom empathy is felt is complicated by gender, which then bleeds into our discussions on feminine monstrosity. Those discussions still subscribe to outdated (practically prehistoric!) language—language that facilitates wrong assumptions about women and their motivations, thus denying them empathy. This disconnect between the definitional meaning of certain words (like hero and monster) and the cultural meaning attached to those words is important as it serves as historical context for what happens next. These language gaps are only part of the linguistic trap we've set for ourselves when it comes to discussing feminine monstrosity.

Material Girls Living in a Material World

If there is a shift between definitional meaning and cultural meaning for certain words, then how has this shift evolved (or not evolved) over time? In the early 1960s, an English professor named Marshall McLuhan wrote two books that introduced the idea that media influences, even shapes, human and cultural experiences. "The medium is the message," he said and gestured grandly, I imagine. Our wizard of Oz. What he meant by that was media is not just a means for disseminating information but a way to shape the meaning or understanding of that information (Stille 2000). McLuhan is, shall I say, a polarizing figure in academia, but his idea that media can (and does) influence narratives is one that helps me understand how a word's cultural meaning might be conflated with its definitional meaning and what that looks like in modern times.

In thinking about stories like *The Odyssey* the medium for communicating that story was through written text. Any discourse surrounding *The Odyssey's* messages took place through written and verbal communications. This allowed for a streamlined way of consuming information (read information → discuss information → information spreads/becomes known). Television and the internet changed all of that. Say it's 200 BC. *The Odyssey* is all the rage, but you read it, and you think Odysseus was a hack. You were rooting for Charybdis to eat his ship like a Big Mac. How you communicate those critiques is pretty limited to word-of-mouth (book clubs pre-Christ must have been savage). Maybe you put pen to paper, but the odds of boosting that message to the masses are slim. New media provided a way to amplify those messages. Now you can blast Odysseus in a TikTok, make #OdysseysSucks trending on Twitter, and write a think-piece that reaches 100K people before lunch. And while the reach of the message has grown, the language used to communicate those messages is still operating on an outdated level.

Symbolic interactionism, an offshoot of McLuhan's original media theory, may help explain this tension with language. Its main idea is that the self develops through human interaction. The way you act towards something is based on the previously understood meaning you have about that thing. For example, I walk my dog on the same route every day. One afternoon, I'm walking, and I see a black snake slithering across the pavement. My response in that moment is to scream and vow never to walk down that street again. Why? Because the meaning I've attached to snakes is that they're bad and scary, and the reason I have menstrual cramps when men don't. In a way, symbolic interactionism echoes what Govers Hopman's posited in her research on the mythical monster Scylla: we communicate through shared cultural symbols (2013, 8). Symbolic interactionism posits that the media uses these shared symbols to influence an individual's sense of self or a community's understanding of a concept (Jansson-Boyde 2010, 59-62). Logically, I know that black snakes are relatively harmless. They aren't even venomous or particularly aggressive. But I still associate the snake with its cultural meaning of dangerous and evil. I still walk the other way when I see one coming.

In that way, media has not changed all that much in the centuries since *The Odyssey*'s publication. Media continues to use easily digestible narratives and symbols to conflate cultural meaning with definitional meaning. What has changed are the goals of that messaging. The angel/monster paradigm that historically plagued women's narratives has expanded to fit the capitalist underpinnings of modern society. Women aren't monsters anymore, they're consumers. They aren't demonic whirlpools of yore but money-hungry mistresses. Materiality is the lens through which we view modern women's stories, a shift generated by the popularization of television and film. Madonna even came out with a song in the 1980s that spoke directly to this sentiment of material girls living in a material world. Dorothy Daniels also voices something similar in *A Certain Hunger:* "As a girl, when you grow up, you become delectable. As a woman, when you grow old, you turn immaterial" (Summers 2020, 250). Both Madonna and Dorothy associate femininity with materiality, something that is not real but, at the same time, tangible and commodifiable. "What big teeth you have, grandmother," Little Red Riding Hood once whispered in horror, but in a post-TV and internet era, the monsters are armed with daddy's credit card; they're clutching quiet luxury in their fists.

Prior to the invention of film and television, ideas of materiality and femininity were linked but less aggressively so. I believe it was Aristotle who came up with the fun masculinist fantasy wherein men are allowed to "transcend their bodies as 'disembodied minds'" and "leap out of the marked body to a conquering gaze from nowhere" (Davis 2021, 388). His fantasies of gender essentially trap women within their bodies, tying their wants and desires entirely to that of their flesh. Art and activities of the mind, these "leaps" from the marked body, are male endeavors, not female ones. And what of these bodies that we're tied to? It's not just that women are thought to be constrained to their flesh, but that flesh has also been objectified, and that objectification has become a cultural symbol. In Laura Mulvey's work on film and the male gaze, she posits that the "[pleasure] in looking has been split between active/male and passive/female" (1989, 18). Again, we see hints of Aristotle's sexist sentiments. Men are active participants in pleasure, leaping, if you will, into the frame as "subject." Meanwhile, women are likened to set pieces, their bodies "simultaneously looked at and displayed" (19). They are objects, their bodies not wholly their own but rather owned by and purposed for male pleasure.

While Mulvey's work focuses primarily on film, the male gaze is something that extends beyond the purview of a screen. In fact, one could argue that the screen is *the reason* for the expansion of this gaze. It's bled into how women act, dress, and behave—all meant to please our patriarchal-dominated society. Our resident maneater, Dorothy Daniels, seems to understand these rules of femininity and performs them outwardly. As she says, "it's not important that [femininity] is real. It's important that it's tasty" (Summers 2020, 35). I mention this line specifically because it hits on a certain point I'm trying to make. Textually, Dorothy is constantly telling the audience all the ways she subverts traditional femininity. Cooking, a historically feminine role, she distorts by making meals out of the various body parts of men: "To eat people is to get the taste of a Titan... But then again, I am an excellent cook" (94). She engages in cis-hetero relationships, even claims to love those relationships, but twists the power dynamics so that she never gives up control to her male partners: "I didn't fuck anyone I couldn't ruin" (41). Lastly, while outwardly she submits to the male gaze by being sexually attractive, she is actually violent and angry (traditionally masculine traits). She manipulates the male gaze to both hide her true nature and engineer outcomes that benefit her own desires over male desire. And yet, reviewers talk about this subversion in buzzy terminology, reducing the complexities of her character to "tasty," digestible bites. Dorothy once said that "women have an emotional wiliness that shellacs us in a glossy patina of caring" (26). I take that observation one step further by positing that the way women are talked about works just as hard to "shellac" us into seeming more patriarchally pleasing, to coat even our most monstrous forms in a glossy exterior.

If women are materials living in a material world, "objects," as Mulvey asserts, then it makes sense that the capitalist framework would manifest in our lexicon with materialistic, surface-level terms. In Amanda Montell's work on sociolinguistics, she suggests language and gender exist in tandem. Gender, we know, is linked in most cultures to power and, so too, is language. Language that objectifies is meant to reinforce certain existing power structures (men as subjects, women as objects) and reduces female power by linking women to three specific categories: edible, nonhuman, and sexual entities (Montell 2019, 31). Think about the insult *tart* or the positive endearment *peach*. Both are edible items that are gendered feminine and used to describe women. Tart began as a word to describe a small pie or pastry before morphing into an innocuous compliment for women. This quickly spiraled until the word was specified to mean a *sexually desirable* woman, and then, in the 19th century, a woman of immoral character or a prostitute. Likewise, the word peach is quite literally synonymous with female genitalia. If these are words that serve as both positive and negative descriptors of women, what does this say about women? That they are "sweet, single-serving items meant to be easily snapped up" (35). This is important because it reinforces a certain narrative about women's worth, mainly that we are consumable, pleasurable objects and not human enough to warrant empathy. The empathy part of this argument is important because it shows not only that our current lexicon reduces and objectifies but also that it weaponizes certain words to deny empathy. Emphatic responses while reading simulates critical thinking. Fiction, in particular, "disarms readers of some of the protective layers of cautious reasoning," which, in turn, can create a "prosocial outcome through interfering cognition" (Keen 2006, 212-213). Meaning: if we are able to empathize with a character in a book, we have the capacity to act on that empathy in real life.

There are certain narrative techniques that writers use to enhance empathy. For example, first-person narratives are more effective in creating empathy than third-person narratives (Keen 2006, 215). I find this interesting because women-centered stories—especially *first-person* women-centered stories—are often discounted and given less urgency in critical conversations. Author Emma Jane Unsworth notes in a *Guardian* article that monstrous men have a place in serious fiction that gets "generally cataloged as 'tales of the human condition,'" while female characters of similar moral (or immoral) standing are not (Unsworth 2014). Outside of the literary world, first-person, women-centered stories are equally discounted as compared to first-person, male-centered stories. Take the Brock Turner rape case that dominated news cycles in 2015. Turner, then a college swimmer at Stanford University, was convicted of sexually assaulting an unconscious woman. Despite a guilty verdict and national outcry over the case, the judge only sentenced Turner to six months of jail time (of which he served three). Before sentencing, the judge listened to a first-person statement from the woman Turner assaulted as well as a statement from Turner's father. "I don't want my body anymore," the victim said. "I was terrified of it… I wanted to take off my body like a jacket and leave it at the hospital with everything else." In contrast, Turner's father called the assault a "steep price to pay for 20 minutes of action out of his 20 years of life" (Fantz 2016). The victim's statement was first-person and compelling. Brock Turner didn't even voice a statement; his father did. And yet, the judge agreed with this second-person, male-centered story.

This goes back to my original point about symbolic interactionism and how the media's amplification of certain cultural symbols affects public empathy. Brock Turner—blond, blue-eyed, collegiate athlete—symbolizes what we value as American successes. In contrast, the woman Turner assaulted symbolizes a challenge to those values. Interestingly, the woman in this case, Chanel Miller, was referred to as "Emily Doe" throughout the trial; her identity was kept secret even during sentencing. Turner's face and body were on display, which allowed the media to impart meaning to that face and body, something they couldn't do with the anonymous Emily Doe. But there were still these facts: she is a woman with a body; "20 minutes of action." "Woman with a body" is its own symbol, and that symbol is often not something worthy of empathy. In this instance of he-said/she-said-and-the-jury-believed-without-a-doubt, the judge saw two symbols and chose to empathize with the one he understood as valuable.

Beyond first-person narratives, character identification is another narrative technique associated with building empathy. Character identification relies on language for things like "naming, description, indirect implication of traits, reliance on types, [and] relative flatness or roundness [of characters]" to create empathy (Keen 2006, 216). If this sounds familiar, then good, it should. Let's recall Dorothy's critical reception where she was called "naughty," "sexy," and— my personal favorite—"preternaturally hot" (for a woman of 51, anyways). Even at her most monstrous, she's reduced to a sexual entity, flattening her character and making it reliant on a certain type of femininity. This reduction does a few things: first, it diminishes the subversiveness of her actions. She's no longer a woman defying traditional female norms and besting men at their own game; she's just a sexy lady doing sexy lady things. She becomes a caricature of a monster instead of an actual monster. Second, it reframes the conversation into the subject/object dichotomy. Instead of the text being about Dorothy's pleasure, it's about how Dorothy can be pleasurable *to us*.

The urge to talk about Dorothy's character by dressing monstrosity up in materialistic language is just an updated version of the linguistic trap that's stalked our discussions of feminine monstrosity for ages. The angel/monster paradigm has evolved to meet our current capitalistic landscape. The cultural symbol for "flawed woman" no longer takes the shape of a watery vortex; it doesn't lash out at you with fangs or claws. Instead, it takes the shape of Manolo Blahniks, red lips, a woman with dollar signs in her eyes. The language has evolved too. The object-first language shrouding femininity is now glossy and candy-coated—*tasty*, as Dorothy so eloquently put it. But that evolution still weaponizes certain words and tropes (tart, bitch, slut, maneater, monster) to stunt emphatic responses, granted in more superficial ways. While the symbols and the language have evolved to match the capitalistic moment, the original design flaw is still present. We still haven't solved the equation for how to talk about feminine monstrosity without falling into the linguistic trap of using language that denies women empathy.

Oh-Oh, Here She Comes, She's a Maneater

When I think about *A Certain Hunger,* I can't understand how this progressive, darkly hilarious, disturbing novel could be so critically misunderstood. Then I remember these facts: *A Certain Hunger* was published in December 2021. That's almost two years into the COVID-19 pandemic, a pandemic that resulted in 5.2 million American women losing their jobs (Clay 2022). That's five years after Donald Trump, a man who was accused of multiple sexual assaults during his presidential run (among other crimes), was elected to the highest office of this country while at the same time, the #MeToo movement, a movement dedicated to women trying to reclaim the narrative, swept the nation. When I think about it that way, it makes sense that Dorothy's character would be reduced to harmful narrative binaries. For as far as we've come as a culture, we still can't conceptualize a world in which women can be both.

This is especially true for women who operate outside the bounds of traditional femininity, such as Dorothy, Charybdis, and Amber Heard. These women are consumers of men—and not just any men, but *powerful* men. Dorothy made her own personal Restaurant Week out of the body parts of New York's elite. Charybdis swallowed a fleet full of men whole and belched up their innards in a wave of sea spray and salt just because she could. Amber Heard ate Hollywood's golden boy for brunch. They are gold diggers and monsters; manipulators and psychos; maneaters, and femme fatales. Of course, these women are not *just* those things. Dorothy is a successful woman who refused to age into obscurity and a homicidal sociopath. Charybdis is either a mindless vortex of hunger or a woman cursed by a male god to live without her body for eternity (or both!). Amber Heard is a victim of domestic violence and a perpetrator of domestic violence. But when we have critical conversations about these women, we're quick to section them off as either an angel or a monster without allowing the possibility for dualities.

The possibility for dualities is important because it allows for the creation of empathy. I've argued that Dorothy's character has not been empathized or romanticized in the same was as other monsters of similar character. In arguing for her romanticization, I don't mean to romanticize a cannibalistic serial killer, only to emphasize that we are already doing that with male characters. "Kidnap me pls" wrote one Twitter user about Joe Goldberg, the "good guy" serial killer at the center of Netflix's *You* (@MalikaPlays 2019). "He's cool," *Village Voice's* Mark Dery wrote about Hannibal Lecter, "coolest of all, his pulse doesn't top 85, even when he's tearing out your tongue and eating it" (1999). Violent, abhorrent behavior in men has been so normalized we often don't even acknowledge it when we discuss their monstrosity. Monstrosity in men is not shocking because it's expected. In moving past that initial shock value it allows for deeper analysis and critical conversation.

Why do we do this? Why can't we have similar critical discussions about feminine monstrosity? Monsters are supposed to destabilize norms and interrogate culture. They pinpoint certain cultural anxieties and function as a warning—either against the creature itself or of our treatment of it. Cohen writes, "the monster's destructiveness is really a deconstructiveness: it threatens to reveal that difference originates in process rather than fact" (Cohen 1996, 15). By "process," I think he means the cultural process of how we create narratives and dole out empathy. Narratives are not created in a vacuum, and neither is our empathy. We use cultural symbols to create and communicate meaning. These symbols, for better or for worse, are then reinforced by the media. The language the media uses to emphasize these symbols then provides a model for our discussions of them. The problem is that language is drenched in patriarchal power structures, so much so that it fractures definitional meaning from cultural meaning, coating our discourse in inaccuracies.

Symbolic interactionism helps us understand this fracture, especially as it pertains to twenty-first-century discussions of women. Through symbolic interactionism, we see the following life cycle take place: information is read/learned/absorbed, and a cultural symbol takes root → the media amplifies that symbol and gives us a template for discussion → that template distorts our understanding of the symbol and undermines our discussion of it. Let's bring it back to my fear of snakes. The evolution of that fear might look something like this: the Bible says snakes are bad and evil and the reason I have menstrual cramps. I watch a commercial for a movie about a plane infested with snakes; lots of screaming ensues. Kim Kardashian enlists a hate campaign against Taylor Swift, and her followers leave snake emojis on Taylor's social feeds. I see a snake on my walk and walk the other way. But what if the commercial I saw was for a movie about a snake's journey to becoming an emotional support animal; lots of crying ensues. What if Kim Kardashian posted a bunch of snakes on social media to applaud Taylor Swift's ability to evolve musically? What if I read about the Bible thing, but it was just one outdated version of a snake that was drowned out by a million other snake stories. What then?

I'll let you in on a secret: I did not expect to like this book as much as I did. I've read hundreds of stories about lady psychos: wives who set up their husbands for murder, mistresses who exact revenge on the men who wronged them, and cheerleaders engaging in girl-on-girl warfare. The list goes on. There's always something sad going on in those stories. The villainess was abused or discarded or suffering from mental health issues. She's burdened by femininity or societal expectations. The beauty of Dorothy is that she's not broken. She's just that twisted. The power emanating from her through the pages of *A Certain Hunger* was stunning to read. I keep coming back to the words Stephen King wrote about Hannibal Lecter in his *New York Times* review: "he is not a joke" (2021). And neither is Dorothy. The critical conversations surrounding her character flatten her power into a caricature of itself. Reading those reviews, I pictured a Bond woman or Rocky & Bullwinkle villain. Suddenly, she wasn't a bemouth of feminist energy but a thing with which the male gaze could find pleasing.

Dorothy exists beyond the bounds of femininity and challenges those notions. But if we can't empathize with her, then how can we empathize with real women who do the same? Because the conversations we have about fictional monsters bleed into our conversations about real "monsters." Reviewers were quick to equate Dorothy to a sexual entity, as Brock Turner's father did with Emily Doe and the media did with Amber Heard during the Depp/Heard defamation trial. Keen suggests that emphatic responses often start with fiction first before extending outwards into our own reality. More than hunger, more than power, more than romanticization, that's what I want people to take away from *A Certain Hunger*. I want people to read Dorothy's character and not go for the low-hanging fruit, to challenge themselves to look at the woman beneath the monster and to unlearn the vocabulary that dressed up her monstrosity in a more pleasing outfit. I want them to see clearly the linguistic trap presented before them and sink their teeth into it instead. Watch out, world, we'll chew you up.

Bibliography

(@MalikaPlays). 2019. "@PennBadgley kidnap me pls." Twitter, January 9, 2019, 1:32 p.m. https://twitter.com/MalikaPlays/status/10830690451 61820161?ref _src=twsrc%5Etfw.

Branigan, Anne, Heller, Karen, and Maloy, Ashley Fetters. 2022. "Depp-Heard verdict will have chilling impact on #MeToo, advocates fear." *The Washington Post*, June 2 2022. https://www.washingtonpost.com/arts-entertainment/ 2022/06/02/me-too-amber-heard-johnny-depp/.

Clay, Rebecca A. 2022. "Millions of women have left the workforce. Psychology can help bring them back." *American Psychological Association*, 53, no.1, (2022), 66. https://www.apa.org/monitor/2022/01/special-workforce-losses.

Cohen, Jeffrey Jerome. 1996. *Monster Theory: Reading Culture*. University of Minnesota Press: ProQuest Ebook Central. https://ebookcentral.proques t.com/lib/uncw/detail.action?docID=310376.

Corbet, Holly. 2022. "#MeToo Five Years Later: How The Movement Started And What Needs To Change." *Forbes*, October 27, 2022, https://www.forbes.com/ sites/hollycorbett/2022/10/27/metoo-five-years-later-how-the-movement- started-and-what-needs-to-change/?sh=2f08a4485afe.

Corrigan, Maureen. 2020. "Sure, You May Be Grossed Out, but 'A Certain Hunger' is a Naughty Pleasure." *The Washington Post*, December 11, 2020. https://www.washingtonpost.com/entertainment/books/sure-you-may-be-grossed-out-but-a-certain-hunger-is-a-naughty-pleasure/2020/12/10/01ba b f78-3a49-11eb -bc68-96af0daae728_story.html.

Davis, Kathy. 2021. "Reclaiming Women's Bodies: Colonialist Trope or Critical Epistemology?" *Feminist Theory Reader: Local and Global Perspectives*, 5th ed., edited by Carole R. McCann, Seung-kyung Kim, and Emek Ergun, 385-395. New York: Routledge.

Dery, Mark. 1999. "Brain Food." *The Village Voice*, June 15, 1999. https://www.villagev oice.com/1999/06/15/brain-food/.

Donegan, Moira. 2022. "The Amber Heard-Johnny Depp trial was an orgy of misogyny." *The Guardian*, June 1, 2022. https://www.theguardian.com/com mentisfree/2022/jun/01/amber-heard-johnny-depp-trial-metoo-backlash.

Doyle, Sady. 2019. *Dead Blondes and Bad Mothers*. Brooklyn, New York: Melville House.

Fantz, Ashley. 2016. "Outrage over 6-month sentence for Brock Turner in Stanford rap case." *CNN.com*, June 2 2016. https://www.cnn.com/2016/06 /06 /us/sexual-assault-brock-turner-stanford/index.html.

Gilbert, Sandra M., and Gubar, Susan. 2020. *The Madwoman in the Attic: The Woman Writer and the Nineteenth-Century Literary Imagination*, 17-82. New Haven: Yale University Press. Accessed November 9, 2021. ProQuest Ebook Central.

Hopman, Marianne Govers. 2013. *Scylla: Myth, Metaphor, Paradox*. Cambridge: Cambridge University Press, ProQuest Ebook Central. https://ebookcentral .proquest.com/lib/uncw/detail.action?docID=1057532.

Jacobs, Julia. 2022. "Jury Reaches Verdict in Johnny Depp-Amber Heard Trial: What to Know." *The New York Times*, August 9, 2022. https://www.nytimes. com/2022/04/21/arts/johnny-depp-amber-heard-trial.html.

Jansson-Boyd, Catherine. 2010. *Consumer Psychology*, 59–62. New York: McGraw-Hill.

Kapach, Avi. 2022. "Charybdis." *Mythopedia.com*, March 22, 2022. https://my thopedia.com/topics/charybdis.

Keen, Suzanne. "A Theory of Narrative Empathy." *Narrative* 14, no. 3 (2006): 207–36. http://www.jstor.org/stable/20107388.

King, Stephen. 2021. "Review: 'Hannibal,' by Thomas Harris." *The New York Times*, October 21, 2021. https://www.nytimes.com/2021/10/21/books/re view/review-hannibal-by-thomas-harris.html.

Kirkus Reviews. 2020. "Book Review: Move Aside Brett Easton Ellis, A Certain Hunger by Chelsea G. Summers." kirkus.com, August 15, 2020. https://www. kirkusreviews.com/book-reviews/chelsea-g-summers/a-certain-hunger.

Online Etymology Dictionary, s.v. "hero, n.1," June 8, 2023, https://www.Ety monline.com/word/hero.

Oxford English Dictionary, s.v. "monster, n., adv., & adj.," September 2023. https://doi.org/10.1093/OED/3193780999.

Oxford English Dictionary, s.v. "hero, n.," September 2023, https://doi.org/10. 1093/ OED/3716012876.

Oxford English Dictionary, s.v. "heroine, n.," July 2023, https://doi.org/10.1093/OED/2271411813.

Montell, Amanda. 2019. *Wordslut: A Feminist Guide to Taking Back the English Language*. New York: HarperCollins.

Mulvey, Laura. 1989. "Visual Pleasure and Narrative Cinema." *Visual and Other Pleasures: Language, Discourse, Society.* London: Palgrave Macmillan. https://doi.org/10.1007/978-1-349-19798-9_3.

Palfy, Cora. 2016. "Anti-hero Worship: The Emergence of the 'Byronic hero' Archetype in the Nineteenth Century." *Indiana Theory Review*, 32, no. 1 (2016), 161-198. https://doi-org.liblink.uncw.edu/ 10.2979/inditheorevi .32.2 .05.

Stille, Alexander. 2000. "Marshall McLuhan Is Back From the Dustbin of History; With the Internet, His Ideas Again Seem Ahead of Their Time," *New York Times*, October 14, 2000. http://www.nytimes.com/2000/10/14/arts/marshall-mcluh an-back-dustbin-history-with-internet-his-ideas-again-seem-ahea d.html.

Silverberg, Amy. 2020. "Why Can't Women Be Serial Killers, Too?" *The New York Times*, December 1, 2020. https://www.nytimes.com/2020/12/01/books/rev iew/a-certain-hunger-chelsea-g-summers.html.

Summers, Chelsea G. 2020. *A Certain Hunger*. Los Angeles, California: The Unnamed Press.

Thorslev, Peter L. 1962. *The Byronic Hero: Types and Prototypes*. Minnesota: University of Minnesota Press.

Unsworth, Emma Jane. 2014 "Readers Love a Good Anti-Hero—So Why Do They Shun Anti-Heroines?" *The Guardian*, November 17, 2014. https://www.theguardian.com/books/booksblog/2014/nov/17/readers-anti-hero-anti-h eroines-fiction.

Zimmerman, Jess. 2021. *Women and Other Monsters*. Boston: Beacon Press Books.

Chapter 10

Trans/futurities: Queering the Cyborg as a Strategy of Transgender Disidentification

Sheridyn Villarreal

Independent Scholar

Abstract: In her 1994 essay, My Words to Victor Frankenstein above the Village of Chamonix: Performing Transgender Rage, scholar and transgender studies theorist Susan Stryker evoked the first cyborg, Frankenstein's Monster, when she declared: "the transsexual body is an unnatural body. It is the product of medical science. It is a technological construction. It is flesh torn apart and sewn together again in a shape other than that in which it was born." As a transgender woman herself, Stryker co-opts the oppressive cisheteronormative discourse of "the monstrous other" to claim affinity between the cyborg figure and the transgender experience. Throughout the 20th century, representations of the cyborg figure in mainstream media have historically been deployed to dehumanize and vilify queer communities, especially transgender identities, for their perceived transgression or corruption of binary norms. Applying scholar Jose Esteban Munoz' theory of disidentification in dialogue with writings of post-feminist theorists Susan Stryker and Donna Haraway, this essay analyzes three contemporary works of visual art as acts of transgender disidentification, which subvert and transform the signification of the cyborg within visual culture. Artists Julia Ducournau, Tabitha Nikolai, and Arca work across disciplines of film, music, and immersive digital media to excavate the cyborg; exploring queered notions of gender, the body, and sex within a culture increasingly mediated by technology. The works of these artists' grapple with the implications of the cyborg figure as a creature of fiction and social reality. Through an examination of these three contemporary artists' practices, I propose that by co-opting the oppressive discourse of the monstrous cyborg figure, there exists the potential to subvert its oppressive power and re-inscribe its cultural meaning to signify a radical self-determinacy and transgender euphoria.

Keywords: cyborg, transgender, disidentification, posthumanism, gender transition, gender euphoria

***

The sheen of sweat and metal — Synthetic bodies, augmented by hormone hacking, implants, and prosthetic sensory interfaces — Beings that transform the conditions of their embodiment at will and operate, sometimes undetected, within society every day. Defying conceptions of "natural" order, the cyborg transgresses reified binaries of organic and synthetic, human and machine.

A wholly modern monster, the figure of the cyborg emerged from the chimeric hybrids of myth in response to the discoveries of enlightenment science, which upended traditional conceptions of the natural world; and the rise of industrialization, which saw the replacement of hand tools with power-driven machinery. As discoveries in medicine, physics, and engineering propelled the increasing integration of technology into human society, the phantasm of the cyborg became ever more menacing. Twentieth-century popular culture, including cinema, literature, and visual art, featured a greater number of cyborg antagonists representing not only the fear of oncoming technological omnipresence but also that of the destabilizing cultural "other," such as immigrants, religious or racial minorities, homosexuals, sex workers, or gender non-conforming individuals (Benesch 1999).

In her 1994 essay, *My Words to Victor Frankenstein above the Village of Chamonix: Performing Transgender Rage*, scholar and transgender studies theorist Susan Stryker evoked the first cyborg, Frankenstein's Monster, when she declares:

> The transsexual body is an unnatural body.[1] It is the product of medical science. It is a technological construction. It is flesh torn apart and sewn together again in a shape other than that in which it was born. (Stryker 1994, 238)

A transgender woman herself, Stryker draws affinity between the transgender experience and that of the cyborg, both of which are demonized for their destabilizing threat to the reified belief in fixed genders and transgression of stable binaries (ibid).

Despite its use by the cisheteropatriarchy as a symbol by which to demonize queerness, considered "sexual deviancy" or the "perversion of nature," there exists a well-documented affinity and reclamation of the cyborg among the transgender community in particular. During a time in which explicitly trans

---

[1] In her essay, Stryker utilizes the term transexual/transsexuality to refer to a culturally and historically specific transgender practice/identity through which a transgendered subject enters into a relationship with medical, psychotherapeutic, and juridical institutions in order to gain access to certain hormonal and surgical technologies for enacting and embodying itself.

subject matter was and continues to be absent in mainstream visual culture, one of the only circumstances in which gender-nonconforming individuals could see elements of their lived experiences represented in art was through these fictionalized depictions of the cyborg. In the centuries that have passed, this situation has undergone a crucial shift.

In 1990, feminist theorist Judith Butler published her essay, *Performative Acts and Gender Constitution*, whose supposition that distinct modes of gender are constructed and reaffirmed by perpetual performative acts, upended the common conceptions of gender as the expression of innate biological sex characteristics. Butler defined gendered performance as:

> ...a stylized repetition of acts...instituted through the stylization of the body and, hence, must be understood as the mundane way in which bodily gestures, movements, and enactments of various kinds constitute the illusion of an abiding gendered self. (Butler 1988, 519)

The implication being, if gender is constituted through the performance of gender itself, then it is formed instead of born, fluid instead of fixed. Therefore, gender as performed by a trans subject is no less authentic than as performed by a cisgender subject.[2] It is from this theoretical foundation that an affinity between the transgender experience and the cyborg figure becomes apparent. Like the cyborg, many transgender individuals who chose to undergo a medical transition, whether that be hormone replacement therapy or gender-affirming surgery, "stylize" and maintain their performance as gendered subjects through technological augmentation, thus transmuting the condition of their embodiment. If modes of gender are constituted by the stylization of the body, then the cyborg body, likewise constituted from a stylization of form, gestures, and movement, represents the utmost posthuman philosophical interpretation of Butler's theory of identity constitution.[3]

---

[2] Cisgender refers to an individual whose gender identity corresponds with their sex assigned at birth.

[3] Post-humanism refers to a set of ideas which emerged during the 1990s, departing from the humanist philosophies which relied upon the notion that humans are and always will be the only agents of the moral world. Post-humanists refute this, and argue that in our technologically mediated future, understanding the world as a moral hierarchy and placing humans is erroneous. Sometimes referred to as transhumanists, posthuman philosophy claims that in the coming century, human beings will be radically altered by implants, bio-hacking, cognitive enhancement and other bio-medical technology. These

Whereas openly transgender individuals had never before been the author of their own representation, solely subject to it as defined by the cisheteropatriarchy; contemporary artists benefiting from increased visibility and alternative methods of disseminating art consequent of the internet age, have increasingly become the creators of their own image in visual culture. Given this greater power to combat harmful depictions of gender-nonconformity with rehabilitative ones, it may come as a surprise that rather than distance themselves from posthuman aesthetics, a growing number of artists have embraced and even reveled in such associations between notions of the cyborg and transgender subjectivity.

Presently, the transgender community is both more visible than ever before and yet continues to endure violent oppression, exclusion, and erasure from both the cisgender queer community and dominant cisheteronormative culture. Just as 2021 became the deadliest year on record for transgender and gender non-conforming people in the United States, with at least 50 documented murders (a gross under-representation of the number of people whose bodies are never found or misgendered after their death), an unprecedented 222 "anti-trans" bills have been either introduced or passed within the year 2022 (Human Rights Campaign n.d.). Such legislation proposes to criminalize access to life-saving, gender-affirming healthcare, civil protections, and full participation in society for trans individuals within the United States.

Given this dire context, my following analysis will consider three contemporary works of art that evoke the cyborg to explore ideas of gender, sex, and the body in a world mediated through technologies and will seek to answer the following questions: why would an already demonized subject embrace or otherwise willingly align their position with that of monstrosity? What social or political strategies are at play, and what outcomes, if any, are at stake?

Pursuing this line of inquiry, I will analyze works of art created by Julia Decornau (French, b.1983), Tabitha Nikolai (American, b.1984), and Arca (Venezuelan, b. 1987) as acts of political disidentification. The theory of disidentification was first proposed by the scholar of queer studies, José Esteban Muñoz, to explain how subjects whose identities are outside the racial and sexual mainstream may negotiate the dominant culture — neither aligning themselves totally with or diametrically against exclusionary works of art (Muñoz 1999). Instead, such subjects may choose to position themselves within the oppressive discourse so that they may subvert and reinscribe its meaning for their own cultural purposes (Muñoz 1999). I will apply this

---

enhancements will lead us to "evolve" into a species that is completely unrecognizable to what we are now (Ethics Centre).

theoretical framework to the aforementioned works of art to propose their significance as acts of transgender disidentification that co-opt the oppressive discourse of the monstrous cyborg figure and reclaim it as a symbol of radical self-determinacy and trans/gender euphoria.

Corrupting Gendered Embodiment

Titane is a 2021 independent feature film by the French writer and director Julia Ducournau (b. 1983). Infamous for its portrayal of transgressive acts against the body, the film offers a visceral exploration of gender, lust, and the intimacy that connect people and machines (Scott 2021). Utilizing a painterly visual style of naturalistic lighting, claustrophobic composition, and fluid tracking shots; the film feels at times hyper-real, with each sense heightened. Its title refers to the titanium plate implanted into the skull of its protagonist, Alexia, in the aftermath of a near-fatal car crash she survives as a child during the film's opening sequence.

Alexia's operation draws comparison to that of Frankenstein's Monster, who, like her, is reanimated from [the brink of] death through mechanical intervention. The side of her head is disfigured by the scars of surgical incision, thus rendering her a hybrid of flesh and metal, a cyborg organism. What follows is a deliriously grisly depiction of a now adult Alexia, a formidable erotic dancer who grinds atop hot-rods at motor shows and an indiscriminate serial murderer. She impersonates the identity of a missing boy, Adrien, in order to evade arrest by the police, who have discovered her trail of bodies. In writing the character Alexia, Ducournau aimed to create an ostensibly female character that was outside the archetype of victimhood, which dictates that women who enact violence must themselves be driven by violence enacted against them, saying:

> ...ultimately, trying to find an excuse for this to exist is also a way to deny it, to say "don't worry, before this, she was a victim; she was that victim you want her to be..."When you make movies, you also create figures — and these are the kinds of figures I want to go against. (Bunbury 2021)

In addition to her homicidal compulsion, Alexia is motivated by an erotic fixation for metal, such as when she nearly bites the titanium nipple piercing off of fellow dancer Justine and two separate sexual encounters with motor vehicles, the first of which results in a pregnancy which is not entirely human. Alexia's transgressions of natural order render her monstrous, occupying the role of a dangerous and destabilizing explicitly queer "other" within society.

Fleeing from the police, Alexia discovers that a sketch of her appearance has been broadcast on local news. Realizing she must disguise herself, she quickly identifies a poster of the long-missing boy, Adrian Legrand, alongside a facial composite of what the now teenaged boy may look like. Viewers watch in horror as Alexia locks herself inside a public bathroom and proceeds to mutilate the feminine attributes of her body; trimming her long hair, binding her breasts and pregnant belly with medical gauze, and brutally cracking the bridge of her nose against a porcelain sink basin to disfigure her appearance to resemble that of male Adrien. The binding of the chest is both a practical act within the context of the plot and one with loaded significance to the trans-masculine experience.[4] Chest binding, or compressing the chest tissue, is a common practice among trans-masculine individuals that can alleviate gender dysphoria by reducing the appearance of a conventionally feminine chest contour.[5] Alexia continues to bind as they become further embedded into the identity of Adrien, compelled to negotiate a convincing performance of masculinity for fear that the failure to do so will have dangerous consequences.

Vincent, the missing boy's devastated and lonely father, bafflingly accepts Alexia's impersonation despite obvious skepticism from the police. Determined to mold the strange and intense boy into his ideal son, he inserts Adrien into the all-male crew of young firefighters he captains. The firefighters vie for Vincent's mentorship and distrust the sudden appearance of the effeminate Adrien. When performing womanhood, Alexia is intimidating, weaponizing her body to seduce and disarm her victims. When performing manhood, Adrien is awkwardly mocked for his inability to conform to the social script of masculinity demanded of him.

When called to answer a reported overdose, Vincent brings Adrien along to observe. While on the scene, the victim's mother collapses from shock, and Adrien successfully resuscitates her. Having proved [his] masculinity and earned the respect of the crew, they tentatively accept him. In a gesture of affection, a proud Vincent shaves Adrien's face to induce the hair to grow. While impersonating the missing boy's identity began as a means of survival, Alexia's willingness to receive the shave, thereby causing a lasting masculinization of the body, implies that they just might prefer living as Adrien.

However, Alexia is not the only cyborg lurking in *Titane*. The aging Vincent's preoccupation with his son's masculinity mirrors his own, as he is shown obsessively exercising and dependent on anabolic steroids to retain his hyper-masculine physique. In one particularly arresting scene, Vincent calls on Adrien's help to inject a dose of testosterone. When Adrien asks whether he is

---

[4] Trans-Masculine refers to individuals assigned female at birth who identify with and present as conventionally masculine. This term may encompass transgender men, gender-fluid, and non-binary individuals.

[5] Gender dysphoria the condition of distress or discomfort induced by the discrepancy between an individual's gender identity and their sex assigned at birth (Jarrett et al. 2018).

sick, he replies simply, "I'm old." Continuing the metaphor of gender transition, these acts draw an immediate comparison to hormone replacement therapy (HRT), which is a gender-affirming treatment regimen in which sex hormones and other hormonal medications are administered to transgender or gender nonconforming individuals for the purpose of aligning their secondary sexual characteristics with their gender identity (Unger 2016). The fact that it is cisgender Vincent who is portrayed in this context reveals the labor required of all subjects to maintain supposedly innate modes of gender.

At the same time that this domestic drama unfolds between father and son, Alexia's unwanted pregnancy is developing at a preternatural speed. They begin to lactate black motor oil and frantically bind their growing belly to conceal the pregnancy, which is incompatible with their new life as Adrien. Profoundly uncomfortable in their body, Alexia scratches and tears at their skin as it stretches apart, revealing a chrome subsurface. Continuing to work against the female archetype, Ducournau depicts the pregnancy as a nightmarish hijacking:

> It's still kind of [a morally] unacceptable idea that a woman can find pregnancy horrid! But, it [can be] horrid! The pregnancy is painful, [and] scary, and, for a long time in the film, she rejects it. (Nolfi 2021)

Though the inability to biologically conceive can be a source of heartbreaking anguish for many trans-feminine individuals who long to be parents, the unwilling experience of pregnancy and the onslaught of feminine gendered expectations it entails can induce acute gender dysphoria among trans-masculine individuals.

Titane's dizzying climax arrives as a frightened Alexia, undergoing excruciating labor, crawls into the bed of sleeping Vincent and kisses him. Having already discovered and accepted their true sex prior to this event, he is more so enraged by their transgression of the father-son relationship he has so obsessively built. Before he can reject them entirely, Alexia cries out, and Vincent jumps to action, encouraging and aiding in the child's delivery. The offspring of human and machine, the infant cyborg is born with visible titanium embedded in its temples and spinal cord. This scene is the final culmination of Ducournau's conceptual vision, as she stated:

> the idea was to [portray the creation of] a new humanity that is strong because it [is] monstrous — and not the other way around. Monstrosity, for me, is always positive. It's about debunking all the normative ways of society and social life. (Kohn 2021)

Though *Titane* does not portray a literal depiction of a transgender protagonist undergoing transition, it does operate from a consciously queer world view to probe notions of embodiment, gender performance, and the construction of individual and social identities. With its frequent invocation of acts significant to the trans-masculine experience, it contains ample material to enact a strategy of transgender disidentification. As an artist concerned with cinematic figures, Ducournau employs the cyborg precisely because of its ability to transcend gender by disturbing reified binaries and revealing their arbitrary construction. Echoing the artist's abiding interest in mutation and metamorphosis, *Titane* succeeds as an act of transgender disidentification by identifying its protagonist with the oppressive script of monstrous gender and sexual deviancy ascribed to trans subjects with an unabashed fervor. Instead of merely rejecting the ascribed script in favor of a sympathetic rehabilitation of the deviant "monster," Titane corrupts expectations, championing transgression as a force of emancipatory transformation.

Reclaiming Monstrosity in the Virtual Realm

Shrine Maidens of the Unseelie Court is a 2018 immersive virtual reality environment created by American multi-media artist Tabitha Nikolai (b. 1984). Inspired by her lived experience as a transgender woman, the work of art relates feelings of isolation and the simultaneous affirmation and toxicity to be found in alternative communities formed online. The work of art functions as a single-player PC game, which viewers may interact with using only a mouse and keyboard, and whose graphics are rendered in a low fidelity style akin to the 3D Flash games of the late two-thousands. Though upon first glance, it may appear as a standard video game, viewers soon discover an experience that does not include the usual conventions of that medium. There are no objectives, enemies, or puzzles to solve, instead, users explore and interact with a remote and surreal post-cataclysmic environment.

Players first spawn at the edge of a clearing within a dense misty forest, its sole paved road in or out being obstructed by invasive blackberry brambles. Gargantuan tarantulas infest the clearing, skittering across the ground over upturned abandoned police vehicles and crawling in the cobweb-filled tree canopy overhead. Shelter appears in the form of a single-story house, however, as the user approaches, it appears every bit as menacing as the forest. All of the structure's doors are flung open, seemingly unoccupied if not for the bathroom from which a neon green glow emanates. Users may explore eerily sterile or derelict interior rooms of the house, each of which instills a foreboding sense of mystery. The artist modeled the house and its rooms from memories of her upbringing in stiflingly conservative Salt Lake City, Utah, especially the typical Mormon homes whose pristine exteriors conceal mundane middle-class clutter.

Figure 10.1. Tabitha Nikolai's immersive virtual reality environment, *Shrine Maidens of the Unseelie Court.*

Upon finally entering the brightly lit bathroom, users discover a freshly drawn bath filled with a strange black liquid. Climbing the wooden ladder within the bath seamlessly transports the player to an underground grotto, wherein an enormous waterfall conspicuously resembling a vulva pours into a crystalline pool. Nikolai conceived of the work of art as containing two worlds: the exterior, symbolizing the hostile, physical world; and the interior, representing the psychological or intangible world (Nikolai 2022). This break from material reality is signified by the ladder, which irrationally ascends to then descend. The artist refers to the grotto as a "sanctuary," protected from the dangers posed to trans or gender-nonconforming individuals by cis-heteronormative society (ibid).

Figure 10.2.   **Figure 10.3.**
Tabitha Nikolai's strange black liquid   Tabitha Nikolai's a crystalline pool

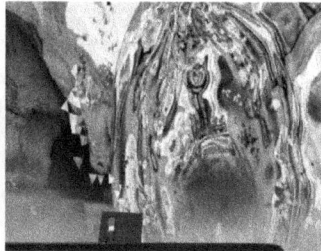

Within the sanctuary, a lone free-standing room sits atop a jutting rock formation. From this point onward, the environment becomes further entwined with the personal history of the artist. Recalled from memories, the room's interior resembles a shabby adolescent bedroom: stained mattress, junk snacks, and haphazardly placed posters. Though innocuous at first, the content of the posters reveals the artist's own interest in the genres of science fiction and fantasy, video games, electronic music, and biomorphic machines, the likes of H.R. Geiger.[6] Each of these intrigued the artist because they contained elements of transformation that resonated with ineffable desires she would not come to realize until years later. On the affinity between the transgender experience and notions of the cyborg, she said that "when your experiences are not being represented in the media that you see, you begin to identify with whatever you find which does reflect aspects of that experience, no matter how abstracted" (ibid).

In the corner of the room, a desktop computer monitor beckons the user to investigate an active chat room as a new message appears, "lol, look who's back online. I thought you kys [killed yourself]?"[7] This is the first and only encounter with another intelligent being within the environment, reinforcing its social isolation. The work of art meta-narratively references itself as users interact with a virtual computer to communicate through the chat room format of selecting from multiple predetermined questions, which will prompt different responses from the entity. When questioned as to the state of the frightening world outside the sanctuary, they reply conversely in taunts and cryptic answers. The entity, whose username is "Orp4n3_d4rlIn6" identifies itself only as a member of the Unseelie Court, a reclusive sect of transgender women forced into hiding because of violent persecution enacted against them. The in-game chat establishes the fictional over-world, in which the artist's memory and artifacts of nostalgia are grafted onto a dystopian alternative history. The persecution of the Unseelie Court is implied to be the first of many targeted eradication of groups deemed dangerous to society, a repressive ideology that leads to its eventual collapse. In its aftermath, the displaced and isolated Unseelie Court communicate and inhabit their identities as women through the internet. In this regard, the *shrine maidens* are also cyborg organisms; beings whose interaction within the world is inextricably mediated through technologies such as virtual networks, online communities, and digital avatars.

---

[6] H.R. Giger (b. 1940, dec. 2014) was a Swiss artist and designer known for his nightmarish science-fiction motifs. Giger is best known for his book Necronomicon (1977), as well as his design work for Ridley Scott's 1979 feature film "Alien." Giger's subjects were portrayed in a unique visual style of surreal hybrid organisms which seamlessly blended organic and technological elements (Artnet.)

[7] Common abbreviation of "laugh out loud" or "laughing out loud" used on the internet.

Figure 10.4. Tabitha Nikolai's Response from Entity

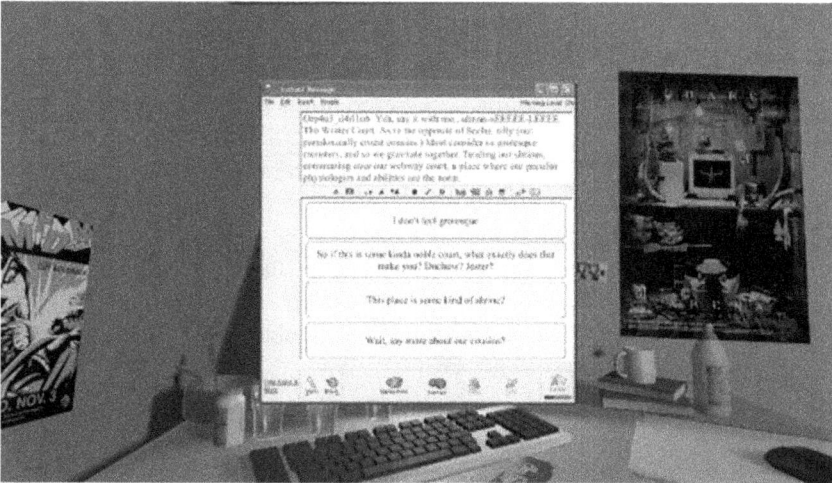

To the generations born of the Internet Age, virtual gestures can constitute social reality to the same extent as natural gestures, further dissolving the barrier between organic and synthetic.[8] Nikolai's adolescent experiences online gave her access to information and communities she otherwise never may have encountered. Online, she was exposed to ideas outside of the dominant ideology regarding gender and identity, remarking that "[on the internet] you can be anything you want, there is space [and community] for anything" (ibid).

In online forums dedicated to the transgender experience, the young artist was able to achieve some modicum of community and solidarity, affirming her gender identity during a time when she was otherwise unable to do so openly. Despite these positive attributes, Nikolai became wary of these spaces because of their potential to induce emotional harm. While the deregulation and anonymity of online forums such as 4chan were the very reason why socially marginalized individuals choose to congregate there, it also allowed for unchecked toxicity within the community. The artist created *Shrine Maidens of the Unseelie Court* in part to address this complex dynamic, saying that:

> eventually I became aware that many of the people who populated these
> spaces were themselves deeply traumatized from the experiences of

---

[8] The time period, (1984 - present) since the modern Internet was created and became widely available to the public for general use, which resulted in fundamental changes to the nature of global communication and access to information.

transphobia, oppression, and violence; compounded by other conditions of marginalization. (ibid)

The character Orp4n3_d4rlIn6 is a manifestation of this toxicity, who, suffering under transphobic persecution, disallowed from counter-identifying with supposedly "real womanhood," revels in the vilification forcibly imposed onto trans subjects and evokes what Susan Stryker conceives as "transgender rage:"

> Like the monster, I am too often perceived as less than fully human due to the means of my embodiment; like the monster's as well, my exclusion from human community fuels a deep and abiding rage in me that I, like the monster, direct against the conditions in which I must struggle to exist. (Stryker 1994, 283)

In *Disidentifications: Queers of Color and the Performance of Politics*, Muñoz warns that while the total alignment by marginalized subjects within oppressive discourses threatens to reaffirm them, so too does its binary opposition in the form of counter-identification. By instead occupying a position both within and against oppressive discourse, a tactical misrecognition of the social scripts ascribed to minority subjects contains the potential to subvert and reinscribe their meaning to that which is devoid of harm (Muñoz 1999, 83). Stryker echoes this sentiment, applying the strategy of disidentification to the political situation of transgender subjects, saying,

> I am a transsexual, and therefore I am a monster. Just as the words "dyke," "fag," "queer," "slut," and "whore" have been reclaimed, respectively, by lesbian and gay men, by anti-assimilationist sexual minorities, by women who pursue erotic pleasure, and by sex industry workers, words like "creature," "monster," and "unnatural" need to be reclaimed by the transgendered. By embracing and accepting them, even piling one on top of another, we may dispel their ability to harm us." (ibid, 240)

In conversation with the artist, Nikolai cites Stryker as a significant influence on her mode of thinking and artistic practice (Nikolai 2022). *Shrine Maidens of the Unseelie Court* is the crystallization of a moment at the intersection of lived experience, personal identity, and political act. As relayed through its fictionalized world, the work of art probes the effect of virtual spaces on social reality and its potential utility to marginalized subjects as a tool of resistance. Nikolai co-opts a discourse of monstrosity through the metaphor of cybernetics to occupy space within the dominant culture and thereby normalize gender deviance or aberration.

Cyborg subjects/Engineering gender

Released in 2020, *Nonbinary* is a short film and music video by Venezuelan interdisciplinary musician, producer, and performance artist Alejandra Ghersi (b. 1989), professionally known as Arca, to accompany the eponymous song off of her fourth album, *KiCki*. Created in collaboration with Belgian multimedia artist Frederik Heyman (b.1984), the video is composed of real footage overlaid with photorealistic sequences of animated photogrammetry; a process by which sophisticated three-dimensional digital models can be created from still photographs or videos and then manipulated (Powell 2018). *Nonbinary* and its accompanying album was Arca's first major release after beginning her trans-feminine gender transition in 2018, coming out as a nonbinary trans woman that same year.[9] Explaining to fans about her decision to transition, she said that she found herself returning to the same question over and over:

> What kind of body do I want to leave behind? …Tides come and go, but our body is the only thing I consider to be one's own — the most intimate canvas one can modify to express some criteria of beauty or some faith or some hope. (Moen 2020)

Given this context, Nonbinary as a comprehensive work of art incorporating sound, lyrics, and visuals, proffers a manifesto on being gender nonbinary as both an identity and philosophy of embodiment.

In the film, Arca occupies surreal set pieces that steam and glisten, augmenting organic elements with prosthetics, valves, wires, and machinery. The invocation of a post-human aesthetic is a frequent motif of the artist's oeuvre, saying that "working with these themes of body and technology is something that I've been drawn to aesthetically since as long as I can remember" (Herrera 2021). Arca's fascination with cybernetics was inspired first by her love of anime, high

---

[9] Trans-Feminine refers to individuals assigned male at birth who identify with and present as conventionally feminine. This term may encompass transgender women, gender-fluid, and non-binary individuals; an adjective describing a person who does not identify exclusively as a man or a woman. A non-binary person may identify as being both a man and a woman, somewhere in between, or as falling completely outside these categories. While many non-binary people also identify as transgender, not all do. Non-binary can also be used as an umbrella term encompassing identities such as agender, bigender, genderqueer or gender-fluid (Human Rights Campaign).

fantasy video games, and the science fiction novels of Ursula K. Le Guin, and would eventually introduce her to the genre of electronic music.[10]

Sonically, the two-minute English-language track features a cadenced vocal monologue layered atop hard-hitting percussion, electronic beats, and discordant metallic tones, culminating in a climax of dramatic, echoing melodies. Arca's monologue addresses the listener directly, recounting both her good fortune to be able to share her art but also the difficulties she's faced as a diasporic Venezuelan and transgender woman.

> Ask me how I got here
> Bitch, I worked hard
> Ask me about my luck
> Yeah, I've been lucky
> And I've been unlucky
> It's both
> Don't put your shit on me
> Bitch, I'm special,
> you can't tell me otherwise
> That'd be a lie

She then implores the listener to "speak for your self-states," a mantra which reflects the artist's belief in being nonbinary, in that it recognizes the presence of "…multifaceted, distinct elements of an individual while simultaneously representing a single unit or whole" (ibid).

This philosophy echoes that of posthuman feminist scholar Donna Haraway in 1991's *A Cyborg Manifesto*. In the essay, Haraway describes the cyborg as both "a creature of social reality as well as a creature of fiction" and purports that the cyborg figure is of great importance to contemporary society and even has the ability to alter our lived experience by modeling the transformation induced by our inextricable relationship with technology (Haraway 1991, 149). Haraway applies this concept to the political situation of women, proposing that by embracing hybrid identities and coming to terms with our cyborg-ness, there exists the potential to dismantle the coercive social forces of gender regulation and control.

---

[10] Ursula K. Le Guin (b. 1929, dec. 2018) was a prolific American author of speculative fiction novels, short stories, essays, and poetry. Her works were known for her treatment of gender (*The Left Hand of Darkness*, *The Matter of Seggri*), political systems (*The Telling*, *The Dispossessed*) and explorations of difference/otherness in any other form as informed by the field of anthropology, philosophy, and cultural studies.

The film's opening sequence depicts the artist lying atop a smoldering rock pierced by enormous metal shears, evoking both the operating table and surgical incision. Unobscured by garments, her cyborg-ness is made evident by both fictional exoskeletal implants and the presence of male and female sex characteristics as induced by hormone replacement therapy. Despite the fact that the transgender body has long endured lurid fixation by the cisgender gaze, which demands intimate knowledge of said individuals' genitalia, any such depiction of authentic trans bodies remains taboo. As a necessity of survival and social acceptance, transgender subjects are expected to conceal any feature that does not align with the correct performance of their gender identity. In effect, in order to be recognized as legitimate and not gender impostors, these subjects are required to erase any indication of their transgender identity. This tactic is referred to as passing, as in "passing for cisgender." While passing is and can be an important method of evading violence, a milestone in one's gender transition, and highly beneficial to emotional well-being, it is also coercively enforced by cisheteronormative society. Arca addresses this dynamic, saying:

> there is a particular kind of skepticism or cynicism in the face of the modified body, as if there was a shame to the transformation of the body. (Americo, 2021)

Arca resists these assimilationist pressures by laying bare the condition of her unabashedly trans embodiment and embracing a state of flux between binary conceptions of gender.

The sequence also inspires association with the Western art historical canon, especially portrayals of the mythical Hermaphroditus, whom Ovid's *Metamorphoses* identifies as the intersex offspring of the ancient Roman deities Venus and Mercury (Ovid 1893, 133). The lesser-known Italian marble *Sleeping Venus/Hermaphrodite* (ca. first-second century AD) depicts a nude Hermaphroditus reclining on a rock covered by loose drapery, similar to Arca's pose in *Nonbinary*.[11]

This interpretation is supported by another possible allusion to Hermaphroditus, that being a later sequence that recreates Sandro Botticelli's

---

[11] While the present-day sculpture appears as a conventional Venus, it originally depicted a hermaphroditic figure whose male genitalia, in addition to two suckling infants, were removed during restoration by eighteenth-century British collector of antiquities Henry Blundell. The sculpture's title was changed by Blundell to reflect the alterations until sketches of its original state were recovered in the Townley Collection of the British Museum (Howard, 1968.)

iconic 1485 painting, *Birth of Venus*. As reimagined by Ghersi and Heyman, Arca assumes the role of the newly-born goddess of love and beauty as she emerges from the sea. Even as Arca aligns herself with divinity, she never forsakes monstrosity as symbolized by the cyborg. The enormous sea scallop, which serves as the vehicle for her arrival, has been augmented by articulated robot arms and electrode implants, signifying the condition of her birth made possible by technological intervention such as HRT or cosmetic surgery. The blossoms that spring forth from her limbs suggest notions of transformation and the elation of gender euphoria as embodiment finally aligns with mind and soul (Moen 2020).

The conceptual throughline of corporeal and spiritual transformation is elaborated further in the following sequence, which portrays a heavily pregnant Arca within a futuristic delivery room. She reclines on a luxurious birthing bed, her distended stilt prosthetics supported by stirrups. Attending to her needs are three cyborg midwives. Appearing more machine than human, their bodies are constructed of robotic armatures that support and encase biological organs, including intestines and the brain. A translucent membrane or synthetic "skin" covers their torsos, complete with humanoid breasts reminiscent of silicone implants; yet another technological augmentation at times used to enhance the bodily performance of gender identity.

While they may appear passive at first, the midwives are active agents and vital to understanding the significance of the impending birth. The cyborg at Arca's head waves two futuristic candelabras in tandem as those on either side carry flares, performing a cleansing ritual commonly practiced throughout Latin America that combines indigenous Venezuelan and colonial Catholic beliefs. This ritual does not merely dispel negative energy, it transmutes it into that which is positive.

Understanding this ritual is vital to appraising its utility to a philosophy of transgender embodiment. Arca is not implying that purification begets transformation, instead, she is proposing far more radically that transmutation of elements equal parts monstrous and divine is what will induce posthuman evolution beyond binary limitations.

By evoking the cyborg as a metaphor for the experience of transgender embodiment, Arca lays claims to the discourse of monstrosity that has been leveled against her by cisheteronormative ideology. The artist enacts a strategy of transgender disidentification by identifying herself within the oppressive discourse, so that she may subvert and neutralize its meaning. Reinscribing the cyborg figure from dehumanizing corruption of natural order to an emancipatory expression of transmuting gender as we know it. As the artist states, "that's where a nonbinary mode of thinking feels really fertile. It opens possibilities rather than collapsing things. Allowing for change without resisting it" (ibid).

Conclusion

The cyborg figure, as popularized in the visual culture of the twentieth century, has undergone a radical political operation. Once a modern bogeyman deployed by the dominant culture to dehumanize subjects, which threatened to destabilize the cisheteronormative social order; the cyborg figure has been co-opted and reclaimed by the very same marginalized subjects it has been weaponized against. Utilizing a strategy of disidentification, artists including Julia Ducournau, Tabitha Nikolai, and Arca invoke notions of the cyborg to engage the oppressive discourse of monstrosity, which has been historically ascribed to demonize trans and gender non-conforming subjects. These works probe questions of embodiment, identity, and community within the contemporary technologically integrated era and propose speculative visions of its transformative effect on the relationship between humans, machines, and the gendered body. By doing so, they neutralize the oppressive rhetoric of the cyborg figure and reinscribe its meaning as an emancipatory expression of gender/euphoria, which transcends binary regulation and control.

Bibliography

American Civil Liberties Union. 2022. "Legislation Affecting LGBTQ Rights across the Country." Accessed April 8, 2022. https://www.aclu.org/legislation-affecting-lgbtq-rights-across-country.

Americo, Lara. 2021. "In Her Battle for Self, Arca Reaches Euphoria on 'Kick Iiiii'." Remezcla, December 6, 2021. https://remezcla.com/features/music/arca-reaches-euphoria-kick-iiiii-album-review/.

Benesch, Klaus. 1999. "Technology, Art, and the Cybernetic Body: The Cyborg as Cultural Other in Fritz Lang's 'Metropolis' and Phillip K. Dick's 'Do Androids Dream of Electric Sheep?'" Amerikastudien / American Studies 44, no. 3 (Body / Art): 379–392.

Bunbury, Stephanie. 2021."Her Movie Makes People Faint but Julia Ducournau Says 'Monstrosity Is Always Positive.'" The Sydney Morning Herald, November 25, 2021.www.smh.com.au/culture/movies/her-movie-makes-pe ople-faint-b ut-julia-ducournau-says-monstrosity-is-always-positive-20211122-p59ayl.html.

Butler, Judith P. 1988. "Performative Acts and Gender Constitution: An Essay in Phenomenology and Feminist Theory." Theatre Journal 40, no. 4 (December): 519–531.

Haraway, Donna J. 1991. "A Cyborg Manifesto: Science, Technology, and Socialist Feminism in the Late Twentieth Century." In Simians, Cyborgs, and Women: The Reinvention of Nature, 149-181. New York: Routledge.

Herrera, Isabelia. 2021. "Arca Once Made Electronic Music. Now She Builds Worlds." New York Times, December 5, 2021. https://www.nytimes.com/2021/12/03/arts/music/arca-kick.html. Accessed 11 Feb. 2022.

Howard, S. 1968. "Henry Blundell's Sleeping Venus." Art Quarterly 31: 405-420.

Human Rights Campaign. n.d. "An Epidemic of Violence: Fatal Violence Against Transgender and Gender Non-Confirming People in the United States in 2021." https://reports.hrc.org/an-epidemic-of-violence-fatal-violence-against-trans gender-and-gender-non-confirming-people-in-the-united-states -in-2021.

Jarrett, Brooke A., et al. 2018. "Chest Binding and Care Seeking among Transmasculine Adults: A Cross-Sectional Study." Transgender Health 3, no. 1: 170–178.

Kohn, Eric. 2021. "Palme D'or Winner Julia Ducournau on Groundbreaking 'Titane': 'I Don't Want My Gender to Define Me.'" IndieWire, July 17, 2021. www.indiewire.com/2021/07/julia-ducournau-interview-palme-dor-titane-1234652010/.

Moen, Matt. 2020. "Arca: Embracing the Flux." PAPER, April 7, 2020. https://www.papermag.com/arca-transformation.

Muñoz, José Esteban. 1999. Disidentifications: Queers of Color and the Performance of Politics. Minneapolis: University of Minnesota Press.

Nolfi, Joey. 2021. "'Titane' Director Reveals How She Made a 'Monstrous,' Metal Car Baby via Car Sex." Entertainment Weekly, October 7, 2021. ew.com/mo vies/julia-ducournau-titane-car-baby-pregnancy/.

Nikolai, Tabitha. 2022. Interview by Sheridyn Villarreal, March 16, 2022.

Ovid. 1893. "Salmacis and Hermaphroditus." In Metamorphoses, translated by Henry T. Riley, 133-136. London: George Bell & Sons.

Powell, Grace. 2018. "In Conversation with Frederik Heyman: Visualising a Better Future." Dust Magazine. Accessed February 11, 2022. https://www. glamcult.com/articles/in-conversation-with-frederik-heyman/.

Scott, A. O. 2021. "'Titane' Review: Auto Erotic." New York Times, September 30, 2021. https://www.nytimes.com/2021/09/30/movies/titane-review.html.

Stryker, Susan. 1994. "My Words to Victor Frankenstein Above the Village of Chamonix: Performing Transgender Rage." GLQ: A Journal of Lesbian and Gay Studies 1, no. 3: 237–254.

Unger, Cécile A. 2016. "Hormone therapy for transgender patients." Translational Andrology and Urology 5, (6): 877-884. doi:10.21037/tau.2016. 09.04.

Chapter 11

Boulet Brothers' Drag Supermonster:
Goth, Macabre, and Queer Excellence

Charlito O. Codizar

Sacred Heart School Ateneo de Cebu, Philippines

Abstract: Drag, as a revolutionary art form, continues to unnerve and fascinate people through its display of heightened reality under the lens of the sensational and the grotesque. Despite efforts of mainstream media representation over the years, a subculture within this subculture remains. Unlike the much-accepted pin-up glamorous drag, horror drag leaves much to be desired. The interplay of terror and beauty creates an ambivalent revulsion that elevates an "otherness" invoking a response that vacillates between abhorrence and allure to suspend real-life sensibilities. This paper resituates the identity of a Drag Supermonster as a form of an afterlife through the lens of goth aesthetic juxtaposed with performative demonstrations of macabre art resulting to queer excellence. Taking these multi-faceted aspects as discussion points, the perspective of a Boulet Brothers' Dragula content consumer is looked into with reference to the show's re-definition and re-construction of fear as observed from the creation and curation of a monster that ultimately provokes one to surrender into the ultimate fright fantasy incarnate.

Keywords: *Boulet Brothers' Dragula*, Horror Drag, Drag Culture, Media Representation, Identity, Subculture, Otherness, Afterlife

Drag as a Revolutionary Art Form

In a song released in 2014, RuPaul Charles famously sings the line "we're all born naked and the rest is drag" which is popularly taken to mean that the clothes one wears ultimately bring up ideas of identity and individuality. True to its meaning, drag is a gender-bending art form as instituted by men, women, transgender, genderqueer, and cisgender people (Tombs 2018) that provides varying levels of gender renditions to both the artist and audience (Rupp et al. 2010).

Hearkening back to history, playing gender roles that do not adhere to communal standards dates as far as the ancient Grecian rituals to Shakespearean theater (Garcia 2018). From then, drag has evolved into a cultural force that evokes hyper-realistic sensibilities to challenge gender-specific perspectives (Clendenen 2020). Its transcendental nature continues to push boundaries as drag artists use themselves as a canvas to produce a Warholian pop art mirage through makeup, wigs, and fashion side by side with the performative aspects of theater and music, which more often than not result in avant-garde productions.

Despite the more beloved entertainment aspect of drag, the act in itself is a form of revolution as it gives social and political commentaries on issues of the day. After all, it is once considered a "crime" for one gender to dress like the other (Arias 2020). Drag becomes a compelling and formidable symbol for queer activism that pushes to continue fighting for LGBTQIA+ rights and visibility. As such, drag artists have always been front and center in movements against discriminatory heteronormative societal norms. They play a pivotal role in bringing the limited rights of those who are considered marginalized into the consciousness of the greater community (Ozeel 2021).

Drag, at its very core, is entertaining, but through its bout of entertainment productions that display heightened realities of the sensational and the grotesque, comes the underlying message that continues to challenge oppressions at any level of society pertaining to the polarizing spectra of gender, identity, and sexuality.

The Repercussion of "Drag Race" Fame

Recent years have seen a meteoric rise in drag popularity. Its stronghold on mainstream media opens an invitation to everyone at a cross-dressing fete (Williams 2022). Although this prominence comes with a multitude of issues, especially on representation and diversity, its impact, as shown in how it booms in cities across the world, is a measurable criterion of how far the art form has come. Perhaps, one of the prominent instigators of this movement is the *Rupaul's Drag Race* franchise. As of the time of writing, it already has 14 seasons, 5 spin-offs, and 14 international versions. This series is a game-changer for queer television (Diaz 2021).

While the franchise has ultimately become an institution that has open doors leading to countless opportunities of conspicuousness, it should not be treated as the be-all and end-all of drag (Hoeffner 2022). Its mainstream success brings with it an uncomfortable adverse effect wherein one part of a multi-faceted art form is taken to represent the whole (Wallace 2019). Ever since its inception, the show pushes the more palatable pin-up, glamorous aesthetic. The pageantry and allure of perfectly symmetrical bodies in haute couture are given more gravity and significance. This threatens to discount the contribution of the other less-known and less beloved styles of drag.

This phenomenon has caused a descriptive imbalance in the art form, especially in that contemporary perspectives easily point to the stunning cover girl persona as the visual of how drag is supposed to be when it's not. In effect, this resulted in the creation of a subculture within a subculture.

The Subculture of Horror Drag

Horror drag, from the name itself, is a merger between the peculiarities of the horror genre and the intricacies of drag as an art form. It provides a venue where the vulgar and edgy facets of queer culture meet the decadence and excellence of traditional drag (Watson 2019). The intermingling between drag and horror is not new. What most people fail to consider is the truth that drag has always had a connection to the horror genre (Varrati 2020). One can argue that what makes horror characters so compelling and effective is their element of drag that goes beyond just costume presentation. It is the embodiment of a persona that presents a temptation that transcends what is perceived to be haunting yet enchanting all at the same time.

Horror drag takes inspiration from the horror genre in alluding to terrifying situations and destructive chaos to create hyper-realistic tendencies. These tendencies, added with drag glamor, can create a reciprocity between terror and beauty. This ultimately elevates an "otherness" that creates an all-powerful ambivalent revulsion that can ultimately become a vessel for a fantasy so creepily overwhelming it can send a message across ten times over. It is for this very reason that horror drag elicits reactions and responses from audiences across different stages.

The complete look for horror drag often references hideous and monstrous creatures abreast with terrorizing and intimidating propensities (O'Bergh 2022). These horror drag characters are never one-dimensional. They go beyond mere aesthetics and performances such that they become capable of creating an "afterlife" in which they very much exist as their own entities. Even with this promising premise, the art form is not given due recognition because of its deviant and atypical approach. It is often sidestepped and relegated to the sidelines, only to be admired come Halloween.

Boulet Brother's Dragula

What started as an underground "horror punk rock drag party" has evolved into a reality competition for mainstream TV. *Boulet Brothers' Dragula* carves the proverbial path for drag artists whose craft dwells in the altar of filth, leather, and piercings, among many others, that would result in a spooky eleganza cleverly juxtaposed with blood-doused or sludge-covered performances (Goodman 2019). It opened up opportunities for those whose drag is never included in what is considered to be the commonly accepted standard. Diverse drag representation has been at the forefront of the show as it boasts drag artists from an inclusive gender identification – queer men, trans people, lesbians, and non-binary people (Damshenas 2021).

Swanthula and Dracmorda Boulet envision the show to become the home of "alternative drag" (Summan 2022). Over the years, it has turned into a pool of talent and creativity full to the brim, with drag artists demonstrating their expertise in special effects makeup and their unprecedented aptitude for intricate costume construction. There is no room for conventional beauty as their clothing is purposely ripped, their makeup artistically smudged, and facial or bodily hairs are triumphantly embellished. *Boulet Brothers' Dragula* provides another layer of seeing how homonormative "realness" is situated when the "monstrous" queer becomes visible (Prins 2021).

Drag has always been radical, so it refuses to be placed in a box. Through *Boulet Brothers' Dragula*, with four seasons under its belt, the art form continues to refuse to be dumbed down, whitewashed, and beautified for straight audiences (Lusky 2020). It champions drag artists who can counter queer complacency. Loud and unashamed queer visibility should be held in the highest regard (Leavell 2018). Monsters in every shape or form, as inspired by dark fantasies, cult films, and iconic villains with a tinge of glamor and peril, are already out of the closet (Holden 2020). Let them come into the light as they sashay in their celebrated runways.

Drag Supermonster

Boulet Brothers' Dragula understands that the "otherness" brought about by the horror genre, as supplemented by unapologetic queerness that is no longer implicit, can be quite threatening to people who do not understand the art form. For this reason, the show is not just formatted to give a reality TV, documentary-like presentation of events. There are heavily scripted parts in each episode to weave a strong narrative akin to celebrated horror films. The ultimate goal is for the audience, whether for or against the art form, to be on the edge of their seats with anxiety all the time (Bramesco 2021).

The format of the show is established to produce content that can shock and engage people. It promises to give a wild, fun, terrifying ride (Sim 2022). Each episode starts with an orchestrated scene that cleverly integrates the Boulet Brothers's explanation of the theme and challenge for the week. The competitors will work on the challenge with or against each other, depending on the parameters given. They are tested on their ability to astound and disturb the judges (Emory 2017). The challenge will culminate with a "Floor Show" where the competitors present their finished look and performance on the main stage. The competitor who scored the highest is chosen as the winner, while two competitors who scored the lowest are going to face an "Extermination Challenge." These challenges are fear-based physical and psychological tests. They can range from being buried alive in a coffin, pierced with gauged needles, skydiving, eating intestines, to spending a night at an extremely haunted house (Villareal 2019).

To be called the ultimate winner is no easy feat. One must showcase world-class horror drag while surviving contrived horror situations designed to test limits. For this reason, the winner of the competition must constantly push the envelope in order to harness the strength of crossing boundaries, elevating peculiarities, and celebrating authenticity. With this, the title Drag Supermonster is bestowed on the chosen one.

Method and Methodology

To extensively discuss *Boulet Brothers' Dragula* and put things in an academic mindset, the "aca-fan" (academic fan) analysis perspective is utilized. This is a familiar designation for scholars who are also fans of the community they are studying. The rationalized position of an aca-fan provides an operative framework for research that facilitates the integration of knowledge between the fandom and the academe (Cristofari and Guitton 2016). Inside information, along with passion and fondness, can provide much data for analysis as there are many things that one could not fully comprehend from the outside looking in. The treatment of subcultural intelligence as part of what makes a scholarly work cognizant and accomplished is the main goal of the aca-fan perspective (Jenkins 2011).

This reality in media and cultural studies provides a movement that needs careful attention especially in methodological responsibilities (Hermes and Kardolus 2022). These are the parameters that need underlining to fully grasp the scope and limitations of the study: (1) there may be a cultural disconnect in the inquiry since the researcher is an Asian fan of a Western reality TV show; (2) the researcher has no extensive knowledge and first-hand experience in drag politics with their multi-ethnic, multi-gendered affairs outside the realm of the show; and (3) the researcher is working on his own viewer experiences that are interspersed and influenced by the conversations and comments read on the internet.

With this range of introspection, autoethnography is used as a research approach. The structure of the study opens the notion that the researcher is front and center of the sense-making process while being mindful of the different risks this method may signify (Arnold 2020). Further, the researcher invokes his own experiences and initiates an analysis that would draw out any type of references and ramifications, whether cultural or personal. In effect, he will be able to present findings and narratives that cannot be captured through more traditional methods.

This study will resituate the identity of a Drag Supermonster in reference to the *Boulet Brothers' Dragula's* re-definition and re-construction of fear. The researcher, as a content consumer, looks into the performative demonstrations of the following winners: Vander Von Odd (Season 1), Biqtch Puddin' (Season 2), Landon Cider (Season 3), and Dahli (Season 4). Their runway presentations, challenge accomplishments, and overall performances are explored through these discussion points: (1) goth, (2) macabre, and (3) queer excellence. The scrutiny will showcase how these drag artists create and curate a monster that has the ability to provoke one to surrender into the ultimate fright fantasy incarnate.

Through the aca-fan logic and autoethnographic research method, definitive narratives on how these Drag Supermonsters strive to become one of the rightful representatives of the complex art form is put to light. This is in accordance with keeping inclusivity and visibility of those who are part of the drag community.

Ultimately, this paper reinforces the idea that horror drag can stand side-by-side with pageant drag in the panoramic view of the art form. With its complex inventiveness and compelling effect, it deserves to be represented properly and not downgraded to just becoming one of the alternatives.

Indulgence of Goth

By its very definition, goth as a movement is the appreciation of all things considered by many as ominous, sinister, apocalyptic, and mystical. Its association with things that are deemed negative gives the biased impression that it is notoriously evil (Hodkinson 2002). To put things in perspective, the movement places much emphasis on the dark to remind humanity that even though the light is held in a much higher regard, the two will always co-exist. They are all part of life. Denying one is denying an entire half of life. The goth philosophy is centered on the idea of embracing life holistically. Honor the good and the bad, the happy and the sad, the beautiful and the ugly, in consonance with the light and the dark (Saccomanno 2019).

Historically, this design movement is considered as a rebellion against classical elegance. In fact, the word itself is derogatory as it is used to describe barbaric, unrefined, and impure art (S.U 2022). Because of this, it garnered undue criticisms from classists due to the way it changed the standards of refined style. In the same spectrum, the goth aesthetic is marked by the post-punk music scene and the love for anything occult-related (Fischer 2019). It has distinctively dark, cryptic, antiquated, over-the-top, garish, even borderline blasphemous, bedeviled features.

Goth, translated to fashion, is structured around two looks: ethereal and flowy (velvet, silks, chiffon, and lace) or bound and restrained (vests, corsets, and chokers). Typical makeup consists of smoky eyes, dark lips, and teased hair. The overall look is inspired and cataloged as a punk version of the Romantic, Victorian, Edwardian, and even Elizabethan ensemble demonstrations. Over the years, goth fashion has sprouted various substyles, however, all of them connect to the very elements that shaped the crusade (Zander 2022).

Goth's movement, philosophy, ominous aesthetic, and rebel roots provide a holistic and necessary push for horror drag to thrive. It offers a bedrock to which the foundation of the art form begins to take shape and grow. The thought process behind a structured look and the persona it connotes stem from the indulgence of the dark, mysterious, even suspenseful decadence of goth.

Looking into the 4 Drag Supermonsters of *Boulet Brothers' Dragula*, goth is omnipresent both in their didactic and tangible standpoints. Here is a rundown of their remarkable drag:

Vander Von Odd, all throughout season 1, is consistent with her well-curated and aesthetically pleasing, albeit shocking, drag presentations. However, it is her genuine character and tenacious spirit that shine through in her journey as a competitor in the reality show. Goth is often referenced in the way she styles her looks for the runway. Most notable are the following: 1.) Wickedest Witch Look [S1 E1]; 2.) Zombies in Death Valley Look [S1 E3]; and 3.) Horror/Finale Look [S1 E6].

Her looks are inspired by medieval and Elizabethan influences. Ruffles are prominent fixtures in her dresses paired with puff long sleeves with fabrics in varying silks and laces. She also favors heavy and theatrical special effects makeup to complete the look. Through all these, she is able to present an "elevated" monster that is quite horrifying but not completely hideous. A touch of glamor is skillfully added to make it more drag. With this, Vander Von Odd continues to shock and mesmerize audiences with her showcases of monstrosity as reflected through her refined artistic lens.

Biqtch Puddin' did not start well in season 2. She often finds herself at the bottom in the first few episodes. At the beginning of her journey in the competition, her competitors did not see her as someone worthy to compete with. However, she persisted, and as the season progressed, so did she. Her powerhouse performances have given her a sure win. Although goth is very much present in her looks, she often integrates it with filth and grime references to create an outrageous storyline. Most notable are the following: 1.) Rock and Metal Look [S2 E3]; 2.) Gothic Brides Look [S2 E6]; and 3.) Horror Look [S2 E10].

Her looks are in consonance with the restrained and sharp characteristics of the goth aesthetic. She is seen wearing paneled corsets, shapely dresses in silks and laces with leather accents, and long, billowy sleeves. Her accessories are often pointed and larger-than-life. She incorporates religious artifacts, metallic trinkets, and pearls in her costume presentation. Her makeup is done in dark tones and deep colors. Her artistic take on filth and grime is often showcased through special effects manipulation on her overall appearance.

Landon Cider made history when he, a drag king, won the third season. All throughout his stint, he has proven well and good that kings can reign in the drag scene as much as queens. His track record is impeccable. Episode after episode, he has shown his exceptional make-up and costume-designing skills. His performances are always on the extreme side of the spectrum of gruesome and incredible. Goth is front and center in his polished looks. His costume presentation is always next-level. His runways have efficient storylines with appropriate references. Most notable are the following: 1.) Punk Rock and Heavy Metal Look [S3 E3]; 2.) Finale Glam Look [S3 E8]; and 3.) Crowning Look [S3 E10].

Although still keeping up with the goth aesthetic, he elevates his looks further by making them appear luxurious and classy. Rhinestones, studs, and glitters accentuate his costumes for a more opulent and ostentatious effect. He favors the body-hugging restrictive gothic cut with corsets and laces as part of the overall design. To provide movement, he incorporates the use of velvet fabrics. His accessories are mostly inspired by Victorian pieces, especially on stonework and pointed crowns.

Dahli's experience in season 2 is less than ideal. She has been perceived as lacking both in drag and personality. However, when she is brought back in season 4, she has shown audiences just how much she has grown since then. Not only has she transformed into someone who is exceptional in her drag, but she has also become an endearing figure to the other queens. Despite painting her face with special effects makeup to look monstrous, it is still very evident that goth is referenced in her costumes. Most notable are the following: 1.) Nosferatu Beach Party Look [S4 E2]; 2.) Ghostship Glamour Look [S4 E5]; and 3.) Finale Glam Look [S4 E10].

Dahli's costume presentation is influenced by formal goth. She utilizes tuxedo cuts and shapes with bowler hats and pleats to give the otherwise manly look a feminine touch. She also references Elizabethan designs, as seen in her ruffled sleeves. Different types of laces are also incorporated into the look to give a daintier effect. Over-the-top and pointed pieces of jewelry are integrated to give off a regal impression. Her looks have this unique tension of contrasting visions, but somehow, she is able to make them work and appear elevated, even polished.

The strong presence of goth exhibited in the analysis of *Boulet Brothers'* *Dragula's* Drag Supermonters' runway looks further prove its significant connection to horror drag. This is powerfully showcased in their costume presentation, narrative context, and overall performance (Jones 2019) in order to conceptualize and create a fully realized drag character. Armed with their drag interpretation of creatures of the dark, these artists become a force to be reckoned with as they elevate fear into becoming the motivation and inspiration of their inventive sensibilities.

Macabre Theatricality and Artistry

Now that the philosophy and the looks of a drag persona are taken care of, the next step is to elevate everything into a production worthy of transcending into an afterlife. This is quite tricky because this aspect should not only display horror and scandal for shock value, it must also carry a message that aims to push boundaries as well as provide intellectual support (Shelton 2022). Macabre influences are incorporated into these performances to achieve the end goal successfully.

Macabre is described as anything gruesome and morbid because of its association with details and symbols pertaining to death, injury, suffering, and violence. If anything, macabre as a movement depicted through theatrical and artistic nuances strengthens the idea of mortality (Rogers 2022). Death is an inevitable occurrence. It is a meditative reality that has the ability to unite and equalize the greater majority. Rather than something to be feared, it should become a catalyst to live life to the fullest, as everything in life is ephemeral (Bernard 2022).

Macabre elements are characterized by the use of grotesque yet artistic symbols portraying atrophy and decay. Dying transient objects are highlighted and made beautiful through creative illustrations. Torn limbs, gouged body parts, rotten fruits, worms, and vermin are presented with flowers and glitters to showcase a discomforting strain between what is considered beautiful and acceptable to what is appalling and taboo. These are seen in artworks from different artists across timeframes, from Memling, Bosch, and Caravaggio, to Rubens, Gericault, and Dali (R 2016).

Macabre, then, becomes a fertile platform for horror drag artists to play around and build a performative demonstration that teases and blurs the line between one's perceived reality and one's idea of the afterlife (Barquin 2022). It is a space that's neither here nor there, where the otherness brought about by the art form lives and breathes. Through this, fear is now re-defined and re-constructed into something one can surrender to if only to fully go through and live out the temptation of a fantasy in monstrous proportions.

Boulet Brothers' Dragula did not shy away from macabre elements, as shown in the following rundown of the 4 Drag Supermonsters' macabre-infused performances.

In *Wickedest Witch* [S1 E1], Vander Von Odd has to act out the death of the Wicked Witch of the West while donning her first-rate witch costume. In her performance, she is seen writhing on the floor as if tortured by the bucket of water thrown at her, all the while looking absolutely amazing amidst the pain that's clearly put on display. In *Zombies in Death Valley* [S1 E3], as an enticing Mexican zombie, she has to attack an unsuspecting passerby and simulate her eating away the victims' insides, complete with blood and guts as props. In the extermination challenge, she has to swallow as many pig brains as she can stomach – brain juice, saliva, and vomit notwithstanding. In the end, Vander Von Odd stands beautiful and polished amidst the grisly circumstances.

In *Cenobites* [S2 E2], Biqtch Puddin' starts strong when she struts the runway in her nude illusion drag, with half of her body peeled and torn as if subjected to acid. Despite sporting seemingly fresh wounds, she managed to look elevated and captivating. The extermination challenge for *Welcome to Wasteland* [S2 E7-8] has given a platform for the remaining queens to fight each other with reckless abandon. They are deliberately trying to torture and physically hurt each other in order to keep their places in the competition. Beauty and strength are displayed onscreen despite the utter chaotic mess shown in the Thunderdome. In the *Finale* [S2 E10], she has shown her love of the macabre when she deliberately puts on a performance when a pail of blood is used to douse her entire body as a means to announce that she has won the season. The display of gore is at its peak, and her demonstration is beyond extraordinary.

Landon Cider pushes the envelope with his drag both in the looks and performance department. In *The Operating Theater* [S3 E6], he has graced the runway with his interpretation of a mad doctor, complete with an exposed brain and sticky goo, bloodstained hands, and syringes with different liquids that he injects himself with. He portrays the interdependent connection between agony and sickness effortlessly. For *Le Freak* [S3 E7], he is seen eating shards of glasses onstage until his mouth bleeds. As the oozing blood meshes into the final look, the act becomes both unnerving and addicting to watch. In *The Grand Finale* [S3 E10], he literally dismembers someone from limb to limb and eats the insides. For the final touch, he devours the heart with much fervor and gusto. In the strictest sense, he has captured the essence of macabre in an excruciating display of questionable and, to some extent, fatal behavior. His presentations, though pre-planned, are always properly executed so that they appear effortlessly realistic and mind-blowing.

Although very much a representation of horror drag, Dahli's demonstrations are a little bereft of macabre elements. Nevertheless, the idea of death and violence are still very much referenced all throughout. In *Nosferatu Beach Party* [S4 E2], his vampire look is every inch creepy and ominous. He pays homage to gore and carnage as blood is used to elevate the look into something more sinister and malevolent. *Exorcisters* [S4 E7] has given birth to a next-level performance of dark magic and exorcism. The idea of dark creatures and evil spiritual elements that can haunt and kill is celebrated in a thrilling and rousing manner. In *Killer Clowns* [S4 E8], he portrayed the character in a way that the audience will immediately see the intent to kill and inflict harm. Despite her looking sublime, there is something perverse just waiting to be freed.

Performances with macabre elements are the language of horror drag. When executed right, these help intensify the art form into becoming a powerful tool to outrage, overwhelm, and even offend people if only to unsettle them with realities so often brushed away under normal circumstances. As properly depicted in *Boulet Brothers' Dragula*, more than the sensationalized productions, these queens/kings are making people leave what they know to be right and wrong and enter a new world where inhibitions are abandoned, fear is romanticized, temptation is surrendered, and death is exalted. Horror drag promotes drag artists who are not just there for aesthetic purposes. They have a message to share and a score to settle, perhaps connecting to parts that most people have conveniently hidden away (Soit 2023). When this is reached, the drag persona has successfully transcended into an afterlife.

Revered Queer Excellence

The goal of drag is quite simple. Dissociate with one's known identity and take on another's. Through the creation of a new persona, a transformation of character and appearance is done to completely embody a compelling fantasy (Moya 2022). It is over-the-top and larger-than-life. While it is true that anyone can do drag, this art form has a strong history with the LGBTQIA+ community, and with it comes queer excellence that is deemed worthy of respect and validation.

In their respective seasons of *Boulet Brothers' Dragula*, Drag Supermonsters Vander Von Odd, Biqtch Puddin', Landon Cider, and Dahli have become an unstoppable force of representation for underrepresented drag styles in the community. They have made waves in the scene in order to appropriately announce their presence and claim their rightful places on the proverbial drag table. The so-called subculture within the subculture is blurred as they stand for their version of beauty and glamor. It might not be conventional nor standardized, but their penchant for blood and gore sends out a message that is also authentic, compelling, and important. These drag artists have legitimized their own art and, by their rights, legendary (Jackson 2018).

All throughout their journey from the lens of reality television, they have shown audiences their brand of queer excellence as translated in their drag, conviction, and position. Here is a rundown of their drag's overall impact and significance:

Vander Von Odd outlines opposing forces in her drag. Her looks are always a juxtaposition of what is perceived to be visually enticing and simultaneously disconcerting. She revels in the clash of the beautiful and the ugly to send a universal message of inclusivity. Her drag proves that the art form is definitely not a one-size-fits-all box (Megarry 2017).

Biqtch Puddin' is too much in the best sense of the word. The way she presents her drag to the audience feels a little too staggering to take in at first, but when one gets past that overwhelming sense, one would soon begins to see the strong meaning behind the act and the vitality behind the grotesque. Live an authentic life, whatever that means, is the inspiration for her drag narratives (Shatto 2022).

Landon Cider has perfected the "glamdrogynous" artistic brief. There is no one proper direction for his drag. His approach to it has always been to find ways and means to support and uplift the queer community (Opie 2022). He taps every genre, every style, and every trope. As a drag king, he reiterates that there is no one way to be a man; there is no one way to be anyone. For this reason, versatility is what fuels his all-inclusive craft.

Dahli's prime drag motivation is to spite people who box one in. Her art form is her stand against those who are not expanding their horizons when it comes to what is perceived as normal and acceptable. Her drag has always been somewhere in between looking masculine and feminine (Earp 2021). Being a non-conformist gives her so much freedom to explore the world in its true, authentic form.

As the push for horror drag to become mainstream continues, these queens and kings celebrate the divergent yet all-embracing queer culture by becoming trailblazers of their polarizing art. While it is true that horror drag is an acquired taste, its gravity and merit are indisputable. It empowers those who are in the peripheries of mainstream society (Salazar, 2023). The aggressive and unapologetic approach by these artists further establishes their supremacy that transcends barriers and transforms mindsets.

Conclusion

The word "monster" connotes an extensive anthology of interpretation and understanding. The descriptions vary from the outright gruesome to the absolute phenomenal. However, the rationale stands that it is a proposition of something that departs from what is distinguished to be the conventional or the traditional. It is in this expansive domain that horror drag flourishes. It augments monstrosity and gives a visual spectacle highlighting what is regarded to be absurd and bizarre in a way that blurs the line that separates reality from fantasy and ordinary from extraordinary.

Because of its unorthodox approach to drag as an art form, horror drag is relegated as an alternative. It is treated as a lesser option in terms of stylistics and popularity in comparison to pageant drag. However, it continues to make its presence felt in the community by showcasing frightening fantasies that make audiences feel both disturbed and enthralled at the same time. Its performative demonstrations become a platform to arouse conversations that are difficult to be had under normal circumstances. It is disconcerting as it is political, just like how drag should always be.

With this, *Boulet Brothers' Dragula* provides a ticket for these artists to break into the mainstream as they search for the Drag Supermonster who can represent the art form to the world. The contestants in the reality show have to subject themselves to different physical and psychological challenges in order to redefine and re-construct fear. This fuels their understanding of goth and macabre, which proves useful when they create and curate the monsters that are front and center in their drag.

Vander Von Odd, Biqtch Puddin,' Landon Cider, and Dahli have established queer excellence in the way they represented the art form as means to educate people of its inception, motivation, direction, and purpose. Their presence is a revolution as it starts discourse and debates that animate the LGBTQIA+ community in its quest for a more balanced and equitable representation. As such, they have become the rightful artists to harness the power of horror drag such that it can stand side-by-side with other styles of drag and erase the notion of a subculture within a subculture.

Drag is multi-faceted and multi-dimensional. It is inclusive as it is aspirational. It provides a phenomenal reverie that pushes high-level cognizance to things of great consequence. This paper proves that horror drag has earned its right to be acknowledged alongside other styles of drag in the greater vista of the art form. It is and will always be at the core of queer culture, for when it comes to queer culture, QUEENS and MONSTERS should have equal right to be heard and honored.

Bibliography

Arias, Jacqueline. 2020. "Friendly Reminder: Drag has always been Political, #periodt." Preen.ph. Last modified February 5, 2020. https://preen.ph/105493/drag-queens-political-2020.

Arnold, Lydia. 2020. "Doing Collaborative Autoethnography." Lydia Arnold. Last modified August 6, 2020. https://lydia-arnold.com/2020/08/06/doing-collaborative-autoethnography/.

Barquin, Juan. 2022. "Bored of Drag Race? Dragula Awaits with Open, Blood-soaked Arms." AV Club. Last modified February 18, 2022. https://www.avclub.com/dragula-boulet-brothers-rupaul-drag-race-1848548559.

Bernard, Daisy. 2022. "How Art History's Most Macabre Genre Carries an Optimistic Message." Mutual Art. Last modified August 16, 2022. https://www.mutualart.com/Article/How-Art-History-s-Most-Macabre-Genre-Car/A57B018677AAF14D.

Bramesco, Charles. 2021. "The Boulet Brothers have Turned 'Dragula' into Truly 'Combustible' Tv." DECIDER. Last modified November 3, 2021. https://decider.com/2021/11/03/dragula-boulet-brothers-interview-shudder/.

Clendenen, Dustin. 2020. "How Drag become a Modern Pop Art Movement." KCET. Last modified July 23, 2020. https://www.kcet.org/shows/southland-sessions/how-drag-became-a-modern-pop-art-movement.

Cristofari, Cecile & Guitton, Matthieu. 2016. "Aca-fans and Fan Communities: An Operative Framework." *Sage.* 17 (3).

Damshenas, Sam. 2021. "The Boulet Brothers on Dragula Season 4 and How 'Queerness and Horror go Hand in Hand.'" Gay Times. Last modified October 25, 2021. https://www.gaytimes.co.uk/drag/exclusive-the-boulet-brothers-on-dragula-season-4-and-how-queerness-and-horror-go-hand-in-hand/.

Diaz, Eric. 2021. "The Continuing Impact and Legacy of Rupaul's Drag Race." Nerdist Last modified June 30, 2021. https://nerdist.com/article/rupauls-drag-race-legacy-impact-lgbtq-culture/.

Earp, Catherine. 2021. "The Boulet Brothers' Dragula Star Dahli Responds to Criticism over their Drag Style." Digital Spy. Last modified December 18, 2021. https://www.digitalspy.com/tv/reality-tv/a38549168/boulet-brothers-dragula-dahli-criticism-drag-style/.

Emory, Lukas. 2017. "Why You Need to be Watching Dragula." Odyssey. Last modified August 2017. https://www.theodysseyonline.com/dragula.

Fischer, Rachel. 2019. "The Gothic Aesthetic: from the Ancient Germanic Tribes to the Contemporary Goth Subculture." *Reference and Server Users Association.* 58 (3).

Garcia, Lucas. 2018. "Gender on Shakespeare's Stage: A Brief History." The Writers Theater. Last modified November 21, 2018. https://www.writerstheatre.org/blog/gender-shakespeares-stage-history/.

Goodman, Elyssa. 2019. "Blood, Guts, and Glamour: How Dragula Made Drag Dangerous Again." Them. Last modified August 26, 2019. https://www.them.us/story/dragula-competition-show-season-three.

Hermes, Joke & Kardolus, Michael. 2022. "The Rupaul Paradox: Freedom and Stricture in a Competition Reality Tv Show." *Javnost – The Public.* 29 (1), 82-97.

Hodkinson, Paul. 2002. Goth: Identity, Style and Subculture. Oxford: Berg Publishers. ISBN 978-1-85973-600-5.

Hoeffner, Joe. 2022. "'Rupaul's Drag Race' is a Blessing, but it shouldn't Define Drag." Collider. Last modified June 24, 2022. https://collider.com/rupauls-drag-race-blessing-but-shouldnt-define-drag/.

Holden, Steve. 2020. "Halloween: How the Boulet Brothers' Dragula Blends Drag and Horror." BBC News. Last modified October 31, 2020. https://www.bbc.com/news/newsbeat-54712624.

Jackson, Jhoni. 2018. "These 5 Performers Came Up without 'Drag Race.'" Paper. Last modified May 30, 2018. https://www.papermag.com/5-performe rs -without-drag-race-2573633520.html#rebelltitem1.

Jenkins, Henry. 2011. "Acafandom and Beyond: Week Two, Part One." Henry Jenkins. Last modified June 20, 2011. http://henryjenkins.org/ blog/2011/06/ acafandom_and_beyond_week_two.html.

Jones, Anna. 2019. "The Boulet Brothers' Queer Horror Empire." Wussy. Last modified August 27, 2019. https://www.wussymag.com/all/the-boulet-bro thers-horror-empire.

Leavell, Jeff. 2018. "'Dragula' is Loud, Weird, and Pisses on Heteronormativity." Vice. Last modified January 18, 2018. https://www.vice.com/en/article/vbyj m3/dragula-is-loud-weird-and-pisses-on-heteronormativity.

Lusky, Bridget. 2020. "Hello Uglies: The Boulet Brothers' Dragula – A Mix of Horror and Glamour." Film Daily. Last modified November 28, 2020. https:/ /filmdaily.co/news/dragulas-drag/.

Megarry, Daniel. 2017. "Vander Von Odd Believes there is Power in Sticking Out." Gay Times. Last modified 2017. https://www.gaytimes.co.uk/originals/dragul a-champion-vander-von-odd-believes-theres-power-in-sticking-out/.

Moya, Jovi. 2022. "Drag is a Powerful Art Form." Tatler. Last modified August 01, 2022. https://www.tatlerasia.com/lifestyle/entertainment/brigiding-drag-is -a-powerful-artform.

O'Bergh, Jon. 2022. "Drag Queen Horror." Divination Hollow. Last modified June 2022. https://divinationhollow.com/reviews-and-articles/drag-queen-horror.

Opie, David. 2022. "Landon Cider on Call Me Mother, Dragula, and Fighting Misogyny as a Drag King." Digital Spy. Last modified December 22, 2022. https://www.digitalspy.com/tv/reality-tv/a42308059/landon-cider-call-me-mother-dragula/

Ozeel, Alexia. 2021. "*The Politics of Drag*." Juncture. Last modified May 30, 2021. https://www.junctureuom.co.uk/post/the-politics-of-drag.

Prins, Kai. 2021. "Monsters Outside of the Closet: Reading the Queer Art of Winning in the Boulet Brothers' Dragula." *QED*, 8 (2), 43-68.

R, Maria. 2016. "Terrifying and Dark Paintings by Famous Artists." Widewalls. Last modified October 29, 2016. https://www.widewalls.ch/magazine/dark-paintings.

Rogers, Kaitlin. 2022. "A Tale of Macabre in Art History." ART. Last modified October 31, 2022. https://art.art/blog/art-history-101-a-tale-of-macabre-in-art-history.

Rupp, L. J., Taylor, V., & Shapiro, E. I. 2010. "Drag Queens and Drag Kings: The Difference Gender Makes." *Sexualities*, 13 (3), 275–294.

S.U, Zoeanna. 2022. "Art Movement: Gothic Art." Rethinking the Future. Last modified 2022. https://www.re-thinkingthefuture.com/architectural-comm unity/a6058-art-movement-gothic-art/.

Saccomanno, Sarah. 2019. "Goth: Going Beyond Black Lipstick." Medium. Last modified April 14, 2019. https://sarah-saccomanno.medium.com/goth-goi ng-beyond-the-darkness-ff27c25915a8.

Salazar, David. 2023. "How Drag Duo the Boulet Brothers are Building a Queer Horror Empire." Fast Company. Last modified May 06, 2023. https://www.fastcompany.com/90888315/boulet-brothers-drag-horror-empire.

Shatto, Rachel. 2022. "Biqtch Puddin' on the Power of Video Games, Playing with Gender, and Surviving the Bullies." Pride. Last modified September 09, 2022. https://www.pride.com/geek/2022/9/09/biqtch-puddin-video-games-playing-gender-surviving-bullies.

Shelton, Kiana. 2022. "Understanding the Joy of Drag." Mindpath Health. Last modified June 29, 2022. https://www.mindpath.com/resource/understanding-the-joy-of-drag/.

Sim, Bernardo. 2022. "Boulet Brothers and Shudder Announce Dragula Season 5, Spinoff, and More." Out Magazine. Last modified August 15, 2022. https://www.out.com/television/2022/8/15/boulet-brothers-shudder-announce-dragula-season-5-spinoff-more.

Soit, Honi. 2023. "I'm the Big, Scary Drag Queen They Warned You About." Honi Soit. Last modified May 16, 2023. https://honisoit.com/2023/05/im-the-big-scary-drag-queen-they-warned-you-about-2/.

Summan, Yasmine. 2022. "How the Boulet Brothers, Venus Envy, and More are Breaking Boundaries of Drag." Alternative Press. Last modified May 27, 2022. https://www.altpress.com/alternative-drag-artists-boulet-brothers-venus-envy-interview/.

Tombs, Jen. 2018. "Drag is an Art Form and a Political Statement." The Boar. Last modified Feb 25, 2018. https://theboar.org/2018/02/drag-lgbtua-political-statement/.

Varrati, Michael. 2020. "Drag Me to Hell: An Incomplete History of the Intersection of Drag and Horror." Gayly Dreadful. Last modified June 17, 2020. Https://www.gaylydreadful.com/blog/pride-2020-drag-me-to-hell-an-incomplete-history-of-the-intersection-of-drag-and-horror.

Villareal, Daniel. 2019. "One of Tv's Biggest Drag Competition is Finally Getting a Drag King." Dragaholic. Last modified August 9, 2019. https://www.queerty.com/one-tvs-biggest-drag-competitions-finally-getting-drag-king-20190809.

Wallace, Megan. 2019. "Drag is so Much More than High-glamour Queens." Hunger. Last modified November 6, 2019. https://www.hungertv.com/editorial/drag-is-so-much-more-than-high-glamour-queens/.

Watson. 2019. "Kim Petras, Horror Drag, and the Glamorous World of Gore." Blendmag. Last modified October 25, 2019. https://blendmag.online/new-blog/2019/10/24/kim-petras-horror-drag-and-the-glamorous-world-of-gore.

Williams, Keegan. 2022. "Mainstream Media Drag and the Future: Despite Major Strides, We still have Work to Do." OFM. Last modified March 4, 2022. https://www.outfrontmagazine.com/mainstream-media-drag-and-the-future-despite-major-strides-we-still-have-work-to-do/.

Zander, Jynx. 2022. "The Ultimate Guide to Goth, Punk, and Emo Styles." The Political Fashion. Last modified March 25, 2022. https://www.political.fashion/posts/the-ultimate-guide-to-goth-punk-and-emo-styles-pf.

MEDIA REFERENCES

Noyes, Nathan and Varrati, Michael. 2016-present. *The Boulet Brothers' Dragula.* Hey Queen TV (S1), Amazon Prime, OUTtv (Canada), SBS Viceland (Australia), Wow Presents (S2), Netflix (S3), Shudder (Ressurection, S4).

List of Contributors

Yeojin Kim & Shane Carreon

Yeojin Kim is a Professor of Instruction at University at Buffalo/Singapore Institute of Management. She received her Ph.D in the English Department at Binghamton University, State University of New York. She was a Korean Government Honor Fellowship student in 2016. Her primary research interests are cultural studies, transnational cinema studies, transmedia studies, and gender studies. She is a contributor to the book, *Cinematic Women, From Objecthood to Heroism* (Vernon, 2020).

Shane Carreon is Associate Professor in the College of Communication, Art, and Design at the University of the Philippines Cebu. His creative work practice and research interests include writing and literature, multimodal artistic expressions, gender studies, translation, visual culture, popular culture, and decoloniality.

Anson Koch-Rein

Anson Koch-Rein is Assistant Professor in the Division of Liberal Arts at the University of North Carolina School of the Arts, where he teaches gender studies, literature, and humanities classes, including "The Monster as Metaphor." He holds a PhD from Emory University's Graduate Institute of the Liberal Arts with a certificate in Women's, Gender, and Sexuality Studies. His writing on horror and monsters has appeared in TSQ: Transgender Studies Quarterly, LIT: Literature Interpretation Theory, and the anthology TransGothic in Literature and Culture.

Youn Soo Kim Goldstein

Youn Soo Kim Goldstein is Ambrose Amos Shaw Assistant Professor of Localization and Translation in the Department of Foreign Languages at Weber State University, where she teaches translation, localization, and Korean language. She received her PhD in Translation Studies at Binghamton University, State University of New York in 2019. Her research interests include contemporary Korean literature, translation theories, and decoloniality.

Min-Chi Chen

Min-Chi Chen received her PhD in the Comparative Literature Department at Binghamton University (SUNY), USA. Her dissertation focuses on the FBI's criminal profiling techniques and their social influence on crime novels, films, and television series. Her research interests include media studies, cultural studies, crime fiction, and criminology, and has recently published in *Concentric: Literary and Cultural Studies* (2023).

Aarzoo Singh & Angie Fazekas

Dr. Angie Fazekas is an Assistant Professor at the Women and Gender Studies Institute at the University of Toronto. Their research focus is adolescent online engagement and behavior, social media, sex education, and pop culture. In their doctoral dissertation, they considered how teenage fans interact with fanfiction as a mechanism for exploring their sexuality. Their publications include a co-authored chapter in Final Girls, Feminism, and Popular Culture and a chapter in Fandom, Now in Color.

Dr. Aarzoo Singh is an Assistant professor at the Department of Women and Gender Studies at the University of Winnipeg. As an interdisciplinary scholar, her research focuses on the theoretical and experiential connections between storytelling, objects, locations, and displacement for the South Asian Diaspora. Her current research and teaching interests focus on reparative justice narratives, alternative epistemologies, affective and personal archives, and postcolonial subjectivity. She was interviewed on her research for the British Museum of Colonisation's platform Paper Trails and her published work can be found in *DisClosure: A Journal of Social Theory.*

Joshua Nieubuurt

Joshua Nieubuurt is a PhD candidate in Digital Rhetoric at Old Dominion University. His previous published research has included topics in the realm of post-humanism, mis/disinformation, and New Materialisms. All of which specifically focus on attempting to breach through the anthropocentric lens to consider artifacts and other non-human things as potential agents dwelling alongside humans in the world. He currently resides in the lush subtropical island of Okinawa, Japan in where he holds several adjunct faculty positions in the fields of TESL, Humanities, Writing, and English Studies.

Morgan Kate Pinder

MK Pinder writer and PhD candidate at Deakin University, Australia studying eco-Gothic representation in media. Her research interests are in the intersection of genre, transmedia narratives, and ecocriticism. She writes about nature, video games, Gothic texts, and literary adaptation.

Mychal Reiff-Shanks

Mychal Reiff-Shanks is a Ph.D. candidate in the Moving Images Studies program at Georgia State University. They are a Black queer, non-binary person whose pronouns are they/them/theirs. An avid fan of media all their life, that idle love turned into a critical passion for Media Studies. Mychal's studies focus on aspects of their identity, such as African American, queer, and gender representation in media. They have been published in the journal Studies in the Fantastic by the University of Tampa Press for their work on Lovecraft

Country and the use of historical reenactment within the show as a possible tool for Black cultural healing. The one thing that they hope to accomplish with their career is to inspire and encourage others to think critically about the media they consume and give them the tools to make media criticism accessible for those in and out of academia.

Adam P. Wadenius

Adam P. Wadenius earned his Master's degree in Film Studies from San Francisco State University in 2007. He is currently an Assistant Professor of Film & Media Studies with Cosumnes River College in California, where he teaches film courses on topics of history, style, genre, and director's cinema, as well as media courses on issues of race, sex, and gender representation in the various modes of mass communication. His primary research interests include the work of Julia Kristeva, horror and the abject, postmodern cultural theory, and the concept of the foreigner in post-9/11 America. His current writing project examines the historical tensions between classical Hollywood cinema and art cinema narration as representations of Kristeva's ideas on signifying processes in language, specifically, the dialectic oscillation between symbolic and semiotic structures.

Eleanor Gratz

Eleanor Gratz is a graduate of the M.A. program in the Department of Film Studies at the University of North Carolina at Wilmington. She previously attended the University of North Carolina at Chapel Hill, where she graduated with highest honors. Eleanor's work focuses on representations of the body, the intersection of race, gender, and sexuality in film, global cinema, essay filmmaking, horror cinema, and film aesthetics. She foregrounds these topics in her critical film scholarship, production projects, and role as an adjunct faculty member at UNCW.

Ryanne Probst

Ryanne Probst is a composition and first-year seminar instructor at the University of North Carolina at Wilmington. Her research tends to follow the monstrous—modern-day Medusas and gorgons, the ladies who go bump in the night—and her writing reflects those explorations. She uses feminist scholarship and historical perspectives to complicate the ways we talk about gender, the feminine, and the feminine body. Her work has been published on Betches.com and SheKnows.com, among others. She resides in North Carolina with her dog Buffy: slayer of naps, vanquisher of houseflies.

Sheridyn Villarreal

Sheridyn Villarreal is an art historian and independent curator based in Chicago, Illinois. Their areas of research include intersections of art and technology, queer art, and the art of Latin America and Latinx diasporic communities. They received their BA in Art History from Columbia College, specializing in Modern and Contemporary art movements and theory. Sheridyn's practice is informed by the field of transhumanism, posthuman-feminism, and critical queer theory. They are currently guest curator at the Hokin Gallery, adapting their research on the cyborg figure into a survey of contemporary queer and transgender artists invoking posthuman aesthetics to relate their experiences of gender nonconformity and transition.

Charlito O. Codizar

Charlito O. Codizar is a tenured faculty in the senior high school department of Sacred Heart School – Ateneo de Cebu. He is the current head of the Humanities and Social Sciences strand. He received his bachelor's degree major in English, master's degree in literature, and doctoral degree in Literature and Communication from Cebu Normal University. He is interested in literatures of the marginalized and the minority, magical realism, and historical fiction.

Vukadinović Maja

Professor of Vocational Studies, Novi Sad School of Business, Novi Sad, Serbia) is an individual reviewer of the anthology.

Index

www.ingramcontent.com/pod-product-compliance
Lightning Source LLC
Chambersburg PA
CBHW072123020426
42334CB00018B/1697